FEMINIST REREADINGS
of Rabbinic Literature

HBI SERIES ON JEWISH WOMEN
Shulamit Reinharz, General Editor
Sylvia Barack Fishman, Associate Editor

The HBI Series on Jewish Women, created by the Hadassah-Brandeis Institute, publishes a wide range of books by and about Jewish women in diverse contexts and time periods. Of interest to scholars and the educated public, the HBI Series on Jewish Women fills major gaps in Jewish Studies and in Women and Gender Studies as well as their intersection.

The HBI Series on Jewish Women is supported by a generous gift from Dr. Laura S. Schor.

For the complete list of books that are available in this series, please see www.upne.com

Inbar Raveh, *Feminist Rereadings of Rabbinic Literature*

Marcia Falk, *The Days Between: Blessings, Poems, and Directions of the Heart for the Jewish High Holiday Season*

Laura Silver, *Knish: In Search of the Jewish Soul Food*

Sharon R. Siegel, *A Jewish Ceremony for Newborn Girls: The Torah's Covenant Affirmed*

Laura S. Schor, *The Best School in Jerusalem: Annie Landau's School for Girls, 1900–1960*

Federica K. Clementi, *Holocaust Mothers and Daughters: Family, History, and Trauma*

Elana Maryles Sztokman and Chaya Rosenfeld Gorsetman, *Educating in the Divine Image: Gender Issues in Orthodox Jewish Day Schools*

Ilana Szobel, *A Poetics of Trauma: The Work of Dahlia Ravikovitch*

Susan M. Weiss and Netty C. Gross-Horowitz, *Marriage and Divorce in the Jewish State: Israel's Civil War*

Ronit Irshai, *Fertility and Jewish Law: Feminist Perspectives on Orthodox Responsa Literature*

Elana Maryles Sztokman, *The Men's Section: Orthodox Jewish Men in an Egalitarian World*

INBAR RAVEH

FEMINIST REREADINGS
of Rabbinic Literature

Translated by KAEREN FISH

BRANDEIS UNIVERSITY PRESS *Waltham, Massachusetts*

Brandeis University Press
An imprint of University Press of New England
www.upne.com
© 2014 Brandeis University
All rights reserved
Manufactured in the United States of America
Designed by Vicki Kuskowski
Typeset in Bembo by A. W. Bennett Book Composition

For permission to reproduce any of the material in this book,
contact Permissions, University Press of New England,
One Court Street, Suite 250, Lebanon NH 03766; or visit
www.upne.com

The HBI Series on Jewish Women is supported by a
generous gift from Dr. Laura S. Schor.

Library of Congress Cataloging-in-Publication Data
Raveh, 'Inbar.
[Bi-fene 'atsman. English]
Feminist rereadings of rabbinic literature / Inbar Raveh;
translated
by Kaeren Fish.
   pages cm.— (HBI series on Jewish women)
Includes bibliographical references and index.
ISBN 978-1-61168-607-4 (cloth: alk. paper)
—ISBN 978-1-61168-608-1
(pbk.: alk. paper)—ISBN 978-1-61168-609-8 (ebook)
1. Women in rabbinical literature. 2. Women in Judaism.
3. Feminism—Religious aspects—Judaism. I. Fish, Kaeren,
translator. II. Title.
BM96.9.W7R3813 2014
296.1—dc23

2014014725

5 4 3 2 1

Women are a nation unto themselves
—SHABBAT 62A

Why are women, judging from this catalogue, so much more interesting to men than men are to women? A very curious fact it seemed, and my mind wandered to picture the lives of men who spend their time in writing books about women; whether they were old or young, married or unmarried, red-nosed or hump-backed—anyhow, it was flattering, vaguely, to feel oneself the object of such attention provided that it was not entirely bestowed by the crippled and the infirm—so I pondered until all such frivolous thoughts were ended by an avalanche of books sliding down on to the desk in front of me.
—VIRGINIA WOOLF, *A ROOM OF ONE'S OWN*

CONTENTS

Foreword by Sylvia Barack Fishman   xi
Introduction   xv

1. BACK TO THE BREAST
   An Aspect of Feminine Sexuality in the Imagined World of the Sages   1

2. DESIRE AND DOMINION   40

3. "THEY LET THE CHILDREN LIVE"
   The Midwives at a Political Crossroads   56

4. JUDITH, WIFE OF R. HIYYA
   A Story of Women's Pain   74

5. THE VOICE OF DOUBT
   The Wife of R. Simeon ben Halafta and the Uncanny   93

6. OPEN TO CONQUEST
   Prostitution—Temptations and Responses   100

7. THE MYTH IN THE ATTIC
   The Call of the Deep   116

8. THE CREATION OF WOMAN
   Men Are from Babylon; Women Are from the Land of Israel   145

Notes   157
Bibliography   179
Index   197

FOREWORD

Sylvia Barack Fishman

In this extraordinary feminist literary critical analysis, newly translated from the Hebrew, Inbar Raveh teases out meanings hidden within a critically important genre of rabbinic literature known as midrash. Produced by rabbis from the first century CE through medieval times and widely dispersed, midrash consists of narrative and sermonic rabbinic commentaries, many of which reflect ancient oral traditions that go back millennia. Midrash may be divided broadly into Talmudic midrash from Babylonia and Palestine, which is interspersed with legal discussions in the Mishna and Gemara; midrash halakha—primarily legal works contemporaneous with the Mishna such as the Mekhilta; and midrash aggada (narrative)—nonlegal material providing rabbinic biblical exegesis. Much midrash was not finalized in writing until medieval times. Aggadic midrash was also collected in anthologies such as the Midrash Rabba and Tanhuma, but even in these collections, narratives often do not flow in logical order; rather, they are frequently episodic, meandering, and fragmented, seemingly wandering from one subject to another. Thus, when Inbar Raveh sets out "to examine aggadic literature from an unprejudiced feminist perspective," to unravel how the rabbis felt about women and about femaleness itself, her first and very necessary task is to piece together narrative elements, in order to create coherent sequences of texts.

She succeeds powerfully at both tasks: in *Feminist Rereadings of Rabbinic Literature* Raveh, a self-defined secular Israeli woman, gathers together fragmented subject matter and then insightfully unpacks the explicit and implicit attitudes the narratives reveal. Raveh illuminates a cosmos constructed by the rabbinic imagination, in which males and females are different in their physical, emotional, and spiritual essences and outward manifestations. As rabbinic midrash constructs this cosmos, in human terms and within the human sphere, maleness is seen as superior and privileged in many ways. And yet God, whom the midrash presents as the Creator of the universe and the author of Jewish and human history, incorporates

FOREWORD

into His Torah and into His own divine behaviors and attitudes the essential attributes of human females!

Female breasts, for example, become a subject of extended positive metaphors, not only in the Song of Songs and in the Book of Proverbs but in midrashic treatments of various biblical episodes, including Sarah's geriatric childbirth. As Raveh shows, the rabbinic imagination presents these virtuous women's breasts as symbols of physical and spiritual nurturance as well as sensual gratification. The biblical Sarah first brings up the topic of sensual and sexual decline due to aging as she laughs at the prediction that she will have children: "After I am grown old, shall I have pleasure, my husband being old also?" (Gen.18:12). After giving birth to Isaac, Sarah refers to the nurturing aspects of her breasts: "And she said, "Who [would have] said to Abraham that Sarah should nurse children? For I have borne him a son in his old age." (Gen. 21:6–7) Raveh analyzes a group of midrashim in Genesis Rabba, the Talmudic tractate Bava Metzi'a, and elsewhere, which build upon Sarah's phrase "nurse children." Within these midrashic narratives Abraham hosts a banquet to celebrate the miracle of Isaac's birth, and the public disbelieves that Sarah could conceive and gestate and that Abraham has the power to impregnate; they gossip that Isaac is a foundling whom the aging couple are trying to pass off as their own. The aged Abraham and Sarah appear ridiculous, and this impression interferes with Abraham's ability to disseminate his religious insights. Abraham deals with this disruption of God's plan by urging Sarah: "Uncover your breasts so that all may know that the Holy One, blessed be He, has begun to perform miracles." Abraham himself reveals Sarah's breasts to the guests, "and the milk gushed forth as from two fountains." All the banquet guests bring their children to be nursed by Sarah. Thus, in these midrashim Sarah's breasts, which she has previously assumed to be past the point both of experiencing sensual pleasure and of offering sustenance, become the source of both, and help Abraham spread God's word.

Other midrashim connect breasts with Moses, the Torah, and God, working from breast imagery in the Song of Songs, Proverbs, and elsewhere. The two tablets of the law are compared to two female breasts, as are Moses and Aaron. The Torah is also compared to the breast: "So long as the infant sucks—he finds milk," in that it provides spiritual nourishment; "so it is with the words of the Torah: so long as a person studies them, he finds meaning." In these midrashim, Raveh notes, "the Torah is perceived ... as a metaphorical gushing breast, a good breast that provides the vital requirements of its children." Still other midrashim connect God with the nurturing qualities of the breast (as does the Hebrew Bible). Thus, Raveh argues, unlike traditions that locate all intellectualism in masculine metaphors, the rabbinic midrash seeks "to diminish the conflict between bodily and spiritual needs," and "structure a bodily, material, feminine perception of the Torah."

Raveh's analysis demands "a special type of listening," to the words and the silences between the words, to what is said and what is implied. Analyzing the various midrashim elucidating Eve's curse, "In pain shall you bring forth children; and your desire shall be for your husband, and he shall rule over you," Raveh draws eruditely on both current historical text scholarship and feminist commentary. She shows how readers can learn something about rabbinic attitudes and anxieties by paying attention to the material removed or added by the "active editor" who redacted Genesis Rabba. Demonstrating "cracks" in the narrative as it now stands, Raveh shows how the midrashim comment not only on "the experience of childbirth and the sacrificial offering [of doves] that the mother is subsequently required to bring," but also on male concerns about women's potential lack of enthusiasm for sexual activity with their husbands or, conversely, their potential to betray their husbands through passionate encounters with others. Plumbing "the hidden connections between textuality and sexuality," Raveh demonstrates that the rabbis understood "that a woman's desire for her husband is not, in fact, self-evident," given the realities of pregnancies, childbirth, and mortality during most of human history, and might, under certain circumstances, be experienced "as a punishment and a curse."

Many midrashim have become incorporated over the centuries into popular Jewish interpretations of particular biblical texts. Working masterfully with a large corpus of less-familiar midrashim, Raveh makes explicit what in the midrashic text itself is implicit or partially hidden: the rabbinic text written, transmitted, and redacted -by men is positioned within a male interpretive framework—and yet it can betray ambivalence, anxiety, and sometimes a surprising sensitivity to women's experience. Raveh describes her own research and analysis as "the pleasure of a renewed encounter

FOREWORD

with the dynamic resources of rabbinic culture." I found reading Raveh's perceptive analysis pleasurable in a similar way. The Hadassah-Brandeis Institute has published numerous works on gender and midrash, including, among others, Judith Baskin's *Midrashic Women: Formations of the Feminine in Rabbinic Literature,* and Sharon Faye Koren's *Forsaken: The Menstruant in Medieval Jewish Mysticism.* The directors of the Hadassah-Brandeis Institute are delighted to bring to an English-speaking audience Inbar Raveh's new, nuanced insights into gender and midrash.

INTRODUCTION

I embarked on writing this book as a secular woman involved in literary research on rabbinic literature. For most of my life, I did not consider myself a feminist. This was an ideological label that I avoided, averse as I am to ideologies in general. Many of them—or, at least, the form that they take in our social reality—appear to me to entail a coercive view of their standards as an absolute against which everything is to be measured. My studies at the *Seder Nashim* Beit Midrash Program for Jewish, Gender and Feminist Studies at the Shalom Hartman Institute took me back to my earlier study experiences in study programs for Jewish renewal—pluralistic frameworks for the study of classical as well as modern texts—and reawakened existential questions well suited to my stage of life. I learned that feminism is a broad umbrella, covering many different shades of thought, insights, and values with considerable persuasive power. I found myself in the midst of it.[1]

The desire to engage with the literature of the Sages as a modern reader continues to motivate me, while at the same time my commitment to academic writing represents an obstacle of sorts. For this reason the undermining by feminist thinkers of the traditional demand for a clear distinction between critical and creative writing, between the everyday and academic spheres, between a philosophical text and a literary one, made a profound impression on me.[2] As a reader, I have always felt that "scientific" encounters with rabbinic literature, and the attempt to control the text and extract a coherent and unified meaning, are invariably impeded and frustrated. Teresa de Lauretis defined feminism as "a radical *rewriting*, as well as a rereading, of the dominant forms of Western culture."[3] I confess that I have sometimes been accused by my positivist friends of "rewriting" the rabbinic materials that I study. Indeed, the tension between "research" and "interpretation," or between "reading" and "writing," occupied me in some inchoate form long before I discovered its rich echoes in the feminist theory of literature.

The marginality imposed on me, as a woman and as an academic, brought me both painfully and powerfully to an awareness of the great advantage of the marginal position. In this sense I accept quite happily the role of cultural critic. While I have never regarded my research work as a neutral or objective occupation, familiarity with feminist criticism helped me to define more clearly in my own mind the sort of creative transformation that I was after.[4]

Yeshayahu Leibowitz, regarded by many as Israeli society's "prophet of doom," claimed that the issue of "women in Judaism" is a matter more critical to Judaism than any political problem. He maintained that the failure to address it seriously endangered the very existence of Torah-centered, religious Judaism.[5] I believe that, even today, thirty years since he made this claim, it remains valid and applies not only to the existence of Torah-Judaism, but to the existence of Jewish culture altogether. As I see it, the radical change in the status and role of women in the Western world must find some response that emanates from Jewish tradition and thought, rejuvenating our culture and rendering it richer and more relevant for us.

Recent years have witnessed a great upswing in women's involvement in Jewish studies and its classical sources, and the number of women engaged in the study of rabbinical literature has grown at an unprecedented rate since the last decade of the twentieth century. In my own experience, women's studies and gender studies are changing the academic world, including the sphere of Jewish studies. I hope that the present work will contribute to this very welcome change.

When my book *Me'at mi-Harbeh* appeared, addressing the descriptive poetics of the legends of the Sages, I was interviewed by a local newspaper. The interview offered me a new perspective on my perhaps curious affection for the object of my research. The journalist expressed his surprise at the love and profound connection of a woman like myself toward such a patriarchal textual world. When I described for him my journey to this ancient literature, I understood for the first time the intensity of the effort that I had invested, throughout my studies, to acquire a basic position of identification. Rabbinic literature was, for me, such a remote province that I needed to build a multitude of bridges before I was able to read it in a way that was meaningful to me. Along the way I skipped over many a field of thorns and thistles, allowing no snakes or scorpions to deter me on my path to the bottomless wells of rabbinic culture. The present project heads back to some of those thorn fields, examines the scratches, reveals the thistles at the height of their flowering beauty, and gives an accounting of a love that is accommodating enough to allow for a measure of distance and criticism.

My reading of literature has always been accompanied by an awareness of the place and role of the reader. Since becoming a reflective reader, I have identified with the insights of Hans-Georg Gadamer, who points out that the reader finds himself within the text as an inevitable result of the overall sociopolitical context of which he and the words form a part.[6] When I began to study feminism and gender theories of reading, it seemed natural to view rabbinic literature as a locus where gender knowledge, inter alia, is formed. This represented further proof that commentators always view matters from within their own context, since there is no other way of reading a text.

Feminist literary criticism, as I understand it, is identified first and foremost with the approach of Eileen Showalter, who analyzes the goal of the feminist position in reading, writing, and critique of fiction and other texts.[7] This position focuses on reviewing and decoding the hidden connections between textuality and sexuality; between the generic and the gendered; between sexual psychological identity and cultural authority.[8] The quest is undertaken through a return to the history of Western culture and a reinterpretation of its central texts. Other women intellectuals express similar aims: Virginia Woolf talks about the "rewriting of history"; Adrienne Rich argues that women's writing must start with a new look at the past; Carol Heilbrun suggests that women must reinvent femininity; and Joan Kelly declares that women must be restored to history, and history restored to women.

Orly Lubin's book, *Women Reading Women,* which was preceded by an article with the same title,[9] was the first to propose a feminist history of reading in the Israeli context, and had a decisive influence on the development of literary criticism in Israel. Her book joins the list of outstanding primary texts in this sphere[10] and was one of my main sources of inspiration. In Lubin's view, reading is a tool of survival. She describes a woman for whom reading is not so much a way of life as a way of being submerged in an existential coma. Reading, in this world of concepts, always means critical reading—awareness of the location of the reader in relation to the text and the context in which it is created. My book resonates with

xvii

and connects two identity-forming experiences: the experience of survival, and the experience of reading.

From the new perspective that I have gained, I see that in the past I did not devote enough attention to the gender element of the identity of the reader of rabbinic texts. The proposed readings that appear here relate, from this perspective, to more extensive aspects of my identity. I have not forsaken more established reading perspectives, and therefore this book presents a multiplicity of viewpoints, with constant hopping between them. This, I have learned, is an important principle: in order to sustain a critical political reading, one has to forgo the quest for a homogenous perspective that prefers a unified subject. Thus, with each reading the reader creates a different aspect of subjectivity and renews her active capacity, while still maintaining the critical advantage, because with each new location of her reading, her previous place is submitted to criticism.[11]

Rabbinic literature was written by men, concerns itself mainly with men, and aims to advance men's objectives. Women appear in this literature in secondary roles as wives, mothers, or daughters, rather than as active participants. The attitude toward women, within this corpus, is therefore the product of and subordinate to the perspective of the creators of the literature. This question then arises: Why would a woman such as myself take an interest in this literature?

In the introduction to her work *Playing in the Dark,* Toni Morrison explains why she is drawn to white people's thoughts about representations of "blackness":

> The principal reason these matters loom large for me is that I do not have quite the same access to these traditionally useful constructs of blackness. Neither blackness nor "people of color" stimulates in me notions of excessive, limitless love, anarchy, or routine dread. I cannot rely on these metaphorical shortcuts because I am a black writer struggling with and through a language that can powerfully evoke and enforce hidden signs of racial superiority, cultural hegemony, and dismissive "othering" of people and language which are by no means marginal or already and completely known and knowable in my work. My vulnerability would lie in romanticizing blackness rather than demonizing it; vilifying whiteness

rather than reifying it ... How is "literary whiteness" and "literary blackness" made, and what is the consequence of that construction? How do embedded assumptions of racial (not racist) language work in the literary enterprise that hopes and sometimes claims to be "humanistic"?[12]

In keeping with Morrison's insights and the question of the gaps between myself and the object of my reading, rabbinic literature offers me opportunities to understand the flexibility of gender imagination and representation, their limitations and their power. Based on the assumption that gender identities are cultural products, and the further assumption that these must be learned somewhere, I approach and read rabbinic legends as a locus where such knowledge—among other sorts of knowledge—is generated. I am interested in texts that have molded the Jewish image of "femininity." The purpose of gender-oriented study of rabbinic literature is not to award points to the Sages for their perceptions of women, but rather to discover the answers to such questions as what the Sages thought about women, how they formed and molded their image, and how they created an ancient discourse about women that determined the image, identity, and status of women in society. Which are the ways in which the Sages' gender ideology is molded? Which literary devices are used to turn a social convention into an "absolute truth" whose purpose is to perpetuate the existing situation as a "natural" situation, a matter not up for discussion and impossible to change?

Another aim of my research is the re-creation of the stories and voices of women against the historical and social background in which they lived their lives. This is more than just empowerment of the feminine subject and a way of moving women from the margins to the center. It is also a matter of exposing the devices and methods that perpetuate male hegemony in society, with a view to facilitating an alternative reading. I believe that turning our attention to characters who are usually at the margins of culture, rather than at the center of its discourse, may reveal new aspects within the culture.

Unfortunately, there is no such thing as a text that is feminist by nature. Within any historical and social context, any text can be swallowed up by a hegemonic reading or appropriated as a reading "from the margins."

INTRODUCTION

Feminist readers are charged with turning the struggle over the meaning of a text into an openly declared and pressing item on our intellectual agenda.[13]

Feminist theories pertaining to sex and sexuality arose within the framework of the study of modern society and culture, but increased awareness of the place of sexuality in cultural discourse has led to extensive research of sexuality in classical ancient cultures, such as the Bible, ancient Greece, and early Christianity.[14] The use of gender theories in this book is eclectic, stemming from the treatment of texts and the subjects arising from them, rather than the other way around. At the same time, the distance between ancient traditions and the modern theories that aid in their reading may challenge us to take a critical look at the theories and the knowledge they offer, in view of the encounter with a given cultural world.

Daniel Boyarin's work in feminist gender research of rabbinic literature guided me in this project. In the introduction to his book *Carnal Israel,* he emphasizes the importance of this sphere, stating:

> I argue that a culture adopting the ideological position that sexuality is a benefit given by God to humans, both for procreation and for other positive ends, acquired problems as well as solutions. Indeed, I am arguing that there was much social conflict within the societies which rabbinic Judaism helped form, precisely owing to the strength of this position, for the insistence on embodiment and sexuality as the foundational primitives of human essence almost ineluctably produces gender and sex-role differentiation as dominant characteristics of the social formation.[15]

I share his view of sexuality and gender as fundamental subjects of Jewish culture. The specific forms in which this knowledge is molded are worthy of careful scrutiny, and it is clear to me that the insights to be gained in this area will influence our understanding of this cultural totality.

Although the study of gender in rabbinic literature is a relatively new area of research, distinct trends have already become apparent.[16] The first step entailed mapping the material in rabbinic literature that dealt with women, and presenting its underlying assumptions. This stage of research focused mainly on the question of the "attitude" toward women. A different trend, which developed during the 1990s, was characterized by a transition from the focus on women to a focus on gender relations and gender identities. The first half of the 1990s saw the publication of works by Daniel Boyarin, Admiel Kosman, David Biale, Howard Eilberg-Schwartz, and Michael Satlow. These writers centered their research on the question of where and how rabbinic culture structured gender.[17] Since the late 1990s some scholars have engaged in in-depth and critical reading of specific, complete rabbinic texts,[18] while others explore different topics and their appearances throughout the literature.[19]

My perspective on rabbinic literature is literary and philosophical. I offer readings of rabbinic legends and the ways in which feminine gender is molded through them. Zunz's distinction between *halakha* and *aggada* may aid us in understanding the realm of expression of the latter: "[Aggada] is the fruit of free individual study, while halakha arises from the grave authority of the establishment ... What halakha develops is a tangible thing which is manifest in practical life ... while aggada aspires more to recognizing the value of an idea."[20] It is my belief that "aggada as literature," dealing as it does with that which is worthy and desirable, may reveal much to us about the values and ideals that guided the Sages in all areas.[21]

Each chapter of this book is devoted to a separate subject. The "feast" presented here is therefore a tasting that allows the reader to appreciate the rich contribution of a gender perspective on readings of classical Jewish texts. I address midrashic texts attributed to both Tannaim and Amoraim, as well as sources in the Talmud and the Yalkutim, with the recognition that rabbinic culture develops over time and space, and that a historical view of traditions may be of value in advancing our understanding of different topics. Owing to the limited scope of the present work, it focuses on prominent gender issues in rabbinic legends. The discussions exemplify various aspects of refraction through the prism of gender: the body; sexual desire and sexual relations; childbirth; exploitation of loopholes in the patriarchal system; the feminine voice representing suppressed truths; gender liminality; feminine myth; gender and cultural context; Babylon versus the Land of Israel, and more.

Ishay Rosen-Zvi, in reviewing the development of gender research of talmudic literature, concludes that relevant and "proper" research is committed to the norms of philological research of the text; it deals with

INTRODUCTION

limited subjects or texts, and it dwells on their subtleties in an attempt to understand the gender mechanism as it operates in rabbinic literature.[22] The readings proposed here deviate from the conventions of the philological-historical approach. Philological research has long regarded exegetical activity with suspicion.[23] The inductive structure of writing in this tradition often allows writers to evade the exegetical task and thereby to approach, as it were, "scientific" or "precise" norms. I enclose these terms in quotation marks, owing to my fundamental misgivings toward any approach, especially in the humanities, that attempts to conceal its subjectivity and its assumptions.[24]

The readings presented in this study are most definitely the fruit of interpretation. Interpretation, as Ruth Lorand points out, comprises two aspects:

> a. The interpreter seeks to protect the value of the object and to show it at its best, out of a belief that the object is indeed worthy. In this sense, interpretation relies on the object, and serves as one of the means of preserving its value and status as something that is relevant.
>
> b. The object is co-opted into the service of the interpreter, and by means of it he expresses and reinforces his values and beliefs. The interpreter discovers in the object elements or aspects which conform to his own tendencies and views, and presents those conforming elements as substantive and essential to the object. In this sense, the object of interpretation becomes a tool in the hands of the interpreter.[25]

The corpus of rabbinic legends, in my view, is an artistic creation. Any artistic creation processes raw materials from the different strata of life experience, in such a way as to shed new light on them, revealing new qualities and meanings. The emotional position is certainly a primary motivation of textual interpretation.[26] To interpret means to love the object of interpretation and to protect it from anything that appears to diminish its value.[27] It is important to me to emphasize this consciousness of love, since a feminist reading of the classical texts taxes them significantly, as we shall see below.

Can a woman reader identify with the esthetic and moral values arising from such androcentric works as those comprising rabbinic literature? How can a woman reader, who experiences herself as a subject, enjoy homiletic texts in which women are given the role of silent objects? Patrocinio Schweickart points to the power that some of the canonical texts exert, even over resistant readers, and urges feminist readers to ask important questions. Among them: From where does the text draw its strength to lure us into its net, and how is it that many of the most blatantly sexist texts succeed in mesmerizing us, even after they have been subjected to detailed feminist criticism? In light of the complexity of this reading situation, she argues that certain texts require a dual commentary: a negative reading that exposes their complicity in the injustices of the patriarchal ideology, and a positive commentary that recaptures the core of their emotional and esthetic power.[28] I embrace the bifurcated approach that she proposes, one that responds to concurrent urges in relation to the text. The acts of interpretation proposed here testify, I believe, to the ability to simultaneously identify emotionally, oppose morally, and respond to esthetic beauty. I hope that good and effective interpretation might persuade readers that the object is richer and more complex than they had previously believed, or that its structure and meaning are different from what they had originally assumed. As in other feminist works, I hope to illuminate aspects of the sources that thus far have remained unexposed. That which has not been the focus of attention was not necessarily deliberately hidden; rather, it might simply have been ignored, or labeled as irrelevant.

In conclusion, I believe that there is great value in exposing gender issues in rabbinic literature to a wide audience in the Jewish world. As Scott demonstrates, the sphere of gender seems fixed and unchanging, but in fact its meaning is subject to competitive forces and is constantly changing.[29] Gender research of rabbinic literature may create new perspectives on old questions and turn women into visible and active participants in the constantly renewed definition of gender. I have no doubt that the path to a more egalitarian cultural experience in the present passes through an understanding of the gender constructs we have inherited from our ancestors. Rabbinic literature is one of our most important spiritual foundations and cultural assets. The Sages of the Mishna and the Talmud defined, to a considerable extent, what would and would not be included within the Jewish tradition to be handed down to future generations. There is a purpose in reading this literature from modern and postmodern perspectives, even though it is clear that its point of departure cannot meet the criteria and demands of twenty-first-century feminism. We are able to approach the teachings of the ancient Sages with a greater awareness of the unconscious motives influencing the formation of our systems of beliefs and opinions. As a result of these insights, I hope that we might be able to create more egalitarian social relationships between the sexes, and to grant them Jewish legitimacy. Therefore, the study that I propose here has an explicit ideological and political purpose: I hope that an understanding of covert and sophisticated cultural mechanisms of suppression, silencing, and exclusion will advance us on our path to neutralizing and dismantling them.

Despite the diversity of Jewish worldviews, I find myself identifying with the statement, "Only if we have a past upon which we can lean and a future toward which we can aspire, can we also have a meaningful present."[30] Leaning on the past, as I see it, does not mean agreeing with it or accepting its authority; rather, it means attaining a profound familiarity with it, feeling a sense of belonging to it, and interpreting it in such a way as to produce living meaning.

Many friends and institutions aided me over the course of writing this book; my thanks and blessings to all of them. The Shalom Hartman Institute opened its doors to me and allowed me to devote a significant portion of my time to research, and my *Seder Nashim* colleagues taught me precious lessons about learning in a women's group. Thanks to my Hartman Institute seminar colleagues: Prof. Ron Margolin, Prof. Noam Zohar, Dr. Eli Sheinfeld, Dr. Hizky Shoham, Dr. Orit Avneri, and Vadim Kelebeyev. The Program for Gender Studies and the Dafna Yizreeli Center for Women and Gender Studies at Bar-Ilan University offered me a postdoctoral fellowship, thereby facilitating the conclusion of the project. My thanks to Prof. Vered Noam, whose friendship and special generosity are an inspiration to me; to Prof. Ishay Rosen-Zvi, who read the manuscript of this book and shared some of the breadth of his knowledge with me; and to Prof. Elisheva Baumgarten, whose comments enhanced the text. Thanks to Noam Zion, a most stimulating study partner, and to my old and beloved friends, Rotem Wagner and Dr. Yair Lipschitz, whose insights and comments are always refreshing and welcome.

I dedicate this book to Yoni, who handled the not-always-agreeable presence of feminist thought in our home with characteristic dignity and humor. My thanks to him for always giving me freedom and encouraging me to be, fully, who I am.

≋ 1 ≋

BACK TO THE BREAST

An Aspect of Feminine Sexuality in the Imagined World of the Sages

For Grandmother Shoshana, of blessed memory

A DISORDERING ORGAN

In the beginning there was the breast. That was the first object; the maternal organ whose significance in the life of every newborn—certainly in the ancient world—was critical. When artists of the ancient world molded the human form, breasts usually signified a woman. They were different, sometimes, in form and even in number, but they were almost always clearly visible.

In *The History of Sexuality*, Michel Foucault looks at the human body as the primary signifier of power relations. He argues that the body is the greatest battlefield in human history. In other words, bodily behaviors and physical indicators occurring in or upon the body of the individual signify the power relations between oppressive forces in society and that individual. These power relations are dynamic, for while the body obeys physiological laws, it is also subjugated to the norms forced upon it by the social and cultural order. Foucault refers to these forces as "biopower."[1] He regards their influence as being so great that we can speak of the universal human body only in a limited and trivial sense. The human body is a sort of locus in which discourse is recorded, but its uniqueness lies in the fact that it is also a locus that resists the discourse about it, creating dialogue when force is applied.

Sexual differences and the study of bodily behaviors serve as central axes for the feminist criticism of reasoning, formation of knowledge, and science. In the wake of Foucault, and inspired by radical feminism, feminist scholars have argued that regimentation of the body as a means of control is especially relevant in relation to the feminine body, and they explore the various spheres in which this regimentation is expressed.[2] Contrary to the intuitive sense that the body is a fixed basis for any discussion of sexuality, Denise Riley argues that "'[t]he body' is not, for all its corporeality, an originating point nor yet a terminus; it is a result or an effect."[3]

In this chapter we shall trace the representations of women's breasts in some rabbinic homiletic teachings and show how they reveal a certain view of feminine sexuality, how that sexuality is constituted, and what differentiates it from the sexuality of men, who are the creators of this literature. Thus, our critical reading here will address the politicization of the body and its attendant practices, and thereby open the study of rabbinic literature to new ways of thinking.[4]

The past decade has witnessed a proliferation of academic interest in the Jewish body, a "corporeal turn" surrounded by considerable scholastic controversy.[5] A range of works has mapped the body as a sort of cultural signifier. Many of these do not purport to present an all-inclusive picture of the "Jewish body," or even of the "body in rabbinic literature"; rather, they offer a meticulous reading of texts and an examination of representations of the body in specific literary worlds.[6] This wave of research focuses, for the main part, on those parts of the body whose functions are bound up with the satisfaction of needs—particularly those of nourishment and sex. The aim of our present discussion is to contribute to this discourse and to examine the representations of an organ meant to satisfy these human needs.

Our point of departure will be the association of the breasts with the concept of feminine beauty. Gender distinctions, as we know, have a considerable influence on the perception of human beauty. When the nature of these distinctions changes, the perception of beauty changes accordingly. There is a halakhic discussion in the Palestinian Talmud concerning the types of defects that disqualify a *kohen* (priest) or a woman (that is, the same defects that would render a priest unfit for service in the Temple, are also considered grounds for annulling a marriage to a woman whose defect was not known in advance and agreed to by the husband), noting that the *beraita* lists only those defects that can apply to both sexes.[7]

> A beard is an attractive feature in a man, but a defect in a woman ...
> Breasts are an attractive feature in a woman, but a defect in a man ...
>
> —Palestinian Talmud, Ketubot chapter 7, 31d / law 7 (Academy edition, p. 992, lines 33–35)

This text is not the only rabbinic source that views the breasts as an organ expressing feminine beauty.[8] Elsewhere, the Sages attempt to establish standards for their size and form to serve as criteria of "beauty."[9] Clearly, the breasts are perceived as a central symbol of femininity. The talmudic text quoted above creates an analogy between a beard and breasts, in the context of a discussion of organs that are considered beautiful in one sex but a defect in the other. However, the analogy here is not simple and straightforward. The beard is exposed to view, whereas the breasts are covered; the beard is not governed by the rules of modesty that apply to the breasts;[10] the beard also represents subjective qualities, such as wisdom; and so on.

Luce Irigaray, a French feminist thinker, discusses the introduction of women into the economy of the gaze, the economy of male desire that enjoys looking.[11] Her analysis may help us to understand the importance of the breast in this context. In contrast to the woman's main sex organ, which "represents *the horror of nothing to see*," a "defect in this systematics of representation and desire," a "'hole' in its scoptophilic lens," breasts are prominent organs with a tangible presence. The Sages' contemplation of the breasts in halakhic contexts, and their noting of size and shape, turns the woman into an object for viewing, an object of desire.[12] Needless to say, women have no role in this setting of standards, which remains detached from women's own concepts about their bodies or their desire.

A review of the representation of breasts in rabbinic literature shows that they are molded as organs that disturb a sexual order that is based on oneness: one perspective, one organ. As Irigaray notes, "So woman does not have a sex organ? She has at least two of them, but they are not identifiable as ones. Indeed, she has many more. Her sexuality, always at least double, goes even further: it is *plural*."[13] In Irigaray's theory, the great cultural metaphor of the contrast between the phallus and the feminine sex organ, between the single whole that is visible in its entirety, and that which is hidden and multiple, rests on duality. A twoness that cannot be divided into one and another one becomes something essentially mysterious, unusual, and negative at the root of Western thought. Dualistic existence is not a temporary situation; rather, it is a constant in our culture, and it disturbs the order that rests upon oneness.

In the rabbinic tradition, breasts are esteemed as the vessels producing the milk that is vital for the survival and nurturing of the members of the Jewish nation. One of the strategies for appropriating women's breasts is to mold them in the broader cultural context of nursing. The fundamental assumption is that "everything that gives birth, nurses."[14] In this context the breasts possess "benevolent" significance: they nourish infants—or, in the metaphorical sense, an entire religious community. It is therefore no wonder that in the few places in rabbinic literature where the Sages lend their voices to women who award their breasts a presence and speak about them in the "first person," the breasts are viewed in their maternal, nourishing context.[15] Of course, this role "conceals" the other aspects of the breasts—that of sexual pleasure. Feminine physical pleasure involving the breasts is left outside this world of meanings; even the male attraction to a woman's breasts undergoes substantial cultural sublimation. Women's sexuality is recognized only in the framework of motherhood, which transforms the body into the abode and servant of potential offspring.

One of the most notable rabbinic literary contexts in which mention is made of breasts, highlighting their "disruptive" nature, is the realm of miracles. The elements of a miraculous event are usually familiar to us from our everyday reality. The essence of the miracle is a reorganization of those elements of reality—what the Sages refer to as "a change in the order of Creation."[16] There occurs some overt or covert Divine intervention in nature, disturbing its order and laws in a way that makes a powerful impression on the human consciousness. Most of the miracles in the Bible have some connection, whether directly or indirectly, with life and death—which, of course, are in God's hands.[17]

The maternal function bound up with the breast led to the molding of a rich thematic model that connects the nourishing of an infant at its mother's breast with miracles. It must be emphasized that this connection is in no way self-evident. On the contrary, in many respects there would seem to be nothing more "natural," nothing more firmly entrenched in the fixed laws of biology, than the phenomenon of nursing. Hence, the ties to the realm of the miraculous would seem to arise from the fundamental tension characterizing the Sages' view of feminine sexuality: the dichotomy of order and disorder, embodied, as we shall see, in the theologically fraught relationship between the individual and the collective.

Let us examine the aggadic sources that create a literary link between breasts and miracles, with a view to understanding the underlying tension between the individual and the collective. As we shall see, this tension finds expression at various levels in the talmudic traditions. Sometimes the focus is on the tension that exists in the biblical text itself; at other times a teaching illuminates the tension in the reality of our world. In some instances the tension is a matter of literary style; at other times it reveals a deeply rooted cultural pattern. I propose that the rabbinic sources, in their discussion of breasts in their maternal context, reveal a more comprehensive attitude toward feminine sexuality, its otherness, and its power. The world of the Sages is a rich and diverse one, and it is not my intention to engage in reduction or to offer a one-dimensional description. Rather, I will attempt to offer a conceptual framework that will illuminate something of the structuring of the feminine.

The first sources that we shall examine relate to a miracle involving the breasts of Sarah, the first matriarch of the Jewish people.

> "And Sarah said, God has made laughter for me; all who hear will laugh for me. And she said, Who [would have] said to Abraham that Sarah should nurse children? For I have borne him a son in his old age" (Gen. 21:6–7):
>
> [What is the meaning of the plural,] "that Sarah should nurse *children*"?
>
> Sarah was exceedingly modest. Abraham told her: "This is not the time for modesty; *uncover your breasts* so that all may know that the Holy One, blessed be He, has begun to perform miracles." He *uncovered her breasts* and the milk gushed forth as from two fountains, and noblewomen came and had their children nursed by her,

saying, "We are not deserving of nursing our children from the milk [meant] for that righteous one, Isaac."

—Genesis Rabba, parsha 53[18]

"And she said, Who [would have] said unto Abraham, that Sarah should nurse children? For I have born him a son in his old age" (Gen. 21:7):

How many children did Sarah then nurse? R. Levi said: On the day that Abraham weaned his son Isaac, everyone in the world derided him, saying, "Have you seen that old man and woman, who brought a foundling from the street and now claim him as their son! And what is more, they are making a great banquet to establish their claim!" What did our patriarch Abraham do? He went and invited all the great men of the generation, and our matriarch Sarah invited their wives. Each one brought her child with her, without the wet nurse, and a miracle happened to our mother Sarah: *her two breasts opened up* like two fountains, and she nursed them all.

—Babylonian Talmud, Bava Metzi'a 87a
(according to MS Hamburg 165)

These are variations on the same theme, and the differences between them are deserving of a separate discussion.[19] For our purposes, we will focus on what they share. As Yehoshua Levinson notes, in his inspiring discussion of the version in Genesis Rabba, the central motif of the biblical account here is the transformation of laughter from an expression of a lack of faith, to an expression of recognition of God's power. It must be remembered that the lack of faith, in the biblical story, is attributed to Sarah: "After I am grown old, shall I have pleasure—my husband being old also?" (Gen. 18:12). This motif becomes the central axis of the homiletical story. The biblical verse raises several difficulties. First of all, why does Sarah say that she "nursed children," in the plural? In addition, the text mentions two statements or utterances by Sarah, not just one. Twice we read, "And she said"—although seemingly nothing happens between the first utterance and the second. Furthermore, there is a syntactical problem with the verse, which conveys a quote within a quote: Sarah is talking about a different speaker ("Who [would have] said to Abraham"), but it is not clear who this speaker is, and what his relationship is to those who laughed with Sarah in the previous verse. While previously it was Sarah herself who could not bring herself to believe the news, this doubt is now projected onto an external observer. The solution that the midrash proposes for the exegetical difficulties raised by the repetitions in the biblical text is that Sarah is voicing the words of other characters: it is the noblewomen who hear [of Isaac's arrival] and laugh [in derision], since they cannot believe that Sarah is the mother of Isaac. Therefore Abraham intervenes and urges Sarah to nurse in public, "So that all may know that the Holy One, blessed be He, has begun to perform miracles."[20]

The problem with this seemingly logical explanation of the midrashic dynamic is that it provides no satisfactory explanation as to why the nursing of several babies is necessary to achieve universal recognition that Sarah is the mother of Isaac, when nursing just this one child would surely represent ample proof.

Although it is the plural form ("to nurse children") in the verse that prompts the midrash to adopt this explanation, I believe that behind this rich and grotesque image lies the same tension arising from the multiple and enigmatic sexuality of woman. The derision of the noblewomen relates to Sarah's sexuality. We read that "Sarah had ceased to experience the manner of women" (Gen. 18:11)—indicating her advanced age, well past her years of fertility. In addition, in the previous chapter, Sarah had spent an entire night with Abimelekh, king of Gerar (a fact which, in the eyes of society, calls the paternity of Isaac into question). The noblewomen serve as a mouthpiece for the profound—to my mind, fundamentally masculine—anxiety arising from the Sages' contemplation of sexual difference. The opaque multiplicity in the biblical verse—the multiplicity of children, of speakers, of scoffers—is "clarified," on a certain level, through an outpouring of milk, which, although meant for one single righteous infant, Isaac, nourishes many infants. These are "children" of sorts, since the miraculous revelation of the One God through Sarah's breasts will lead to their recognition of Him.

To my mind, the midrashic depiction of Sarah's mythical nursing expresses an ambivalence toward both miracles and feminine sexuality. The individual at the center of the miraculous occurrence—Sarah—is the object of derision and a fundamental lack of good faith on the part of her environment. The testimony of the miracle exposes the hidden desire to impose order on the woman's body, to regiment it, to understand it—since the very definition of a certain event as a miracle, as something that disturbs the natural order, proceeds from the assumption that the order is known. But is the "natural" order of nursing truly understood? Does it have defined rules? Clear boundaries? Is an abundance of milk really a "stronger" proof of childbirth? Or does the very fact that we declare something a "miracle" demonstrate that we establish a fictitious order that we then declare to be the "order of Creation"?

The structuring of the female body and sexuality in this text should also be considered in light of the insights provided by Mikhail Bakhtin in his description of the grotesquerie of the corporeal body as a victory of life over death. The overflowing breasts of the elderly woman are supposed to prove that "God has begun to perform miracles." In Bakhtin's description of the grotesque, special emphasis is given to the bodily orifices, which present the body as being open, fluid, and in contact with the outside world. Bakhtin discusses various systems comprising the bodily drama[21]—eating, drinking, elimination, perspiration, sneezing, intercourse—and to these we might add lactation as another activity that is carried out on the boundary between the body and the world outside of it. The ambiguity inherent in the connection between fertility and old age, the beginning of life and its conclusion, order and disorder, is conveyed in particularly condensed form in the story of Sarah's breasts. It is the breasts, the plural organs of woman, which create the connection between the One (God) and the many (His many potential followers); it is they that create a new socioreligious order.

It is clear that the story both shapes and reflects a male consciousness. Attention should be paid to the fact that while the biblical Sarah is a speaking subject, in the midrash she becomes an object. The sexual aspect of her breasts, signified by the concept of modesty,[22] is set aside in favor of the interest that drives the story—the familiar masculine interest in proving paternity. Mary O'Brien argues that the patriarchal establishment, in all its forms—society, law, culture—was established as a response to men's experience of uncertainty as to their paternal status.[23] This is not a feminine need, since motherhood is anchored in a woman's body in a way that makes it exceedingly difficult to deny or conceal. Sarah, after nine months of pregnancy and then childbirth, hardly needs to prove anything. The matter of publicizing the miracle, then, arises from the need for evidence, for proof that comes to *demonstrate* the facts, such that afterwards there will no longer be any room for denial. The breast, the visible organ that is part the economy of the male gaze, serves here as the basis of knowledge, of that which will be known from this point onward as fact. Clearly, Abraham proves nothing with regard to his paternity by means of Sarah's nursing, but the puzzling mechanism of the midrash makes sense when understood as arising from the depths of a male consciousness projected onto God.[24] In other words, Abraham's paternity of Isaac is not thereby proven, but God's symbolic "paternity" concerning His "children" certainly is.[25]

Thus the story creates a parallel between the exposure of Sarah's body and the revelation of the miracle, such that the publicizing of the miracle entails the exposure of the body in public. As Levinson notes, the woman's body is the cultural focus for the dramatization of ideological anxieties concerning ethnic identity. The breasts of the matriarch of the Jewish people are the porous membrane that mediates the absorption of those who accept her righteousness and God's miracles. She brings forth milk from her body in order to bring "everyone in the world" into the Hebrew social body.[26]

The Exodus from Egypt and everything related to it represents especially fertile ground for the appearance of miracles. This is another central context in which breasts appear—sometimes naturally, as a matter of course; other times, less so. Below are two midrashic scenes describing miracles wrought by God to nourish the nation of Israel. Both are bound up with the experience of abandonment, which is closely bound up with national birth. The servitude in Egypt and the harsh decrees imposed on Israel are described by the Sages as an experience of a profound abandonment in which the mother—both real and symbolic—is set aside while the function of substitute nourisher is filled by God or His emissaries. The first story describes a concrete situation in which, following Pharaoh's decree, the Israelite children are abandoned in the Nile. The second story depicts a symbolic drama representing God's redemption of Israel after they are abandoned in the field.

At that time the Holy One, blessed be He, said to the ministering angels: Go down from before Me and see the children of My beloved Abraham, Isaac, and Jacob, who are being cast into the river. So they hurried down from before Him, and they stood in the water up to their knees, and they took up the sons of Israel, and laid them upon the rocks, and the Holy One, blessed be He, *brought forth breasts for them* from the rocks, and nursed them, fulfilling that which is written: "And He caused them to suckle honey from the rock" (Deut. 32:13).

—Yalkut Shimoni, parshat Vaera, 182

R. Akiba expounded: As the reward for the righteous women who lived in that generation, the Israelites were delivered from Egypt. When they went to draw water, the Holy One, blessed be He, brought small fishes into their pitchers, which they drew up half full of water and half full of fishes. They would then set two pots on the fire, one for hot water and the other for the fish, and they would carry them to their husbands in the field, and they would wash them, anoint them, feed them, and give them drink, and then they would have relations with them among the sheepfolds, as it is written: "When you lie among the sheepfolds..." (Psalms 68:14). As the reward for "lying among the sheepfolds," the Israelites merited the spoils of Egypt, as it is written: "As the wings of a dove covered with silver, and her pinions with yellow gold" (ibid.). After the women had conceived, they returned to their homes; and when the time for childbirth arrived, they went [and gave birth] in the field beneath the apple tree, as it is said, "Under the apple tree I caused you to come forth..." (Song of Songs 8:5). God sent an angel from the high heavens who washed and straightened the limbs [of the babies] in the manner that a midwife [straightens the limbs of a child]; as it is said: "And as for your nativity, in the day that you were born your navel was not cut, neither were you washed in water to cleanse you" (Ezekiel 16:4). *He also provided for them two round [stones],* one for oil and one for honey, as it is said: "And He caused them to suckle honey from the rock, and oil from a flinty rock" (Deuteronomy 32:13). When the Egyptians noticed them, they came to kill them; but [a miracle occurred on their behalf so that] they were swallowed up in furrows in the ground, and [the Egyptians] brought oxen and plowed over them, as it is written, "The plowers plowed upon my back..." (Psalms 129:3). After they had departed, [the Israelite babies] broke through [the earth] and came forth like the herbage of the field. And when [the babies] had grown up, they came in flocks to their homes, as it is written, "And you increased and grew great and came with ornaments" (Ez. 16:7). And when God revealed Himself at the [Reed] Sea, it was these [children] who recognized Him first, as it is written: "This is my God and I will praise Him" (Exodus 15:2).

—Babylonian Talmud, Sotah 11b (according to MS Munich 95)

In her discussion of the biblical metaphor of national suckling, Ilana Pardes argues that the national experience of leaving Egypt is analogous to the painful process of weaning as experienced by a young child, when the bountiful breast of the nursing mother is withheld.[27] It is this experience of the disappearance of the breast that would seem to inspire these sources. In both instances, the biblical verse, "He caused them to ride upon the high places of the earth, and they ate the produce of the fields, and He caused them to suckle honey from the rock and oil from a flinty rock" (Deut. 32:13), is interpreted as a reference to God's miraculous nursing of the people.

From Freud onwards, psychoanalysis has maintained that the infant's first instinct is feeding, and for this reason the oral stage is the first step in his development. This drive involves sucking or swallowing, and its proper object is the breast. Freud understood, in a way that none of his predecessors had,[28] the psychological attraction to the breast that lasts throughout life. This insight explains something of the molding of God's image as a "nurser" in the rabbinic tradition. The complication of the drama by presenting God in the role of nurser, offering a Divine image that is also the ultimate mother whose milk—whether produced by stones in the midst of the river of death or offered in the field, via alternative breasts—responds to the fundamental human need for and anxiety about food.

The Sages therefore expose a suppressed metaphor incorporated in the biblical text in expressing their wish for closeness to God. In their retelling of the drama of the nation's birth, they are not content with the evidence of God's involvement and concern as manifest through the phenomenon of infants suckling at the breasts of real women—as in the midrashim about Sarah. They go a step further, molding God Himself with a feminine aspect, as nursing from breasts[29]—a graphic illustration of the name *El Sha-dai*.

This description of the image of God raises the thorny theological problem of anthropomorphism. The inclination of most scholars in previous generations, as well as many in the present, has been to deny outright any hint of a depiction of the Divine in rabbinic literature as possessing human traits. Ironically, twelfth-century Maimonidean radicalism has become orthodoxy—in both senses—in modern Jewish studies. This perception fails to address the strongly anthropomorphic expressions in midrashic literature; indeed, some contemporary voices argue that "the perception of the Divine in human form is a foundation stone in the world of the Sages—or, at least, among major groups in that world."[30]

The sources above would seem to suggest a vision of God as possessing a form that is not only human, but also androgynous, corresponding to the creature created in God's likeness: "Male and female He created them, and He called them 'Man'" (Gen. 5:2).[31] The perception of Divine bisexuality is a common religious phenomenon: even the most manifestly masculine gods and the most obviously feminine goddesses are androgynous. The true meaning of this theological formula is the realization of *coincidentia oppositorum;* as Mircea Eliade explains it—the unification of the cosmological principles (male and female) in the bosom of the Divine.[32]

The act of nursing is imbued here with exceedingly positive meaning. What is most notable in these legends is the appropriation of the woman's breasts by the male rescuers of the nation.[33] In the first source, the children of Israel are traced back to their ancestors, God's beloved, and this picture creates a masculine continuity of God-angels-fathers-sons who suckle and nurse in an altogether miraculous manner from the rocks in the Nile,[34] with a complete dispossession of the feminine figures in the story.

The second legend is more interesting from a gender perspective, and creates a different continuum, in which the women initiate the miraculous drama.[35] The rabbinic dictum, "They, too, were part of the miracle," is exposed, in the light of this midrash, as a sort of understatement.[36] God, who cooperates with the righteous women whose actions are wholly oriented toward fertility and the survival and continuity of the nation, is a God with a feminine aspect: He carries out many maternal actions of caring for the infant; He provides "breasts" (in the plural) for His children from the rocks; He feeds them different types of foods (honey as well as oil); and for all of these good reasons, His tens of thousands of children, who cross through the sea in droves, identify Him on that day as having given them life. Everything that a mother does, He does better; it is therefore no wonder that when the time comes, God's children identify and proclaim His uniqueness and oneness: "This is my God and I shall praise Him." These two midrashic sources present the immanent connection between physical dependence and religious loyalty. The commitment of the multitude of children to the One Source arises from the fact that He gave them life in a situation where their survival was greatly endangered.

On the subject of miracles, rabbinic sources also include stories of men who nursed in special situations. For instance, there is "the story of a man whose wife passed away, leaving a son who needed to be nursed. The man lacked the means to pay a wet nurse, but a miracle occurred and his breasts opened, like the two breasts of a woman, and he nursed his son." There is also the instance of Mordecai, who nursed Esther: "R. Judan said: At one time Mordecai went around among all the nursing women, but just then he could not find one for [the infant] Esther. So he himself gave her suck."[37] Admittedly, it is recorded that when one Sage taught this midrash his colleagues began to laugh, but he responded in all seriousness, citing the Mishna in tractate Makhshirin, which states that "the milk of a male is ritually permissible" as proof of the possibility of such a situation.[38] If the Sages could imagine a man possessing breasts and nursing, then it is not so strange that they could have imagined God in a similar way.

However, this transition from the mother to God is not a simple matter. As we shall see in the next source, the appropriation of the woman's breasts, the conviction that the One is preferable to the many, and that the proper order is a hierarchy with the One, Divine, male at the top, is not self-evident. There are sources that reveal the huge cultural effort necessary for the structuring of this consciousness.

Our Rabbis taught: R. Jose the Galilean expounded: At the time when the Israelites ascended from the Red Sea, they desired to utter song; and how did they render song? The infant lay upon his mother's knees and the suckling *sucked at his mother's breast;* when they beheld the Divine Presence, the infant raised his neck and *the suckling released the nipple [from his mouth]*, and they exclaimed:"This is my God and I will Praise Him" (Ex. 15:2), as it is said: "Out of the mouths of infants and sucklings You have established strength" (Psalms 8:3).

—Babylonian Talmud, Sotah 30b
(according to MS Munich 95)

This teaching, offering a close-up shot of the breast, gives a precise rendering of the situation in which the Israelites recognized God at the splitting of the Reed Sea. The image reveals the latent competition between God and mother.[39] In contrast to the more ancient tradition of R. Jose in the Mekhilta,[40] this teaching sharpens the contrast between the competing elements. The breast, the source of food and bodily warmth, is released in favor of song and praise to God. The multiplicity of elements influencing and molding a person's identity throughout his life is funneled, in this midrash, toward God, who is preferred over and above any other figure.

The reading of this midrash may be enhanced by reference to a theory developed by Julia Kristeva, who identifies two identity-forming systems. The first is the semiotic system, representing the pre-Oedipal stage of connection with the mother—a connection marked by undifferentiated and concrete identities. The semiotic is characterized by the harmony of a free flow of emotions and unmediated closeness between mother and child, a closeness that precedes the inevitable severing. The second is the symbolic system, at the center of which stands the logos—logical and clear expression. It is this that molds the individual identity and allows human beings the possibility of social communication. The response to the miracle of the splitting of the sea in the form of song is, therefore, the entry into the symbolic order represented by the father: an entry into the world of words and culture, leaving the mother's breast behind.

R. Jose the Galilean teaches that the Song of the Sea was uttered even by infants who were not yet verbal. The song is molded here as a ceremony of transition, as the moment of entry into culture, entailing the turning of the gaze from the breast to the heavens. It marks a shift from the primal situation, characterized by physical merging with the mother, to enter into a community of believers who turn to God in speech. The infant singing verses of praise is a sort of "child wonder" who illustrates the transition from "nature" to "culture," from the "mother's order" to the "father's order." The miraculous nature of the splitting of the sea is amplified, of course, by the fact that even suckling infants are aware of their Creator and know where their primary loyalty lies.[41]

Once again, however, attention should be paid to the "production" that is required of God in order for the infants to release the mother's breast. This turning away demands nothing less than the splitting of the Reed Sea—a fact that testifies to the natural primary bond. I propose that the anxiety underlying this scene is articulated in the words, "Perhaps, heaven forefend, there are two ultimate authorities" (Hagiga 15a). The midrash reveals the battle lines extending throughout a culture that suppressed the place of the mother. It reveals the overturning of the natural order, and molds a staged scene (this is perhaps the other significance of the miracle) in which infants exhibit perspective,[42] identifying and recognizing the persona responsible for saving and preserving their lives. The metaphorical language of the verse, "Out of the mouths of infants and sucklings You have established strength," is realized and evoked here in a narrative context.[43] God's power, established through the song of His children who release their mother's breast from their mouths, is a gender victory no less than an ethnic one.

In his book *Moses and Monotheism,* Freud assumed that there had, indeed, been some point in human history when a change in social structures took place.

> Under the influence of external conditions—which we need not follow up here and which in part are also not sufficiently known—it happened that the matriarchal structure of society was replaced by a patriarchal one. This naturally brought with it a revolution in the existing state of the law. An echo of this revolution can still be heard, I think, in the Oresteia of Aeschylus. This turning from the

mother to the father, however, signifies above all a victory of spirituality over the senses, that is to say a step forward in culture, since maternity is proved by the senses whereas paternity is a surmise based on a deduction and a premise. This declaration in favor of the thought process, thereby raising it above sense perception, was proved to be a step charged with serious consequences.[44]

Freud, as we see here, confirms and reestablishes the dichotomous hierarchy that identifies motherhood with sensuality, concreteness, physicality, cultural inferiority, and the like, and fatherhood with spirituality, abstractness, logic, cultural advancement, and so on.

The interpretations of the verse, "This is my God and I shall praise Him" (Ex. 15:2) in the story of the righteous women, as well as in the words of R. Jose the Galilean concerning the Song at the Sea, are, to my mind, residual images of the stage of exchange of the mother for the father. I propose that the breast, the organ that provides the infant with his needs during the first period of his existence in the world, be viewed as a metonym for an entire world of connection, which a culture that turned away from woman and her body has relegated to the margins. A reading that discerns that which existed before it was lost may shed light on a system of costs and compensations that Jewish society has carried on its back from antiquity until the present time.

The distinction between motherhood and feminine sexuality, with the various attempts to either unify or separate them, is one of the major topics in feminist theory. As we have seen in the sources cited above, the Sages treated the breast mainly in the maternal context. Ignoring its simultaneous role in women's sexuality is a typically patriarchal strategy. Anat Palgi-Hacker, who studies the absence of the mother as a subject in psychoanalytical theories, describes the breast as an organ that, for women, is a central erotogenic zone in sexual interaction and one that also serves the function of providing nutrition for the infant. The same contact with the nipple is involved both in the sexual act, the fantasies accompanying it, and the pleasure derived from it, and—on other occasions—in feeding a baby. But Hacker questions whether these situations are indeed distinct from one another. A nursing mother is faced, perhaps for the first time in her life, with an inescapable conflict; she comes face-to-face with the taboo of incest. Maternal feelings of giving, nurturing, concern, and the like mingle with the erotic pleasure produced by nursing. The nursing zone—the point of complex interaction between one body and another, one psyche and another, and one erotogenic zone and another—highlights the question of where the psychological and social need arises to separate motherhood from sexuality. The need for this separation, in Hacker's view, arises from the desire to create an image of pure maternal love that consists of infinite giving. The ideal mother is defined as giving to others and nourishing them. In the context of this aspiration, the mother has no sexual desire, nor could she possibly have any, since this would mar the perfection of her existence solely for the sake of others.[45]

A reading of the sources dealing with the links between breasts and miracles responds to the challenge of viewing rabbinic texts as "[necessarily failed] attempts to provide utopian solutions to cultural tensions."[46] The breasts, as described here, are organs that represent, in a covert way, feminine sexuality as viewed from the perspective of the Sages. A discussion of the broader gender aspects of the concept of modesty lies beyond the scope of our present study, but the concept itself pertains to feminine sexuality and the requirement that a woman's body be covered and concealed in the public domain. The modesty that is mentioned explicitly in the midrash in relation to Sarah reveals an inkling of the perception of breasts as a sex organ.[47] Feminine sexuality is viewed as different, separate, other: since it is based on multiplicity, it possesses power and is therefore threatening and competitive. The various attempts to regiment it, to reduce it to the sphere of fertility, and to render it subservient to the order of the One all illuminate the dynamics of its structuring. However, the complexity of the text also contains alternative possibilities, even if they are denied or suppressed. These are exposed through a reading with a gender interest.

BREASTS OF GOOD AND EVIL

An understanding of the breasts as an organ symbolizing a sexuality that is "other," multiple, and disordering, requires us to address further distinctions, no less fascinating, in the Sages' attitude toward this organ. I refer here to the two-faced dimension of the breasts—the good and the evil.

The breast was described by Freud as a sort of model of the Garden of Eden: once we were all satisfied. Then we were separated and removed from the maternal breast, and ever since we are doomed to wander in a breastless desolation. As adults we seek in vain the comfort of the original breasts, finding it occasionally but fleetingly in the sexual union that Freud views as a sort of substitute for that primal pleasure.[48]

The myth that Freud wove around human sexuality draws its power from the Creation narrative and maintains an intriguing relationship with it. We recall that at the very heart of the Garden of Eden stood the Tree of Knowledge of good and evil, of which Adam and Eve were forbidden to partake. Accordingly, the first human sin is eating of its fruit, "and the Tree of Knowledge of good and evil" (Gen. 2:9). The phrase *good and evil* is a merismus—that is, the two opposite poles also include everything in between. Someone who "knows good and evil" is someone who knows everything, like God[49]—as God Himself testifies in stating His reason for expelling man from Eden: "Behold, the man has become like one of us, knowing good and evil" (Gen. 3:22).[50] The younger generation in the wilderness, who will eventually reach the Promised Land, are likewise referred to in their innocence as having "no knowledge of good and evil": "And your children, concerning whom you said, 'They will be a prey,' and your children, who that day had no knowledge of good and evil—they will go into there" (Deut. 1:39).[51]

A reading of the Garden of Eden story as a psychological, developmental myth identifies the original sin as one related to eating—that is, that which is identified in psychoanalysis as the human being's earliest urge—the oral stage. In Britain, where Freud spent the final years of his life, his work was continued by Melanie Klein, a pioneer of object relations theory, which expanded the Freudian view of the first relationship object—that is, the maternal breast. To her view, this object remains permanently in a person's subconscious, like a kaleidoscope picture that is able to assume unlimited forms. Klein's theory will help us to understand the fundamental ambivalence in the Sages' attitude toward this feminine organ.

In rabbinic literature there is an interesting thematic cluster comprising knowledge, wisdom, Torah, and consciousness, which is based on distinctions and contrasts. A midrash describing the symbolic nursing of Moses illuminates the importance that the Sages attached to the breast and to nursing. In contrast to regular babies, who will usually suck at any breast offered to them, Moses turns out to be a fussy baby with clear preferences.

> "And his sister said to Pharaoh's daughter . . ." (Ex. 2:7)—why does Miriam specify "of the Hebrew women"? Was it then forbidden for Moses to imbibe the milk of non-Jewish women? But this is not what we have been taught: a daughter of Israel shall not nurse the child of a Cuthite, but a Cuthite woman may nurse a Jewish child in her possession. So why did Miriam say this? Because she took Moses around to all the Egyptian women, to nurse him, but he rejected all of them. And why did he reject them? The Holy One, blessed be He, said, "Shall the mouth that is destined to speak with Me then imbibe something that is impure?" This is the meaning of the verse, "To whom shall one teach knowledge? And who shall one cause to understand doctrine?" (Isaiah 28:9). "To whom shall one teach knowledge"—"To those who are weaned from milk . . ." (ibid.). An alternative explanation: Why did he reject their breasts? The Holy One, blessed be He, said: "This [individual] is destined to speak with Me; in the future, the Egyptian women will say, 'The one who now speaks with the Divine Presence was nursed by me.'"
>
> —Exodus Rabba 1 (Shinan edition p. 80)

The assumption underlying the midrash is that the milk imbibed by a baby has a decisive influence on the rest of his life.[52] Let us consider the special way in which the midrash molds the relationship between the "quality" of the milk and the suckling infant—who, in this instance, is the future leader of the nation. The exegetical question here is why Miriam specifies, in her offer to Pharaoh's daughter, that she will seek a wet nurse "from the Hebrew women." It is clear from the answer that the intention of the midrash is to use this verse in order to teach a moral lesson about Moses and about the woman who will nurse him. The midrash suggests that Miriam makes her suggestion following unsuccessful attempts to find a wet nurse for him among "all the Egyptian women" (obviously an exaggeration). Despite his young age, Moses knows what is not appropriate for him.[53] The midrash seems to be addressing the assumption, widely accepted in the ancient world, that the profile of the nursing mother is of great importance in relation to the milk that her body produces—and, consequently, on its effect on the baby.[54]

This midrash is interesting in that it cites a halakha in the midst of the hermeneutical teaching.[55] We discover that the specification that the wet nurse be "from the Hebrews" is not halakhically self-evident, since the Mishna (Avoda Zara 2, 1) states that it is permissible for a Jewish child to be nursed by a non-Jewish woman.[56] Why, then, does Moses reject the breasts of the non-Jewish women? To this the midrash provides two different answers:

1. The fact that Moses turns away from non-Jewish breasts and refuses to receive impure milk is an expression of the wisdom with which God has imbued him.

2. The reason for the rejection is God's concern that since Moses is destined to talk with God face-to-face in the future, the Egyptian women will pride themselves on having nursed him, and this will dishonor God.

These explanations highlight the idea that the milk imbibed by the leader of the nation has significance in relation to speaking with God. The first view states that Moses must have milk that is appropriate for him, not milk that is "impure." Attention should be paid to the fact that, despite the explicitly stated halakha, non-Jewish milk is relegated here to the category of "impurity."[57] *Impurity* is meant here in the ideological rather than ritual sense, and is based on a religio-national distinction.[58] Non-Jewish milk is not suitable for Moses because his mouth—the organ used for speech—must not come into contact with anything that is inappropriate from a religious point of view.

A different problem that might arise, were Moses to accept the non-Jewish milk, is that this future leader of the children of Israel, who is destined to speak with God, will be appropriated by a non-Jewish wet nurse—and this will damage the honor and status of God Himself. Here, too, it is speech that stands at the heart of the matter, and the mouth is depicted as an organ that both suckles and speaks. God maintains Moses' spiritual hygiene by guiding him not to suckle from the breasts of the Egyptian women.

In order to grasp the depths of the gender tension underlying this midrash, we must come back to Kristeva's important distinctions. In her study of the relationship between the subject and language, she addresses the reciprocal relations between meaning and language, between meaning and life, and between language and life, and describes a dialectical process that takes place between the semiotic and the symbolic. The *symbolic* is a term used by Jacques Lacan to describe the process of the entry by the individual into the world of language—a process that entails separation from the mother and an acceptance of the law of the father. According to Lacan, at the symbolic stage the subject undergoes a formative process that is made possible only through language. Kristeva, by contrast, argues that the prelanguage experience, which is maternal, does not cease to exist with the acquisition of language, but rather becomes part of the subconscious.[59]

It is possible that the Sages relate the verse, "[To] whom shall one teach knowledge, and whom shall one cause to understand doctrine? Those who are weaned from milk, and drawn from the breasts" (Isaiah 28:9), to Moses specifically because of the verses that follow: "For it is precept upon precept, precept upon precept, line upon line, line upon line, here a little and there a little. For with stammering lips and a different tongue shall one speak to this people" (Isaiah 28:10–11). This series of verses, which on the plain level refer to the prophecy of Isaiah himself, are also strongly suggestive of Moses and his stammering—both because of the repeated words, recalling a stammering style, and because of the explicit reference to "stammering lips." Either way, the verses suggest a relationship between the weaning of the infant from milk, in the sense of removing him from the breast, and speaking and language—the same relationship noted by Kristeva. The suckling Moses, depicted here as an idealized exception, is still at the preverbal stage, but nevertheless already possesses knowledge; that is, the ability to distinguish pure from impure, good from evil. His biography skips over the semiotic stage, as it were; he is presented as belonging, already at birth, to the defined order of the father, the symbolic order.[60]

It is difficult to read this midrash without recalling the testimony of the adult Moses: "And Moses said to God: 'O my Lord, I am not a man of words, neither yesterday nor the day before, nor since You have spoken to Your servant, for I am slow of speech and of a slow tongue" (Ex. 4:10). Moses's stuttering raises the question of whether perhaps beneath the "ideal" story described in the midrash, there lurks the explanation for his disability specifically in the realm of language. It is as though the midrash has unknowingly disclosed a certain understanding that skipping over the semiotic stage and the bond with that which is maternal, exacts a price specifically in the realm of speech and communicative fluency, signified by the mouth.[61]

What emerges from the above is the ambivalence with which the Sages relate to the feminine element. On one hand, the woman's breasts and her milk receive acknowledgment and respect, owing to their important influence on identity. This milk—the maternal influence—is the foundation of identity, and from this point of view it is important that Moses imbibe milk that is "suitable" in religious and national terms. On the other hand, the ideal infant is one who skips the semiotic stage that is bound up with the mother figure. From the outset, he is the iconic representative of Jewish civilization—that is, of the linguistic norms and phallocentric patterns that it has consolidated. This is an infant who has already eaten from the Tree of Knowledge.

Furthermore, it would seem that the Sages, who belong to an oppressed national minority, compensate for their ethno-political weakness by means of a story that turns national hierarchies upside down in an attempt to reoccupy a position of power and strength. As in many other instances, the inversion is accomplished at the expense of women.[62] The story of the *enfant savant* is therefore the story of a symbolic order that devours the semiotic. The exegetical act, the creation of the logos, dispossesses the feminine "other" not once, but twice: once in relation to the "otherness" of the non-Jewish women whose breasts are rejected, and again in relation to the feminine "otherness" that is signified by the semiotic itself.

Hélène Cixous and Catherine Clément criticize the dichotomous-hierarchical model of thinking and its centrality in Western thought. They point to the gender foundation underlying this model, which connects one pole—which is identified with insight, spirit, intellect, and activism, and which is attributed positive value—with "masculinity," while the other—identified with emotion, drives, desires, irrationality, and insanity—is connected with femininity. Their call for a breaching of the solidarity between logocentricity and phallocentricity reminds us that what will ultimately disturb and dismantle the work of the patriarchate is exposure of the structures underpinning it. These are the hierarchical, binary contrasts that weave myths, philosophical systems, and entire social theories.[63] The discussion of this midrash from a gender perspective exposes some of the most basic hierarchical contrasts that organize the culture of the Sages and structure their worldview.

THE GOOD BREAST, OR WHY THE WORDS OF TORAH ARE COMPARED TO A BREAST

The Garden of Eden story is an etiological legend by means of which the culture tells its members that the temptation to eat from the fruit of the tree, the quest for "knowledge of good and evil," distanced man from a different tree—the Tree of Life. Conversely, adherence to the sort of knowledge that is proper for man—that is, the Torah—will bring him life. The Book of Proverbs teaches, "Happy is the man who finds wisdom, and the man who achieves understanding. For its merchandise is better than commerce of silver, and its gain than fine gold . . . Length of days is in its right hand; in its left—riches and honor . . . It is a tree of life to those who grasp it, and happy are those who hold it fast" (Prov. 3:13–18). Similarly, "Wisdom" declares, "Whoever finds me, finds life, and achieves favor of the Lord" (Prov. 8:35).

The Sages, the elite members of a society in which wisdom and Torah scholarship were the most prized assets, molded a strong connection between these central expressions of the symbolic order and the woman in general,[64] and the breasts as a source of spiritual nourishment in particular. This connection is part of the unresolved tension in rabbinic culture between home life, family, and the marital relationship, on one hand, and devotion to a life of Torah study,[65] on the other. In other words, the analogy between Torah and the breast is an expression of something that is fundamentally in strong competition.[66]

> "Let her [wisdom's] breasts satisfy you at all times" (Prov. 5:19)—Why are the words of Torah compared to a breast? To teach that just as in the case of the breast, so long as the infant sucks—he finds milk, so it is with the words of Torah: so long as a person studies them, he finds meaning.
>
> —Babylonian Talmud, Erubin 54b
> (according to MS Vatican 109)

The words of the Torah are compared to a breast, according to this midrash, in the sense of a similarity between the accessibility of the breast as a source of food for the infant, and the accessibility of Torah as a source of spiritual nourishment for its scholars. The Torah is a vital, existential need for those who study it, just as the breast is vital for the infant. The parallel gives rise to a certain interdependence between the vessel and its users: as long as the infant suckles at the breast, he finds milk. If he stops suckling and ceases to demand nourishment, the breast will dry up, and can no longer serve as a source of food. The same applies to the Torah: in order for a person to find meaning in it, he must involve himself in it on a regular basis. Perhaps, then, this midrash actually suggests a more radical message: that the meaning of the Torah is not given "in and of itself"; rather, it is the act of studying and explaining it—the actual interaction between the scholar and the text—that vitalizes it.

> "He caused them to suckle honey from the rock" (Deut. 32:13)—this refers to the Mishna; "and oil from a flinty rock"—this refers to the Talmud; "the butter of cattle and the milk of sheep, with fat of lambs and rams . . ." (ibid. 14)—these are the hermeneutical laws and the responsa, "with the fat of kidneys of wheat" (ibid.)—these are the laws that are the substance of Torah; "And you drank wine of the pure blood of the grape"—these are the narratives that draw a person's heart like wine.
>
> —Sifri, Deuteronomy 317

The verse that is interpreted elsewhere as a metaphorical description of God's wondrous feeding of His people is understood here as a metaphor for the Torah itself. The Torah in its entirety—legal and narrative units alike—is the spiritual nourishment that God provides for His people, and it is this that gives them life.

The allegorical, exegetical approach to the Song of Songs, which views the "Beloved" as God and the "maiden" as the Torah, finds expression in several places in talmudic literature.[67] The verses in the Song of Songs that refer to the woman's breasts are understood as pairings in the context of Torah and its institutions: the spiritual leaders—Moses and Aaron, the scholars and the bearers of the Torah; the synagogues and study halls—the space in which Torah is studied; and the physical appearance of the Tablets of the Covenant—the essence and symbol of the Torah given to Moses at Sinai.[68]

> "I am a wall and my breasts are like towers" (Song of Songs 8:10)— R. Johanan said: "I am a wall"—this is the Torah; "and my breasts are like towers"—these are the Sages. Raba taught: "I am a wall"— this is the entirety of the Jewish people; "and my breasts are like towers"—these are the synagogues and study halls.
>
> —Babylonian Talmud, Pesahim 87a (MS New York אנלאו 271 [Yemenite])

"I am a wall, and my breasts are like towers"—in the text these words are uttered by the maiden in an attempt to relieve the concerns of her brothers, who fear for her innocence. In an exchange that sounds like a parody of the Freudian description of penis envy, the woman assures her brothers that, contrary to their claims, she lacks nothing; on the contrary, she has two breasts as strong and impressive as towers, and she is therefore able to protect her own body with no outside help.[69] Two of the greatest among the Sages interpret this verse in a manner that can be understood, in a political, polemical context as a counterargument to the activist views arguing that the Jewish people must defend itself with the help of military means and institutions. R. Johanan reads the verse as a reference to the Torah and its bearers—the Sages. The wall has a defensive, protective function, and it also divides between spaces (defining who is inside and who is outside) and creates boundaries. Similarly, the Torah protects Israel. The towers that look out over the wall—the breasts, in the imagery of the verse—refer to those who engage in Torah, studying and teaching it.

Raba offers a different reading. The broader allegorical rabbinic reading views the maiden as symbolizing the Jewish people. Raba therefore understands the image of the wall as alluding to the Jewish people as a unified force; a community that is as consolidated and firm as a wall. According to this reading, then, who are the "breasts like towers," whose role is to watch over the wall? Raba singles out two institutions, equal in number to the breasts, which protect the nation and its strength: the synagogues and the study halls. These are the central institutions of worship and of religio-spiritual activity, according to the Pharisee world-view, and the Torah stands at their center.[70]

The next interesting source evokes the ideal of an egalitarian duality in religious leadership.

> "Your two breasts are like two fauns, twins of a gazelle" (Song 4:5)—these are Moses and Aaron, for just as the breasts are the glory and splendor of a woman, so Moses and Aaron are the glory and splendor of Israel. Just as breasts represent the beauty of a woman, so Moses and Aaron represent the beauty of Israel. Just as the breasts are the honor and praise of a woman, so Moses and Aaron are the honor and praise of Israel. Just as the breasts are full of milk, so Moses and Aaron satiate Israel with the Torah. And just as, in the case of the breasts, whatever the mother eats is imbibed by the infant, so the Torah that Moses learned he taught to Aaron, as it is written, "And Moses told to Aaron all of God's words" (Ex. 4:28), and our rabbis taught: He revealed to him God's holy Name. Just as the breasts are equal in size, neither being greater than the other, so it was with Moses and Aaron, as it is written, "These were the same Moses and Aaron . . ." (Ex. 6:27), and it is written, "These were the same Aaron and Moses" (Ex. 6:26): Moses was not greater than Aaron, nor was Aaron greater than Moses, in Torah. R. Abba said: This may be likened to a king who had two pearls. He placed them on a scale, and neither was heavier than the other. Likewise Moses and Aaron were equals. R. Hanina bar Papa said: Blessed is God Who chose these two brothers, who were created solely for the purpose of the Torah and for the glory of Israel. R. Joshua of Sakhnin said in the name of R. Levi: There were two families

of priests in Alexandria; one induced cold and the other heat [in the healing process]. It once happened that the physicians sent for [their wares], and made a *theriaca* [remedy] from them, which they used for healing. Raba said in the name of R. Simeon: A human [physician] does not apply a dressing before he sees the wound, but not so He by Whose word the world came into existence. He first creates the dressing, and only afterwards inflicts the wound, as it is written, "Behold, I will bring it healing and cure . . ." (Jer. 33:6), and it is also written, "When I was to heal Israel" (Hosea 7:1). The Holy One, blessed be He, says: "I came to heal the transgressions of Israel, and [only then] the transgression of Efraim and the wickedness of the Shomron was revealed." But when it comes to the nations of the world, He first strikes at them and only afterwards heals them, as it is written, "And the Lord will smite Egypt; He will smite and heal" (Isaiah 19:22). "He will smite"—through Aaron; "and heal"— through Moses. Happy are these two brothers, who were created for the glory of Israel, and this is as Samuel the prophet says, "The Lord, who made Moses and Aaron" (I Sam. 12:6). Thus, "your two breasts" (Song of Songs 4:5) are Moses and Aaron.

—Song of Songs Rabba, parsha 4

The aim of this interpretation is to consolidate the status of Moses and Aaron as the leaders of the nation and teachers of Torah, and it does so by comparing them to breasts,[71] thereby praising them and associating them with beauty and life. The midrash goes to great pains to emphasize that "just as" in the case of the female paired organ, there is no difference between Moses and Aaron in terms of greatness or importance. This in itself is quite surprising, considering that a discussion of the symmetry—or, more accurately, the discovery of asymmetry—in the actual appearance of breasts is to be found in various halakhic contexts dealing with the development of the signs of feminine puberty.[72] Symmetry expresses order, because it unifies multiplicity within a system. The Sages who observe women's breasts and find many instances of asymmetry, describe a bodily reality that does not conform to the inner wish of the rational observer— to find the natural law that is built on the idea of repetition. In halakhic discourse regarding the symmetry or asymmetry of breasts, what stands out is the need to find unity in multiplicity. Asymmetry mars what is perceived as the traditional formula for beauty: an expression of order.[73]

In response to the quest for order, the midrash molds Moses and Aaron as twins—like the image of the breasts in Song of Songs. This image recalls many myths and legends in which the founding fathers of a city or nation are twins. The importance of twins in different mythologies pertains not only to the birth of human twins, but also to their symbolic essence. They symbolize the most primal form of twinning, one that begins in the womb, and reflect the human yearning for the merging and unification that develop out of equality and understanding. In the study of religions, twins enjoy a place of honor, and this phenomenon—which became a popular subject for study during the 1920s and '30s—is known by the general title of "dioscurism."[74]

It would seem that the midrashic molding of Moses and Aaron as matching, identical breasts, neither greater than the other, responds to one of the central Roman images of twinning,[75] a fundamentally positive image that is related to fertility, material abundance, and harmony. Unlike a different perception of twinning that finds expression in the biblical ethos of twins as opposite entities that are engaged in battle, as well as in the Roman myth of Remus and Romulus, Moses and Aaron stand as a model of the ideal of social concord or *entente,* which played a central role in Roman sociopolitical imagery. During the period of the Republic, this concept represented the commitment of all elements of the country to conduct themselves in harmony and agreement, with an avoidance of discord. The leaders of the generation of the wilderness are, according to the midrash, twins who complement each other, with one striking and the other healing—an image that conveys a wish for multiplicity that is based on harmony and completion.

It is interesting that in Roman mythology, Concordia was the goddess of agreement, understanding, and harmony in marriage (the equivalent of the Greek goddess Harmonia). In other words, the Roman political concept is fundamentally bound up with marriage and with intergender cooperation. One might say that, in a certain sense, Aaron and Moses are molded here as the model of an ideal egalitarian, nonhierarchical relationship.

The midrash maintains a dialogue with the biblical verses in which

Moses describes himself as a mother: "Did I conceive this people? Did I bear them, that You should say to me, Carry them in your bosom as a nurse carries the suckling child, to the land that You have sworn to their forefathers?" (Num. 11:12). The midrash offers a contrasting view of the two brothers jointly as representing a sort of mother with nourishing breasts. Two brothers fulfill the maternal role in nourishing the nation. The milk that they provide is, of course, the Torah, in the same way that the mother's body produces vital food.

> For this reason the Ten Commandments were given, five on one Tablet and five on the other—according to R. Hanina ben Gamliel. But the Sages say [they were given] all ten on each Tablet, as it is written, "These words the Lord spoke to your entire assembly at the mountain, from amidst the fire, the cloud and the thick darkness, with a great voice that was not heard again. And He wrote them on two tablets of stone ..." (Deut. 5:19), and it is written, "Your two breasts like two fauns, twins of a gazelle" (Song of Songs 4:5), and it is written, "His hands are like rods of gold set with emeralds" (ibid. 5:14).
>
> —Mekhilta de-Rabbi Yishmael, Massekhta di-be-hodesh, Yitro 8 (Lauterbach edition, p. 264)

The Torah is God's word; it is the language of God's revelation to His people. The Ten Commandments that are engraved on the Tablets are a symbol of this speech. The midrash describes the material aspect of the Tablets—and the view depicting all ten Commandments on each identical Tablet—by means of the image of breasts that are equal in size and form; they are twins.

In its fundamental opposition to the corporealization of God's image, the biblical text notes the fact that the Revelation was not a visual experience but rather an auditory one: "God spoke all these *words,* saying" (Ex. 20:1); "You saw no form, only a *voice*" (Deut. 4:12).[76] How, then, are we to understand the intention of the midrash in creating such a consistent connection between the Torah, as an abstract covenant of language, and the breasts—the feminine organ with such a prominent, tangible, material presence? It would seem that the Sages, in seeking to diminish the conflict between bodily and spiritual needs—the need to devote one's life to Torah as opposed to the partaking of the life of this world—use the midrashim to structure a bodily, material, feminine perception of the Torah. The masculine abstraction of God and of the covenant with Him is balanced by a view of the Torah as a feminine, bodily entity. Clearly, the identification of the feminine with the corporeal here is based on a strongly internalized system of patriarchal identity of the woman with the "body" and with "nature."[77]

The Torah is perceived, in all the sources cited thus far, as a metaphorical gushing breast; a good breast that provides the vital requirements of its children. It is an object that provides beauty, life, and healing, and assumes diverse forms: "Delve into it, and delve into it, for all is included in it" (Avot 5:22).

THE BAD BREAST

The value duality that arises from the discussion in the midrash of Moses and his refusal to imbibe the milk of the Egyptian women recalls Melanie Klein's contrast between the "good breast" and the "bad breast." Focusing her research on the first years of an infant's life, she concluded that the fact that the mother is the infant's first "object" has very complex psychological ramifications. Her theory comprises both the concrete maternal body, with all its parts, and the rich world of phantasy of the infant. Phantasies of the breast, originating in the first months of life, become part of a person's subconscious, influencing all later psychological processes. Mother's milk, which at first quiets the infant's pangs of hunger, is offered from the breast that he learns to love more and more. The breast acquires an emotional value that is difficult to overstate. The breast and its product, which satisfy first his survival instinct as well as his libido, now represent for him love, pleasure, and security. But not all is rosy. Some element of frustration will necessarily develop in the early attitude of the infant toward the breast, since even a successful and happy nursing situation cannot be a perfect substitute for the unity with the mother experienced in utero. In addition, the infant's yearning for an inexhaustible, ever-present breast arises not only from his craving for food and his libidinous desires; even at the earliest stages the drive to receive constant evidence of the mother's love grows, fundamentally, from anxiety. The struggle between the life instincts and the death drive, and the resulting danger of both the self and the object being terminated by destructive drives, are decisive factors in the primal relationship of the infant toward his mother.[78]

The "I" engages in nascent activities that arise from the vital need to deal with the struggle between the drive for life and the death drive. Inter alia, it tends to "split" itself, as well as its object, because this splitting protects him from his primal anxiety and represents a means for preserving the self.[79] The death drive is the earliest source of the infant's anxiety, which is directed to the first outside object—the breast. Hence the "bad breast." On the other hand, the breast that provides and satisfies, and is connected to the drive for life, becomes the "good breast."[80]

In the midrashim that identify the Torah with the breasts we encounter several texts that express the "good" aspect of this first object, the "giving" side that provides what the infant needs. However, this is only one aspect of the image of the nourishing God. No less worthy of our consideration are other texts, which depict God providing in a way that limits or frustrates the beneficiaries of His largesse.

The midrash describing the striking of the rock by Moses in the Book of Numbers, illuminates the complexity of the metaphorical nursing scene, testifying—quite by accident—to the problem of metaphorizing nursing as a means of appropriating the breasts and their power by a masculine religious community.

> "And the Lord spoke to Moses, saying: Take the staff, and gather the congregation—you and Aaron, your brother—and speak to the rock before their eyes, and it shall give its water. And you shall bring forth water for them from the rock, and you shall give the congregation *and their cattle* to drink" (Num. 20:7–8)—this shows that the Holy One, blessed be He, has consideration for the property of Israel. (emphasis mine)
>
> "And Moses and Aaron gathered the company facing the rock" (Num. 20:10)—this shows that each and every one viewed himself as standing before the rock; in a similar way it is written, "And gather all the congregation, at the entrance of the Tent of Meeting" (Lev. 8:3). Likewise, when they crossed over the Jordan, all of Israel

passed between the two poles of the Ark, as it is written, "And Joshua said to the children of Israel: Come near and hear the words of the Lord your God" (Josh. 3:9), and it is written, "And all of Israel, and its elders, and its officers, and its judges, stood on this side and on that side of the Ark" (Josh. 8:33). Likewise here, all of Israel stood and watched the miracles of the rock.

They began to say, "Moses knows the secret of this rock; if he so wishes, he can bring forth water from it." Moses was therefore placed in a quandary: if he paid heed to them, he would be nullifying the words of God, for the Holy One, blessed be He, "catches the wise in their own craftiness" (Job 5:13). Moses had guarded himself all those forty years so as not to become angered by them, for he feared the oath that the Holy One, blessed be He, had sworn—"Surely not one of those men [of this evil generation shall see that good land]" (Deut. 1:35). [Now, as] they said to him, "This is a rock; just as you wish to draw [water] from this rock—draw it from that one," he shouted at them, "Hear now, you rebels; shall we bring forth water for you from this rock?" (Num. 20:10) . . . "And Moses lifted his hand and he struck the rock with his staff" (Num. 20:11)—He struck it once, and a small quantity of water began to trickle from the rock. This is as it is written, "Behold, he struck the rock, and water issued [*va-yazuvu mayim*] . . ." (Ps. 78:20), like a *zav* who experiences an issue [seminal discharge] in single drops. They said to him, *"Son of Amram, is this water for those who suckle at the breast, or for those weaned from milk?" He then grew angry with them and struck the rock twice,* as it is written, "Moses lifted his hand, and he struck the rock with his staff—twice, and water came forth abundantly" (Num. 20:11), gushing over whatever was in its path, as it is written, "and the streams overflowed" (Ps. 78:20). . . . (emphasis mine)

—Midrash Tanhuma, Hukkat siman 9

The problem at the center of this text speaks to the difficulty of fulfilling the needs of an entire nation. The children of Israel have left Egypt, the land of the Nile, and are now wandering in the arid wilderness, desperate for water. They are numerous, and their cattle, too, are thirsty. Can the One God provide for the needs of this great assembly? The suppressed biblical ethos of nursing in the desert complicates the initial drama—both by placing a father in the role of mother, and in its treatment of the points of view of both the child and the parent. In both the biblical depictions of thirst, in Exodus 17 and in Numbers 20, there is a description of a staff used to strike a rock in the search for water. These are moments of intense conflict between the people and God.[81]

The midrash focuses the relationship between multiplicity and Oneness (which, as we have noted, reflects the fundamental tension between male and female sexuality) on different levels, with alternating gender values. The tangle of symbolic gender identity of the objects participating in the event is part of the conflict that is being described here. The midrash describes the entire congregation standing before a single rock.[82] It creates an analogy between this standing and the standing before the entrance of the Tent of Meeting for the commandment of *hak'hel* (gathering of the entire nation).[83] The rock parallels the Tent of Meeting, a symbolic representation of the opening in the Divine body from which the congregation will imbibe the spiritual nourishment that is vital for its existence. The very parallel between the rock and the Tent of Meeting creates anticipation of the realization of the connection between the congregation and God, between the many and the One. The parallel created by the midrash is reinforced further by another image, which transforms the dualistic model composed of God and the people into a triad: the description of the nation's crossing of the Jordan in between the two poles of the Ark.[84] The three-way model represents God, the nation, and the leader—he who facilitates the connection between God and the people—but who sometimes, as we shall see, also complicates it.

Moses, the same leader who was described in the midrash cited previously as having the ability to distinguish between the "good breast" and the "bad breast," serves here as a mediator who is meant to lead the national drama of weaning. Weaning is in fact managing the infant's relations with the "bad breast." The consequent drama is predictable, and Moses responds in a manner befitting someone who is, literally, stuck between a rock and a hard place. The nation is molded as an aggressor, testing Moses to see whether he will have the strength to fulfill their demands: "They said to him, 'This is a rock; just as you wish to draw [water] from this rock, draw it from that one.'" But for the nation, Moses is God's human representative, and the nation's questioning of him is in fact a questioning of God's ability to meet their needs. The nation's challenge in the face of the rock that oozes just a few drops—"Son of Amram, is this water for those who suckle at the breast, or for those weaned from milk?"—is full of scorn and lack of faith in God's ability, and that of His emissary, to provide. Whether the implied message here is that "those who suckle at the breast" need a great quantity of milk, or whether it is rather "those weaned from milk"—the older children—who require a greater quantity, it is clear that the jeering is meant to convey that this tiny amount is not going to come anywhere close to satisfying the need. It would seem that the midrash relates here to the prophetic verses that are understood as referring to Moses:[85] "[To] whom shall one teach knowledge, and whom shall one cause to understand doctrine? Those who are weaned from milk, and drawn from the breasts. For it is precept upon precept, precept upon precept, line upon line, line upon line, here a little and there a little. For with stammering lips and a different tongue shall one speak to this people" (Isaiah 28:9–11).

Moses, who is familiar with both points of view—that of the mother and that of the infant—is presented in the midrash as a victim of the system. Each side views him as the representative of the other, and he is condemned to be the one who errs or sins by striking the rock instead of speaking to it. The words, "He grew angry with them and struck it twice," describe Moses's aggression, directed toward the two sides in the middle of which he has become entangled.

The rock is, inter alia, a symbolic, metaphorical representation of God, as evidenced by the fact that it He is commonly referred to as *tzur*.[86] The description of the extraction of water from a rock by means of the metaphor of nursing explains the difficulty inherent in the relationship between God and the nation. He whose breasts are hard as rock encounters the aggressive and heretical drives of His children, which are translated into the striking of the rock. The rock is one; breasts are two. It is possible that underlying the repeated striking of the rock is the symbolic battle between the one and the many. It is as though Moses wishes to replicate the rock, making it two, thereby turning it into a mother.

Another expression of the limiting, repressive, and destructive aspect of

BACK TO THE BREAST

the Divine breast is to be found, in my view, in some of the midrashim on the name El Sha-dai, which appears in all the blessings of fertility in the Book of Genesis. A name is a minimal textual unit inviting exegesis.[87] Its interpretation, from biblical literature onward, entails a perception of the word and its power. A name is perceived as expressing the essence of its bearer; all the more so when it is the Name of God.

In Genesis 49 there is a series of blessings that Jacob bestows on his twelve sons as he lies on his deathbed. The blessing to Joseph is, "By the God of your father, who shall help you, and by the Almighty (Sha-dai), who shall bless you, with blessings of heaven above, blessings of the deep that couches beneath, blessings of the breasts (*shadayim*) and of the womb . . ." (49:25). There is a play on words here, with an allusion to the "God of breasts," or the "God who nurses."[88] The idea that the name *Sha-dai* is derived from the word *shad* (breast) has a long history, and in modern scholarly literature it is identified with Albright.[89] Today, most scholars view the name as a derivation of the Accadian *Shadu,* meaning "mountain." The etymological connection between El Sha-dai and the breasts is mentioned repeatedly by Harriet Lutzky, who identifies El Sha-dai with the name of the Canaanite Ashera, goddess of the earth, marriage, and fertility who is responsible for all growth—"Mother Earth." This identification sits well with the fact that in some of its appearances, the name *Sha-dai* is mentioned in the context of fertility.[90] In Lutzky's view, in the ancient Near East the image of breasts has religious significance, symbolizing Divine Providence, such that the name *Sha-dai,* with its feminine suffix, refers, at the very least, to the "Possessor of breasts" (in reference to a goddess) or "Possessor of mountains" (a reference to God).[91] The use of this term may be metaphorical, but its presence is nevertheless surprising.[92]

Of particular interest with regard to the "bad breast" are midrashim in which God's name *Sha-dai* is interpreted as an expression of limitation, alluding to God's repressive and destructive powers: *she- (amar) dai,* that is, He who said to the world, "Enough!"

> This, too, is what Resh Lakish said: "What is the meaning of the verse stating, 'I am El Sha-dai [God Almighty]'?" (Gen. 35:11). [It means,] I am He who said to the world, "Enough!"—and it stopped. Resh Lakish said, When the Holy One, blessed be He,

35

created the great sea, it went on expanding throughout the entire world, until He rebuked it and caused it to dry up, as it is written, "He rebukes the sea and makes it dry" (Nahum 1:4).

—Babylonian Talmud, Hagiga 12a
(MS Munich 6)

This midrash and its image of the Creator who halts the sea in its expansion can be understood within the broader context of biblical parallels among ancient Canaanite legends. The *Enūma Eliš,* the Babylonian creation mythos, includes the war waged by Marduk against the sea and the sea monsters.[93] The gender context is part of the mythos itself: Marduk challenges and defeats Tiămat, goddess of the sea.[94]

The midrash appears not to recognize the etymological connection between Sha-dai and *shadayim* (breasts). Nevertheless, it is interesting that Resh Lakish forges an indirect link between God who is called El Sha-dai and the halting of the spread of liquid. In her chapter on "The 'Mechanics' of Fluids," Irigaray describes feminine otherness as represented by the qualities of fluids.[95] In her research of ancient Greek literature, Anne Carson describes the view that emphasizes the fluid dimension of the feminine entity.[96] In the world of the Sages, too, as in the world of Aristotle and Plato, femininity is perceived as fluid, devoid of form and boundaries.

Thus we see that God the Creator has a restrictive aspect that includes the ability to halt the mechanism of spread and expansion of matter—in this instance, liquid. The command, "Enough!" is, of course, uttered here in a constructive context—meaning that the limiting of the sea facilitates the coming into existence of dry land and the continuation of the Creation. At the same time, this molds the principles of suppression and limitation required for the work of Creation. If the sea is understood as a feminine, fluid element, we might say that the midrash is describing how the primal gender struggle is won by God.

The next midrash we shall examine understands the name El Sha-dai on the basis of this same characteristic of restriction or limitation, but, unlike its predecessor, it speaks explicitly of annihilation.

The Holy One, blessed be He, said to Abraham: When I created My world, I sustained it for twenty generations for your sake, so that you could come and accept [the commandment of] circumcision. Now, if you do not accept circumcision, "I am El Sha-dai" (Gen. 17:1)—I shall say to the world, "Enough; no more," and I shall return it to chaos.

—Midrash Tanhuma, Lekh Lekha 19

The dialogue between God and Abraham is fascinating from a gender perspective. Circumcision is the first commandment given to Abraham and his descendants.

God said to Abraham, You shall therefore keep My covenant—you, and your descendants after you, for their generations. This is My covenant that you shall keep between Me and you, and your descendants after you: every male among you shall be circumcised. And you shall circumcise the flesh of your foreskin, and it shall be a sign of the covenant between Me and you. And he that is eight days old shall be circumcised among you, every male, for your generations: he who is born of your house, or bought with money of any stranger who is not of your descendants. He that is born of your house, or bought with your money, shall surely be circumcised, and My covenant shall be in your flesh for an eternal covenant. And the uncircumcised male, the flesh of whose foreskin is not circumcised—that soul shall be cut off from its people; he has broken My covenant. (Gen. 17:9–14)

Abraham's acceptance of circumcision marks the beginning of the Jewish people, and it has served ever since as a central symbol in the nation's identity and consciousness.[97]

In the midrash, God threatens Abraham that if he does not accept the commandment of circumcision (performed on the male sex organ) and bequeath it to his descendants, God will return the world to its primordial chaos. God wants a sign of His children's commitment to Him. El Sha-dai here is perhaps an instance of the desire to give exceeding the desire to receive. The relationship between the organ of the covenant and the breast, as molded here, embodies the complexity involved in the Jewish view of fertility, nursing, and sexuality. Circumcision, which is "a sixtieth of castration," is linked here to God's power of destruction. In order for the world to exist, the Jewish male is required to remove the foreskin—to limit his sexuality; to mark this limitation in his flesh. The ambivalence embodied in El Sha-dai finds expression in the fact that God creates the world, but is also able to destroy it. The ambivalence is projected here onto the male sex organ, and creates the conditional relationship between the national covenant and the existence of the world.

Klein's work may help us to understand the significance of the aggression embodied in this midrash: "When the baby is hungry and his desires are not gratified, or when he is feeling bodily pain or discomfort, then the whole situation suddenly alters. Hatred and aggressive feelings are aroused and he becomes dominated by the impulses to destroy the very person who is the object of all his desires and who in his mind is linked up with everything he experiences—good and bad alike."[98]

Klein focuses on the perspective of the infant, while the midrash would seem to focus on the perspective of the nursing mother. Nevertheless, we might suggest that the aggression expressed here is an expression of human projection onto an object.

As we have seen, the breast—the feminine sex organ that does not easily conform to the internalized command to conceal the sexual body and its physical prominence—is given a range of cultural representations. The breasts are illustrated in the various midrashim as an arena for rich and tense discourse, with a struggle between multiplicity and oneness, maternity and sexuality, eros and tantus, father and mother, order and chaos, good and bad, the Divine and the human, hierarchy and equality, and more.

The picture that emerges is a complex one that does not submit to simple reduction: the woman and her breasts represent multiplicity, but at the same time they are the channel to unity and Oneness—like Sarah, who nurses many infants who become the children of the One God. The breasts are dual, but they are also one—as we understand from the midrash about Aaron and Moses, whose comparison to breasts is meant to create a unity of equality between them. (It should be noted that Klein's "good breast" and "bad breast" are also one and the same; the split is artificial; it is simply a stage in the infant's development.)

I believe that multiplicity and unity, as a gender topic that seethes below the midrashim that concern breasts, are related to the cultural and theological struggle waged by the Sages against the surrounding cultures. The monotheistic concept of One God, beside whom there is no other, was not formulated during the period of the Sages as a model, but it was in their time that the obligation was introduced to recite twice daily the verse stating, "Hear, O Israel—the Lord our God, the Lord is One" (Deut. 6:4). The idea of absolute unity was understood as the climax of the recognition of God, and faith in Him was expressed in the absolute rejection of any other divinity. Faith in One God is the first principle, and one who denies it is known as a *kofer be-ikkar*—a denier of the first principle (a heretic).[99] By means of the structuring of the perception of the feminine body and sexuality, the Sages address "otherness" in a most primary and constitutive sense of understanding humanity, and confirm their religious worldview. At the same time, the proposal here to "read the body"—to note the connections between it and a certain symbolic world—points to the breasts as a locus of intense imagery, and allows us to sense something of the outlines of that which lies concealed, culturally suppressed: the actual feminine body.

≡ 2 ≡

DESIRE AND DOMINION

IN THE WORLD of the Sages, feminine identity is awarded its fullest representation when a woman becomes a wife to her husband. In this culture, heterosexual marriage is presented as an extremely positive value. The desired matrimonial norm is expressed and reinforced through such statements as, "Any man who does not have a wife, exists without joy, without blessing, without goodness . . . without Torah, without wisdom";[1] "Any man who does not have a wife is not a man, as it is written, 'Male and female He created them, and He blessed them, and He called them *man*, on the day He created them'" (Gen. 5:2);[2] "'In Our image, in Our likeness'—not a man without a woman, nor a woman without a man, nor the two of them together without the Divine Presence."[3] The materials we review here expose the tremendous cultural force that is applied with a view to justifying, establishing, and reinforcing this norm—perhaps because there are different forces that do not "naturally" conform to it.

In her influential work *Sexual Politics,* Kate Millett argues:

> [A] disinterested examination of our system of sexual relationship must point out that the situation between the sexes now, and throughout history, is a case of that phenomenon Max Weber defined as *Herrschaft,* a relationship of dominance and subordinance. What goes largely unexamined, often even unacknowledged (yet is institutionalized nonetheless) in our social order, is the birthright priority whereby males rule females. Through this system a most ingenious form of "interior colonization" has been achieved. It is one that tends moreover to be sturdier than any form of segregation, and more rigorous than class stratification, more uniform, certainly more enduring. However muted its present appearance

may be, sexual dominion obtains nevertheless as perhaps the most pervasive ideology of our culture and provides its most fundamental concept of power.[4]

Millett suggests that the relations between the sexes are the most fundamental model of power-based control in human culture.

This chapter examines the connection structured by the Sages, on the basis of biblical sources, between the woman's sexuality and desire and her husband's dominion over her.[5] Rabbinic literature includes descriptions of the woman as an unrestrained temptress,[6] along with descriptions of her as passive, devoid of desire, her essence being the satisfaction of the man's sexual needs.[7] Various studies have addressed the lack of coherence emerging from the sources in this regard.[8] One of the prominent issues that they address is the question of restraint and control. While the Sages attribute sexual desire to both man and woman, there is a clear difference in the attitude toward the two sexes insofar as the ethos of restraining this drive is directed toward men only, while women are depicted as prisoners of their urges.[9] This being the case, there is a need for an external system of laws to govern and restrain them, directed partly at the women themselves and partly at men, as a cautionary and protective measure. The need to control that which is perceived as uncontrollable produces entire fields of discourse and knowledge whose aim is to create an illusion of control.[10]

According to Genesis 3, desire is originally aroused in woman. The desire for the forbidden "fruit" speaks to both the sexual and the intellectual appetite. She—the active, initiating agent—arouses this desire in the man, following which they both try to deny and evade responsibility. The forbidden desire turns out to carry a heavy price—expulsion from the Garden of Eden.

The punishments meted out to Adam and Eve reflect a manifestly gender-based perception: the man's punishment involves labor, while the woman is punished with the pain entailed in childbirth and subservience to the man. The description of the punishments may be viewed as an etiological mythos underlying gender differences: man is subjugated to the land; the woman is subjugated to her body and to her husband.[11]

The punishment received by the woman is formulated in the biblical verse as follows: "To the woman He said: 'I will greatly multiply the travail of your childbearing; in pain shall you bring forth children; and your desire shall be for your husband, and he shall rule over you'" (Gen. 3:16).

This is one of the most important sources shaping the image, fate, and destiny of woman throughout the course of Jewish culture. It is part of a mythos that reflects fundamentally patriarchal perceptions, and it offers ostensibly theological reasons for the social and sexual subservience of women: feminine suffering and oppression is of Divine rather than human origin. Through its very formulation as a punishment, with the implication of a curse, it represents a situation of breakdown or corruption. The ideal, perfected state of affairs is seemingly indicated by the opposite: painless pregnancy and labor; feminine desire that is not necessarily directed toward her partner; and freedom.

We must ask: What does the pain of childbirth have to do with the channeling of the woman's desire toward her husband, and to him alone? The verse juxtaposes—and thereby connects—childbirth with sexual desire and gender power relations. Attention should be paid to the way in which this connection, which is not intrinsically necessary, becomes internalized and apparently essential. Is the subordination of the woman's desire to a single object a way of channeling her "natural" desire, which is diffuse, in the direction of reproduction? Is this a way of repressing her tremendous childbearing power and the unregulated desire that may arise from it—such as desire toward her children, other men, other women, etc.? Clearly, the juxtaposition in the verse serves to establish the man's control over childbirth, specifically because of the absence of any visible connection to it.

The definition of the pain of childbirth as *the* curse for woman may blur a repressive totality that is concealed here but exposed through the Sages' attention specifically to the second part of the verse—the connection between desire and dominion. As we shall see, the Sages' teachings reveal the perceptions of women in their world and ways in which these are formed, including the internalization of these views by women.

Although a superficial reading of the curse imposed on Eve as punishment for her sin might suggest that it entails only pain in childbirth, a closer look reveals its separate elements. R. Isaac b. Abdimi belonged to the third generation of the Amoraim of Babylon, and was a biblical exegete of such renown that Raba said of him, "Any verse that R. Isaac b.

Abdimi did not explain, has not been properly elucidated."[12] His analysis of the curse breaks it down in such a way that each constituent phrase carries a separate message.[13]

> R. Isaac b. Abdimi stated: Eve was cursed with ten curses, as it is written: "To the woman He said: 'I will *greatly multiply* (the travail of your childbearing)'" (Gen. 3:16): This [dual expression of multiplicity] alludes to the two issues of blood, one being that of menstruation and the other that of virginity; "the travail" refers to the trials of child rearing, "of your childbearing" refers to the trials of pregnancy; "in pain shall you bring forth children" is to be understood literally, "and your desire shall be for your husband" teaches that a woman yearns for her husband when he is about to set out on a journey, "and he shall rule over you" teaches that the man demands [marital relations] verbally, while the wife does so in her heart, this being a fine character trait of women.
>
> —Baylonian Talmud, Erubin 100b
> (MS Vatican 109)

These curses fall into two categories. One includes the "biological curses"; those pertaining to the processes of menstruation, pregnancy, and childbirth. The other includes "social curses" imposed on women: the trials of child rearing and limitations on the realization of a woman's sexual desire.

The sixth and seventh curse enumerated by R. Isaac deal with desire and dominion, and both concern social norms governing sexual relations. The first refers to the fact that men are active in the public domain and are not always available to fulfill their wives' sexual desire.[14] The second reflects norms of modesty that prevent a woman from asking her husband explicitly for sexual intimacy, requiring instead that she ingratiate herself with him and thereby hint indirectly to her wish. Modesty—at least according to this source—is "a fine character trait" specifically in women. A man, by contrast, expresses his wish for physical intimacy openly and explicitly, and this grants him dominion, advantage, and control over her. The limiting of women's verbal expression of desire excludes them, in effect, from discourse about sexuality. This being the case, R. Isaac under-

43

stands these two curses as outlining the limitations on the realization of feminine desire, and as independent from one another.

This structural basis relating to desire recalls the argument posited by Catherine MacKinnon:

> Sexuality is the social process that creates, organizes, expresses, and directs desire—desire here being parallel to value in Marxist theory; not itself the same, but occupying an analogous theoretical location of being the quality that is taken for a natural essence or presocial impetus but is actually *created by* the social relations, the hierarchical relations, in question. This process creates the social beings we know as women and men as their relations create society. Like work to Marxism, sexuality to feminism is socially constructed yet constructing. It is universal as activity yet always historically specific and jointly comprised of matter and mind. As the organized expropriation of the work of some for the use of others defines the class—workers—the organized expropriation of the sexuality of some for the use of others defines the sex—woman. Heterosexuality is its structure, gender is its social process, the family is a congealed form, sex roles are its qualities generalized to two social personae, and reproduction is a consequence. (Theorists sometimes forget that in order to reproduce one must first, usually, have had sex.) Control is gender's issue, also.[15]

In the rabbinic ethos that we are discussing, in any event, the man controls his own desire, while the woman's desire places her under her husband's control.

One might read R. Isaac's teaching as a misogynous view that heaps curses on woman, amplifying her punishment and, accordingly, her sin. Another possibility, no less reasonable, is to understand his statement as an attempt to contract the idea of "your desire shall be for your husband and he shall rule over you" from an all-encompassing control of men over women, to control of the specific realm of woman's sexuality.[16]

Either way, R. Isaac's teaching fails to address the simple and almost self-evident connection between desire and dominion: the fact that, to a considerable degree, the object of a person's desire rules him. In order to learn more about the perception of feminine desire, its identification as a curse, and its connection to the control of women in rabbinic literature, let us turn our attention to a midrash that is organized in a seemingly technical fashion on the basis of the order of the biblical verses.[17]

> "Your desire shall be for your husband" (Gen. 3:16)—there are four [entities] that are "desirous." A woman's desire is for her husband, [as it is written,] "Your desire [*teshukatekh*] shall be for your husband." The desire of the evil inclination is for Cain and his like, [as it is written,] "its desire [*teshukato*] shall be for you" (Gen. 4:7). The desire of the rain is for the ground, [as it is written,] "You visit the earth and water it [*va-teshokekeiha*]" (Ps. 65:10); and the desire of the Holy One, blessed be He, is for Israel: "His desire [*teshukato*] is for me" (Song of Songs 7:11). We are fainthearted, and although we are fainthearted we await God's salvation, and declare His Oneness twice daily, proclaiming, "Hear O Israel, the Lord our God, the Lord is One" (Deut. 6:4).
> —Genesis Rabba 20, 7

> An alternative interpretation: "Your desire shall be for your husband"—when a woman is in labor, she declares, "I shall no longer have relations with my husband," but God tells her, "Return to [the object of] your desire, return to the desire of your husband." R. Berakhia and R. Simon taught in the name of R. Simeon b. Yohai: Since [the woman in labor] experienced a fluttering of heart [that is, entertained the thought "freeing" herself from relations with her husband], therefore [following childbirth] she brings a sacrifice that flutters: "Two turtledoves or two young pigeons" (Lev. 12:8). "And he shall rule over you"—R. Jose the Galilean taught: Can this imply all-encompassing dominion? [Surely not,] therefore it is written, "He shall take neither the nether nor the upper millstone for a pledge" (Deut. 24:6). There was once a woman from the house of Tavarianus, who was married to a highway robber,[18] and her husband used to afflict her. The Sages heard of it and came to her [home] in order to rebuke him. She brought out to them a golden candelabrum with a clay lamp upon it, fulfilling that which is written, "Your desire shall be for your husband."

As various scholars have demonstrated, the redactor of Genesis Rabba is an active editor who plays a significant role in the formulation and editing of the midrashic material.[19] This text focuses on the last two curses discussed by R. Isaac b. Abdimi in Erubin: desire and dominion. We propose that this homiletic unit plays a role in the structuring of heterosexual marriage as a normative institution, in both the social and the religious sense, while simultaneously testifying to the Sages' awareness of the cracks in this structuring. The midrash seems to reflect an acute awareness on the part of its creators that a woman's desire for her husband is not, in fact, self-evident, and it proposes a certain understanding of the necessity of its imposition as a punishment and a curse. Thus, in between the cracks of the midrash there seeps a pervasive anxiety concerning feminine ambivalence toward the heterosexual monogamous institution of marriage whose ultimate aim is childbirth.

The above midrash consists of four units: the first offers a comparative interpretation of four verses that mention "desire" (*teshuka*); the second is a teaching involving a homiletic technique known as *notarikon,* whereby the word in question is divided into parts; the third deals with the experience of childbirth and the sacrificial offering that the mother is subsequently required to bring; and the fourth records an anecdote concerning a specific woman. The first unit, itself comprising four parts, looks at different types of desire. It begins with the assertion that "a woman's desire is for [that is, directed toward] her husband." It appears that this unit was originally a three-part teaching that addressed three biblical appearances of the word *teshuka*: the curse given to woman; God's words to Cain; and the expression of desire in Song of Songs.[20] Later on the verse from Psalms was added by R. Aha, as attested to by a parallel text,[21] in which mention of the rain and the accompanying verse from Psalms are omitted. In our unit this earlier stage is concealed, with the teaching about the rains inserted as the third out of the four types of desire. In other words, the redactor had an interest in integrating this teaching in the service of the unit's rhetorical objectives.

The teachings here illuminate different expressions of desire, including both its darker side (the evil inclination, sin) and its more positive aspect (the blessing of rainfall). Where does the woman's desire for her husband fall on this spectrum? The answer is not clear. However, this desire is tremendously uplifted in the fourth and final teaching, which speaks of the desire on the part of God (the male, as it were) for the Jewish people (portrayed in feminine form). The literary unit creates a framework that connects the first teaching to the fourth—the woman's desire for her husband to God's desire for His people. This association molds a powerful bond between the private sphere of the individual and the religious collective.

However, the closely guided religious existence of the Israelite community and its connection to a woman's desire for her husband is not shaped solely in terms of cause and effect. The next teaching, based on the parsing of the word *teshuka* into two verbs—*tash* (fainting) and *kav* (hoping)—resounds with the ambivalence attributed to women and recalls men's jokes about women and the headaches that they develop under certain circumstances: "We are fainthearted, and even though we are fainthearted we [continue to] hope for God's deliverance." The faintness, the fatigue (caused by the Exile) is a weakness that the Jewish people manages to overcome, as evidenced by the use of the expression *even though*. The twice-daily recitation of the *Shema* shares the same goal of overcoming ambivalence and placing the One, whose Oneness must be declared, at the center of Jewish consciousness. The teaching exemplifies the religious need to regulate feminine desire, with its tendencies toward diffusion and fatigue, and to focus it on "the one."[22]

At least two of the protagonists of desire are clearly masculine, in terms of their Hebrew appellations: the evil inclination (*yetzer ha-ra*), which pursues Cain and his like, and the rain (*geshem; geshamim*) that is directed toward the earth. As noted, the teaching on *tash* and *kav* invokes a verse that speaks of "male" desire (God's desire for Israel), but puts the words in a feminine mouth. In other words, the feminine desire for the male is not unequivocally the subject of this midrash, and this reveals that the Sages are speaking no less about themselves and their own desires, through projection. Perhaps they do not know enough about women's desires, but are concerned that they are not necessarily directed toward their husbands. Moreover, regimenting desire toward "the one" reveals the connection between the patriarchal structuring of sexuality and the patriarchal structuring of monotheism.[23] Pardes reaches this conclusion in her research on the Creation narrative in the Bible: "God is admittedly the Supreme Authority, but this does not prevent man from disobeying Him again and again. Similarly, the man is, formally speaking, master over women, but this on its own is no guarantee that biblical women will accept their husband's authority."[24]

In rabbinic literature, as in the Bible, a tense dialogue is maintained between patriarchal hegemony and the currents undermining it. The above midrash seems less an assertion of the "positive" or "negative" nature of desire than an emphasizing of its natural or cosmic dimension. Desire exists on different cosmological levels: between the sexes; within a single individual; between God and humankind; and between the rain and the earth.[25]

The next unit of the midrash talks about childbirth, thereby returning to the first part of the verse, which is perceived as the principal curse cast upon woman. It should be noted that the syntax of the verse itself, which mentions childbirth before speaking of desire, does not match the feminine consciousness in which sexuality is inextricably bound up with reproduction—certainly in the ancient world, where contraceptives were not widely available. Here the ambivalence attributed to women with regard to sexual relations is channeled into the experience of childbirth: the woman is depicted as swearing, in her pain, that she will no longer have intercourse with her husband. There is a profound fear that now that she has a child, she will no longer fulfill her role in the economy of reproduction—both because her desire will be directed toward her child, and because perhaps she will now maintain celibacy in order to avoid another pregnancy.[26] This concern exposes men's dependency on women's ability to bear children.

But perhaps the pain of childbirth should be understood not as the cause of feminine equivocation, but rather as the last straw on the back of a desire that carries such a heavy structural burden. This iffiness must, of course, be attacked with the heaviest type of ammunition: God Himself tells the woman, "Return to your desire; return to the desire of your husband." The second phrase adds clarification to the first; it defines which desire is proper, and where the woman must return to. This teaching joins together two versions of the biblical formula and shapes them at will.

The verse is translated in the Septuagint (as well as in the Vulgate and the Aramaic translation, Onkelos) as follows: "your return [*teshuvatekh*] shall be toward your husband," and this exchange of "desire" for "return" also appears in the Dead Sea Scrolls.[27]

The sacrifice to be brought by a woman following childbirth is set forth in Leviticus 1–8:

> And when the days of her purifying are fulfilled, for a son or for a daughter, she shall bring a lamb of the first year for a burnt offering, and a young pigeon or a turtledove for a sin offering, to the door of the Tent of Meeting, to the priest, who shall offer it before the Lord, and make atonement for her; and she shall be cleansed from the issue of her blood. This is the teaching for she who has borne a male or a female. And if she is not able to bring a lamb, then she shall bring two turtledoves, or two young pigeons; the one for the burnt offering and the other for the sin offering; and the priest shall make atonement for her, and she shall be purified.

Part of the sacrifice that the woman is to bring to the Temple is a sin offering, and now the reason for this becomes clear. The Sages understand the biblical verses concerning the sacrifice that the woman must bring following childbirth as atonement for some wrongdoing. Their solution to the exegetical difficulty that this raises for them is that the violation of her oath, once the crisis accompanying the birth has passed, is the sin that must be atoned for.

R. Simeon b. Yohai states explicitly that this atonement is "measure for measure," with the nature of sacrifice suited to the nature of the sin: the woman had sought to "flutter her wings" and soar like a bird, cutting herself off from the social chains that hold her; therefore, she must bring a sacrifice that flutters and soars, in order to offer it up and prevent it from taking to the air. To my mind, the symbolic ritual act of the woman's sacrifice is part of the cultural regimentation imposed on anyone harboring rebellious tendencies surrounding the pain of childbirth. While the first units in this midrash were related to the first part of the verse, "Your desire shall be toward your husband," this unit may be understood as already falling under the shadow of the verse's conclusion—"and he shall rule over you," since the element of control, which has both a social and a Divine source, is the power that regulates the sole approved orientation of feminine desire.

Adrienne Rich challenges feminist works that do not criticize what she calls "compulsory heterosexuality" and do not portray it as the headstone of our patriarchal society: "In none of these books, which concern themselves with mothering, sex roles, relationships, and societal prescriptions for women, is compulsory heterosexuality ever examined as an institution powerfully affecting all these; or the idea of 'preference' or 'innate orientation' even indirectly questioned."[28]

Is monogamous heterosexuality indeed the "natural" preference of women, or is this too a "social structure," a political institution, the product of norms and of certain social relations between the sexes?

In contrast to the preceding units, the fourth unit creates an explicit connection between the woman's desire and control over her. In asking, "Can this imply all-encompassing dominion?" R. Jose seeks to clarify whether the husband's control of his wife is, in fact, limitless, extending to whatever degree he chooses. On the face of it, his question addresses the dimensions of male control over a woman's sexuality: Is he entitled to force himself upon her? To rape her, for example?

The verse offered in response, "He shall take neither the nether nor the upper millstone for a pledge" (Deut. 24:6), speaks to the juxtaposition of verses that discuss sexual relations, including the obligation of a husband during the first year of marriage—"And he shall cheer the wife whom he has taken" (ibid. 24:5), with the prohibition against taking the nether or the upper millstone—vessels used in the preparation of food—as a pledge, "for [in so doing] he takes a life for a pledge" (ibid. 24:6). R. Jose's question as to the possibility of unlimited control of the woman receives a negative response: "all-encompassing dominion" in this context is identical with "taking a life for a pledge"—in other words, it is a state of affairs that is unbearable for the oppressed party. Our midrash apparently understands the commandment, "He shall take neither . . . nor . . ." as a prohibition of rape within the framework of marriage.[29]

At this point the midrash cites the story of the woman who was married to a robber. The story, which is cited in the context of R. Jose's teaching, may connect it to the issue of violent sexual relations or rape within marriage. What is the role of this anecdote within our midrash, and how does it relate to the preceding units? Seemingly, from an editorial perspective, its aim is to take the theory of a woman's desire for her husband to an extreme, and to establish that no matter what sort of husband she has, even if he occupies a lower economic, social, and moral status than she does, a woman's desire will always be reserved for him. From this perspective we might view the inclusion of the anecdote within its context as a most blatant sanctioning of the connection between desire and dominion.

Despite the power of the hegemonic norms at the forefront of the text's meaning, a subversive reading of the story reveals questions about these norms. The lack of clarity as to the manner in which this bandit "afflicts" his wife leaves a gap that persists to the end of the story. Different possibilities for understanding her affliction operate here simultaneously, taking into account the mention of the husband's occupation: perhaps, owing to his criminal activities, he is away from home much of the time, thereby withholding marital relations. Or, to suggest a completely different direction, perhaps the fact that he is a highway robber hints at the fact that he is a violent man who is also violent toward his wife.

There are two images that appear in the story. Both involve two objects that work together in a single action. In both images, one object is positioned above the other: in the first image the upper millstone rests upon the lower one; in the second image, the lamp rests upon the candelabrum. It would seem that the background to this midrash is the prophetic verse, "I shall take from them the voice of joy and the voice of gladness, the voice of the bridegroom and the voice of the bride, the sound of the millstones, and the light of the lamp" (Jer. 25:10). The verse suggests that "the sound of the millstones and the light of the lamp" are critically important symbols of life. It should be noted that during the Hadrianic persecutions, when women were married off secretly, so as to escape the notice of the Roman authorities, the sound produced by millstones was the signal that a wedding was to take place, while the light of a lamp signaled that a circumcision was scheduled.[30] Both images represent the coupling of a man and woman. They are borrowed from two different semantic fields—the first from the labor of grinding wheat to prepare flour, and the second from the realm of lighting. We encounter the act of grinding wheat into flour as an allegory for the sexual act in both the Bible and rabbinic literature.[31] Similarly, various midrashim describe marital problems using images from the world of lighting.[32] The candelabrum or lantern, an important household item, was made from different materials; golden candelabra served kings and nobles.[33] The lamp (*ner*—can be either masculine or feminine) joins with the candelabrum, which serves as its basis. In the ancient world, lamps were made either from clay or from copper.[34]

In feminist theory, a subversive reading is one that exposes some infirmity in the text that allows for an alternative understanding, contrasting with the story's normative hegemony. A reading of this sort relies on the textual materials (in keeping with the normative demand of most reading theories) but also exposes how the text is never whole and smooth, and how it always contains that which has been excluded from it, along with the gap between that which is said and that which is left unsaid.[35]

Rabbinic literature, originally an oral, popular literature, is intrinsically different from fictional literature in relation to which the model of subversive reading developed. Fiction is produced by individualists who seek to express themselves and their worldview in their work. This is written, original literature, which exists in one version only. The model that speaks of "cracks" regards the text as a unified crystal, with the various forces acting within it producing cracks that are visible only to a very attentive eye. The subversive reading uses these cracks and gaps for its own purposes: to expose the opposing forces that exist within the text. Rabbinic literature, whose texts exist in multiple form,[36] resembles more closely an organic, botanical item; a tree with many branches. Instead of forces being applied to the text, pulling it in different directions, here the wording of the text itself is split and branches off in different directions. The metaphor of a tree speaks to the significant differences among the versions of a single text. (This in no way negates the existence of cracks within a single rabbinic text as well.)

The variant texts of our story give rise to several weighty questions. According to MS London, MS Rome,[37] and MS Munich, the bringing out of the candelabrum with the clay lamp upon it is a symbolic act by the *husband* whom the Sages have come to rebuke, his intention being to justify and uphold the existing situation. However, the majority of manuscripts attribute the act of bringing out the candelabrum to the wife. Attention should be paid to the gender significance of this difference.

The difference between *hotzi* (he brought out) and *hotzi'a* (she brought out) involves the addition or deletion of a single letter, *heh,* at the end of the word, and as such may be viewed as nothing more than a slight corruption in one manuscript version; this reflects the philological approach that seeks to locate as many versions of a text as possible and through them to arrive at the original "urtext."[38] From a different perspective, this quest for the "original," "authentic" version may be viewed—certainly within the framework of feminist study—as the result of a profound patriarchal structure; as a quest for "the one."

Another possibility is to view the multiplicity of versions of a given narrative as a fact possessing its own exegetical significance. With a view to bringing multiplicity to the fore, we shall examine both options. According to the version that presents the husband as the active party who brings out the candelabrum with the clay lamp atop it, the gesture might be understood as a brazen vindication of the existing situation. The robber-husband is aware of the disparity in status—and perhaps also values and morals—between himself and his wife, yet he defends his position of power in relation to her, which is bound up with his physical supremacy, symbolized by the lamp placed atop the candelabrum. The gesture as a whole displays his defiance toward the Sages, and it offers no message but the symbolic depiction of a situation in which desire and dominion are closely intertwined. In this scene R. Jose's question and the ambivalence that it raises, encounter an almost ridiculing presentation of the attempt at intervention by the Sages. The brute shows them how this situation "works" and why there is no point in them trying to interfere.

I prefer the version in which it is the woman who brings out the candelabrum. Specifically because of the ethical problem that it raises, it seems to me the better literary version of the story. As noted above, it appears that, from the point of view of the redactor, the story is included in the midrash with a view to reinforcing the status of marriage per se. The woman's choice of such a partner, contrary to all expectations, supports this interest. From this perspective it would seem that her gesture represents a climactic victory and vindication of the system. But is this all that is to be gleaned from it?

How are we to interpret the gesture of this woman, who displays a clay lamp atop a golden candelabrum—dramatizing the situation of a woman of high status (the gold candelabrum), whose fiery desire is fulfilled by her husband (the cheap clay lamp)? Her symbolic expression may be understood in different ways. Perhaps "all-encompassing dominion" is masculine behavior that, in fact, arouses desire in women—or, at least, in some women. Perhaps violent machismo can actually be a "turn-on." A critical reading may illustrate the tragedy of feminine cooperation with the patriarchal system and the internalization of the images, positions, and roles that it assigns to women. MacKinnon explains this phenomenon, whereby women's submission undergoes eroticization that is presented as feminine, such that women are in fact aroused by it to some degree. She argues that the resulting situation, in which women actually want male control, is undoubtedly contrary to women's interests.[39]

I sense here the constant presence of a different exegetical possibility. Attention should be paid to the fact that this version of the midrash depicts a woman, pseudo-mute, who illustrates through her gesture the cultural sanction on sexual discourse by women. Perhaps this physical gesture is meant as a show of silent protest against this suppression. The witnesses to her apparent affirmation and validation of her desire are the Sages, representatives of the rabbinic establishment, whose intention had been to rebuke the husband—that is, to defend the woman's interests. Ostensibly, they are intervening on her behalf and for her sake: they are responding to the troubling question raised by R. Jose. However, since the control over the discourse that shapes this story rests exclusively in the hands of men, there is no way of knowing whether they interpret the woman's symbolic statement correctly or not.

In any event, it appears that within the fundamentally nonegalitarian relations between the sexes, which we have referred to here as relations of desire and dominion, there arises an asymmetrical relationship of dependence. The psychological mechanism controlling gender relations is such that not only does desire lead to control, but control also creates desire. This dynamic is illuminated by Simone de Beauvoir, in a work written two generations ago: "Master and slave are also linked by a reciprocal economic need that does not free the slave. That is, in the master-slave relation, the master does not posit the need he has for the other; he holds the power to satisfy this need and does not mediate it; the slave, on the other hand, out of dependence, hope, or fear, internalizes his need for the master; however equally compelling the need may be to them both, it always plays in favor of the oppressor over the oppressed."[40]

As I understand it, this midrashic text is not about feminine desire, but rather about the attempt to control it. Homiletically, one might suggest that "all-encompassing dominion" means concealing or denying feminine desire, on one hand, while controlling it, on the other. Obviously, this entails internal contradictions. If the text focuses on masculine desire and the anxiety that comes with it, then on the contemporary cultural level, now that women are part of the discourse of desire and sexuality, it must be viewed as a call for a cultural reevaluation of these concepts, including the desires of women.

Freud's question, "What do women want?" is one that needs to be posed, first and foremost, by women to themselves. The great perplexity surrounding this question has drawn a wide range of responses in recent decades, and allows us to imagine a future in which feminine sexuality will enjoy a more diverse place in society. Liberation from the web of stagnation and mystification surrounding this crucial realm will benefit not only women, but men, too.

≡ 3 ≡

"THEY LET THE CHILDREN LIVE"

The Midwives at a Political Crossroads

To my Shoshik

IN OUR QUEST for the absent story of birth as a subject in classical Jewish literature, we must remember that this central and important event in the existence of every individual—certainly in the ancient period that we are discussing—was, apparently, the exclusive domain of women. Women had unmediated, personal experience in this area, but since it was not they who wrote the books, what we have has been mediated by the creators and molders of rabbinic culture—men. It is an incontrovertible fact that the act of birth, the concrete, actual childbirth involving the bodies of actual women, has been given very limited space—not to say ignored—throughout generations of human culture, including Hebrew culture. In the Bible, the entire experience is usually reduced to the laconic formula, "she conceived and gave birth."[1]

The Book of Exodus opens with a description of the crushing slavery that Pharaoh, king of Egypt, imposes on the children of Israel. Among other decrees, Pharaoh commands the Hebrew midwives that all male infants born are to be cast into the Nile. The midwives defy the king's order, which violates natural morality, and they allow the children to live. Their motivation in disobeying the decree stems from their devotion to a profession whose essence is helping to nurture life, as well as from the fact of their being women—as I shall explain below. When the furious king summons them and demands an explanation, they lie to him: "for the Hebrew women are not like the Egyptian women; for they are lively—before the midwife comes to them, they are delivered" (Ex. 1:19). Pharaoh becomes an object of ridicule—not just because the midwives manage to fool him, but also because of his fundamental mistake: he believes that it is boys and men who pose a threat to him, but the story proves that, for him, the women are more dangerous.

An examination of the ways in which the Sages read the story of the Hebrew midwives should take into account an important comment by Adrienne Rich: "How have women given birth, who has helped them, and how, and why? These are not simply questions of the history of midwifery and obstetrics: they are political questions."[2] Carol Mossman, too, argues that childbirth was never a neutral sphere. It always functioned in a political context—whether with regard to proof of inheritance rights; in preferences as to the sex of the fetus; in state intervention in matters of reproduction and fertility, and the like.[3] Mary O'Brien presents a systematic and comprehensive discussion of the theories of childbirth in the context of political philosophy. The title of her book, *The Politics of Reproduction,* locates the discussion about childbirth in Marxist terms of relations of power and production, and points to the philosophical and ideological framework within which she examines the birth event.[4] She argues that the process of human reproduction is the zone where the ideology of male supremacy took root. Childbirth, and the feminine birthing body, functioned as productive labor, and were exploited by the patriarchate to achieve that which was considered most precious and essential—continuity, offspring.[5]

The story of the Exodus from Egypt, which occupies the first part of the Book of Exodus, describes the emergence of the nation, and it is not surprising that this process is framed as the story of a birth. This is a typical story about the survival of the weak and oppressed in a situation of cruel domination—a story that is shaped by means of gender discourse. The dominated people is compared to a powerless woman, using guile and cunning in her struggle to survive.[6] The story presents the narrative of servitude and redemption as a sort of guerrilla warfare, consisting of everyday acts of resistance against the ruler.

The Hebrew midwives not only engage in helping actual birthing mothers, but also play a symbolic role in the story of the birth of the nation of Israel. Instead of being a tool in the king's hands and killing the Hebrew infants at birth, they mount a powerful resistance against the repressive and authoritarian forces symbolized by the regime. Their insistence on the perpetuation of life is a revolutionary act in the context of slavery. It demonstrates hope for the future of the newborn and the power to imagine a different future, without slavery and oppression.[7] From whence do the midwives draw the strength to defy this tyrant? The text answers: "The midwives feared God" (Ex. 1:17).

The midwives' refusal to kill the babies is an act of heroism. However, they are not the only "conscientious objectors" in the story. Jochebed and Miriam join their ranks when they place Moses in the basket among the reeds. Pharaoh's daughter becomes part of this group by rebelling against her father and bringing a Hebrew baby, the son of slaves, into the palace; she goes as far as to bring a Hebrew wet nurse for him. Thus, the rescue and adoption of Moses is a women's rebellion, staged in a feminine manner. It involves cooperation between Hebrew and Egyptian women, daughters of slaves along with a princess; uneducated women along with the product of a royal upbringing. Together, they defy the king's authority; they cross boundaries of socioeconomic standing, of education, nationality and religion, in order to save the life of a single boy.

It is difficult to point to any other biblical narrative so full of enterprising women. Feminist biblical scholar Cheryl Exum addresses the extraordinary function of the women in this story. She points out that the text portrays them in an especially positive light, and poses the question: What is the aim of this unusual depiction of biblical women? She concludes that the positive presentation is actually meant to rein in the feminine rebellion, by rewarding the women who support the objectives of patriarchal society. Indeed, we cannot ignore the fact that the story leads to a patriarchal destination: its purpose is to bring Moses, the male savior, into the world. Once Moses appears onstage as an adult, the women disappear: "The Moor has done his work—the Moor may go."[8]

A major shortcoming of Exum's reading of the text, as I see it, lies in her failure to appreciate fully its subversive potential and the ways in which it may give rise to a different gender discourse. Her understanding of the concealed repressive mechanism is especially interesting in the context of the problematization introduced by the Sages in their reading of the story of the midwives. The questions that will accompany us in our reading of the midrashim concerning the midwives will be: To what extent do the women in rabbinic texts serve patriarchal interests? Is their resistance weakened or strengthened in relation to the biblical text? And what new gender insights arise from these midrashim?

A review of the first unit (parsha 1) of Exodus Rabba, with its collection of traditions concerning the Hebrew midwives whose actions introduce the story of the Exodus from Egypt, illuminates the power of women's resistance and its political influence, from a unique perspective. Exodus Rabba is a later midrash, and some of its units have parallels in more ancient midrashic anthologies that serve as its sources. The teachings gathered in Exodus Rabba reveal a radical theme that is unequaled in both its scope and its intensity in the parallel texts. Over the past three decades, research has increasingly been focused on the actual redaction of rabbinic literature. In the wake of this development, some scholars have called into question the clear-cut differentiation between "midrash" and "yalkut."[9] The present study may help to shed light on the work of the redactors who molded and interwove the homiletic traditions in a direction that conforms to a given literary and thematic orientation.

> When Pharaoh saw that they were numerous, he issued a decree concerning the males, as it is written: "The king of Egypt said to the Hebrew midwives ..." (Ex. 1:15). Who were these? Rab said: A daughter-in-law and her mother-in-law: Elisheba, daughter of Aminadab, and Jochebed. Samuel bar Nahman said: A woman and her daughter—Jochebed and Miriam. And Miriam was only five years old; Aaron was three years older than Moses. R. Simeon b. Gamliel said: "She would accompany Jochebed, her mother, and perform duties for her; and she was nimble, for even when a child is young his character may already be discerned—as it is written, 'By his (later) doings, too, a child is recognized'" (Prov. 20:11).
>
> "One of them was named Shifra, and the other was named Pu'a" (Ex. 1:15)—But were they not named Jochebed and Miriam?! Why, then, was Jochebed called "Shifra"? For she would enhance [*meshaperet*] the infant. [And why was] Miriam [called] Pu'a? For she would revive the infant with wine [*nofa'at yayin*] after her mother [delivered it]. According to a different interpretation, [Jochebed was called] "Shifra"—because through her, Israel multiplied and

grew numerous [*paru*]. [Miriam was called] "Pu'a"—because she would cause the baby to coo [*maf'a*] [that is, revive it] when others declared it dead. Yet another interpretation: [Jochebed was called] "Shifra"—because she perfected [*shipra*] her actions before God. [Miriam was called] "Pu'a"—because through her actions she caused [*hefi'a*] Israel to draw close to God.[10]

Another explanation: "Pu'a"—for she was brazen [*hofi'ah panim*] toward Pharaoh and defied him. She said to him, "Woe to this man when God comes to punish him!" Pharaoh became enraged toward her, [seeking] to kill her. "Shifra" [was so called]—for she softened [*meshaperet*] her daughter's words and appeased him. She said to him, "Why do you pay attention to her? She is a child, and knows nothing." R. Jose b. Isaac said: "Shifra"—for she brought Israel before their Father, they for whom the heavens had been created, as it is written concerning them: "By His breath the heavens are serene [*shifra*]" (Job 26:13).

"Pu'a"—for she was brazen [*hofi'ah panim*] toward her father, Amram, who was the head of the Sanhedrin at that time. When Pharaoh issued his decree and said, "Every boy who is born—you shall cast him into the river" (Ex. 1:22), Amram said: "What, then, is the purpose of Jewish procreation?" He promptly sent away his wife, Jochebed, and separated himself from her; and he divorced his wife when she was three months' pregnant. All of Israel then followed suit and divorced their wives. His daughter said to him: "Father, your decree is worse than that of Pharaoh. Pharaoh's decree concerned only the boys, while your decree [will withhold life from] both boys and girls. Pharaoh is an evil man, and it is questionable whether his decree will be fulfilled, but you are a righteous man, and your decree will be fulfilled." He [then] took back his wife, and all of Israel likewise took back their wives. Therefore she is called "Pu'a"—for speaking brazenly to her father.[11]

—Exodus Rabba 1:13, Shinan, p. 56

The midrash starts off by identifying the Hebrew midwives. All of these different traditions view as self-evident that the midwives were themselves

Hebrews, and two hypotheses are raised as to the family connection between them. The first suggests that these women were a daughter-in-law and a mother-in-law; the second—a mother and her daughter. What is the reason for identifying them thus? We recall that these midrashim pertain to the biblical unit that discusses Moses's birth, and the saving of his life. In this process his mother, Jochebed, and his sister, Miriam, play a critical role. The midrash imbues the juxtaposition of the textual units with special meaning: Jochebed, who gave birth to Moses, introducing him into a reality of decrees and mortal danger, is identified here as the same woman who is responsible, along with her daughter-assistant, not just for the birth of the redeemer of Israel, but also for creating the conditions that facilitate the birth and redemption of the nation as a whole. The active rebellion of the mother and her daughter against Pharaoh's decrees of annihilation of the Jewish nation, is conflated, in the midrash, with the rebellion of the midwives against his authority. The identification in the midrash between the two pairs of women causes the story of Shifra and Pu'a to be projected onto the story of Jochebed and Miriam, and vice versa. It expresses the idea that they are two women who operate as one, in complete harmony,[12] and molds the connection between them as the closest feminine bond—a mother and her daughter.[13]

The midrash overcomes the difficulty raised by its chronology, according to which the second midwife, Miriam, is a five-year-old girl (at the time of Moses' birth), by explaining that she served as a sort of assistant to her mother, and was notable for her assiduousness even at this early age.

The Sages often identify anonymous or semianonymous characters—that is, those not elaborated upon in the text—with familiar figures. Notably, aside from the list of members of Jacob's family who go down to Egypt and the names of the two midwives, the early chapters of the Book of Exodus mention few characters by name. There is the "man from the house of Levi" (Amram) who marries "a daughter of Levi" (Jochebed), "his sister" (Miriam), and "Pharaoh's daughter"—none of whom are named. It is perhaps this absence of names of the principal characters in the story that led the Sages to view the names of the midwives as having special significance.

In exploring the meanings of names, the Sages sometimes encounter a name whose original meaning is unknown, its derivation lost in a more ancient period of the language. They follow the example of the biblical text itself, which likewise at times ignores the original meaning of a name, enlisting it instead to express beliefs and opinions.[14] Their interpretations of names are free and creative, unfettered by grammatical rules. They explore the root, add or remove letters, and through homiletic teachings reveal new meanings in the text. The midrashim cited above understand the names Shifra and Pu'a as appellations for Jochebed and Miriam—and, as such, as needing explanation.[15] These are their professional titles, alluding to the nature of their work as midwives.[16] In addition, the interpretations offered disclose character traits and relationships, and evince dramatic narrative scenes.

Let us start with the two teachings that appear in section 13. These homiletic narratives depict a conflict between the midwives (Jochebed and Miriam) and the repressive authoritarian forces—Pharaoh and Amram. They are inspired by a derivation of the name *Pu'a* from the expression *hofi'ah panim,* meaning that she was audacious or brazen.[17] Perhaps the vignettes with Miriam at their center allude to the element of *meri*—rebellion—in her name. Their textual and thematic similarity indicates an understanding of the power of the midwives as a significant political force directed against the patriarchate and its representatives.

In the first story, the young Miriam speaks insolently to Pharaoh, king of Egypt, declaring: "Woe to this man when God comes to punish him!" She confronts this tyrant and threatens him fearlessly. Shifra, her mother, standing at her side, perceives the danger her daughter is in and attempts to tone down her words and soften their impact. She uses Miriam's tender age to excuse her outburst, out of fear for her fate: "Why do you pay attention to her? She is a child and knows nothing." The story presents the close relationship between Miriam and Jochebed as a synergetic system, catalyzing Jochebed's intervention to protect Miriam from the violence of the patriarchate. Attention should be paid to the element of guile manifest in this scene, bearing in mind the preceding series of teachings suggesting that Miriam, despite her youth, is fully cognizant, and serves as her mother's assistant in the special profession of midwifery. Thus, Jochebed "lies" concerning her daughter's nature, in order to save her. Her defensive position in relation to her daughter echoes the deception that they both employ in their defense before Pharaoh concerning their inability to carry out his decree.

The next scene likewise shows Miriam as a brazen heroine who is impudent toward her father, who is the leading Sage of the generation.[18] Notably, Amram is given brief and limited treatment in the text; in the midrashic narrative he becomes a round and developing character. Miriam's place and role in the family are shaped here in relation to her parents. The adult's protection of the child, in the previous image, is now inverted and we see the girl protecting the interests of the adult woman. Miriam is presented as a "parental child"; she takes action and functions as a parental figure toward her parents. Amram's divorce of Jochebed is, to her mind, an act of despair and weakness on the part of the leader of the generation. As Blidstein notes, in contrast to the traditions of the Second Temple Period, the Sages were not hesitant to present Amram as an erring leader whose faith was weak.[19] In Pharaoh's decree concerning the killing of the boys, Amram foresees the end of national existence, and in light of this he views marital relations, meant for procreation, as pointless. For him, conjugal relations have a national purpose, and if that purpose is eradicated then he sees no reason to pursue them. We shall address this connection between childbirth and the establishment of the nation at length below.

Miriam defends her mother against the twofold decree of the patriarchate. She objects to Amram's divorce of Jochebed, and prompts him to remarry her. Her argument derives from a view of reality that is different from that of her father. As she sees it, the results of her father's decision will be even more catastrophic than the effects of Pharaoh's decree, because Pharaoh's decree affects only the sons, while the act of divorce denies life to daughters, too. Miriam also argues that Pharaoh is wicked, and his decree may or may not be fulfilled. Amram, on the other hand, is a righteous man, and his decree will certainly be fulfilled. Miriam's blunt, direct words to her father draw an explicit analogy between him and Pharaoh. She does not bow to his authority, nor qualify her position out of respect. She knows that divorcing a woman who is pregnant is an injustice that must be protested. At this fateful moment she demands of her father, Let faith prevail! Retract your decision!

Significantly, while Miriam's brazen outburst before Pharaoh leads to a situation where Jochebed needs to save her daughter from his fury, Amram not only shows no displeasure at his daughter's directness, but proceeds to act on her advice. He bows to his daughter's vision and performs an act of repair.

In order to understand the radical nature of this scene and its central function in the spinning of the overall homiletic theme, it must be noted that Miriam acts as a woman, based on her feminine perception. She adopts a position of protest and defiance toward her father, not hesitating to express her religio-moral view and to criticize his own. In contrast to the biblical narrative, which casts the conflict as an essentially ethnic one, with the wicked Pharaoh pitted against the Hebrew midwives (who are joined by an Egyptian woman), the homiletic elaboration that places Miriam in confrontation with Amram brings into focus the universal gender aspect of the conflict.

The analogy that the story draws between Amram and Pharaoh, and between Jochebed + Miriam and Shifra + Pu'a, broadens the subversive foundation and the antihierarchical element concealed in the biblical situation. What we have before us is clearly a rebellion against the foundations of the ruling establishment. Alongside Pharaoh, the cruel foreign king who faces a rebellion by the women, we find a Hebrew leader—the head of the Sanhedrin. Miriam is presented as a learned scholar who adopts an a fortiori argument in order to persuade her father to take back what he has done.[20] Furthermore, the act of repair that she brings about goes beyond the family framework, affecting Jewish society as a whole: "All of Israel remarried their wives." These midrashic materials express the utopian aspiration to change reality. They empower the voices speaking out in protest against the creators of the existing oppressive order, along with those who submit to and reinforce it.[21]

> "They let the children live" (Exodus 1:17): If they did not do as [Pharaoh] had spoken to them, do we not already know that they let the children live? Why must the text state explicitly, "They let the children live"? Rabbi Meir said: Can there be a furrow within a furrow? [That is, the phrase appears to be redundant, and must therefore be teaching something else:] Not only did they not fulfill his words [to kill the baby boys], but they went further, performing additional favors for them. Some of the women were poor, and [the

midwives] would go and obtain water and food from the homes of wealthy women, and would come and give it to the poor, so that they could sustain their children; this is the meaning of the words, "They let the children live."

A different interpretation [of the words,] "They let the children live": Some of them were destined to be born lame, or blind, or with some other defect, or would have to have some limb amputated in order to be born; what did the midwives do? They would stand in prayer and say to the Holy One, blessed be He: You know that we have not fulfilled Pharaoh's word; it is Your word that we seek to fulfill. Master of the world, let the child be born whole, so that Israel will find no reason to speak against us, saying, "[The children] emerged maimed because [the midwives] sought to kill them." The Holy One, blessed be He, heard their voice, and [the children] emerged whole. Rabbi Levi taught: Instead of a minor lesson, we may derive a major one: There were some babies who were destined to die as they emerged, or who would endanger their mothers' lives. They therefore prayed to God, saying: Lord of the Universe! Suspend their fate now and grant them their lives, so that Israel will not say, "They killed them." And God heard their prayer. Hence, the words "and they saved" refers to their saving of the mothers; and "the children" refers to the children themselves.

—Exodus Rabba 1:15, 3, Shinan, pp. 61–62

This unit goes even further in praising the midwives. From the seemingly superfluous phrase at the end of the biblical verse—"The midwives feared God, and did not do as the king of Egypt had told them; *and they let the children live*" (Ex. 1:18), the Sages conclude that the midwives did more for the survival of the children than merely ignoring Pharaoh's command and refraining from killing them: "They performed additional favors toward them." The lesson drawn from this textual redundancy is part of the manner in which the midrash expands on the biblical account. The midwives' activities, according to this teaching, included collecting charity for poor mothers so that they would be able to feed themselves and their newborns, as well as praying for the fetuses that were likely to be born maimed, or those that would have died a "natural" death in childbirth or who would have endangered the mothers. The midwives are depicted as righteous women who not only refrain from the crime of killing the infants, but are altogether focused on the humanistic quest to nurture life. They act to change the social and religious reality, to resist the prevailing order and "fate" and to remold them in a life-giving direction. Their description as social and spiritual activists shows them using all possible means to help the birthing mothers and the newborns.

However, there is also a theological radicalism that finds expression here in the inclusion of God—the source of power and authority—within the hegemonic framework populated by men. Indirectly, the midrash hints at a questioning of the absolute goodness of God. We are gently reminded that the process of bringing children into the world is not idyllic, even before Pharaoh's decrees make the situation unbearable. For, if childbirth were indeed idyllic, women and their babies would always come through the experience safe and sound. The expositor uses this opportunity to protest the fact that even at the best of times, childbirth is a process that sometimes seems unjust and unfair. God is, as it were, a partner to Pharaoh and to the men who divorce their wives, rather than being on the side of the women who seek to save and to give life. Pharaoh must be outwitted, but in order to survive and to save lives it is necessary, as it were, to maneuver God as well.

Let us examine the rhetoric adopted by the midwives in their prayers to God. First of all, they attain an initial measure of strength by employing flattery and the well-used strategy of "divide and conquer": "Master of the universe, You know that we have not fulfilled Pharaoh's word; it is Your word that we seek to fulfill." The obsequious appeal to God recognizes His power as Master of the world and creates a clear hierarchy between Him and the human monarch. They then go on to employ the typical feminine "trick" of beseeching the patriarchate for refuge and protection. The request to lead the birthing mothers and their infants safely through the birthing process is presented as being motivated by the midwives' fear of being accused of harming the babies: "So that Israel will find no reason to speak against us, saying, '[The children] emerged maimed because [the midwives] sought to kill them.'" By choosing a shrewd angle that sits well with their defiance of Pharaoh, the midwives advance the feminine interest in their stand before God, as well.

The midwives' negotiations with God recall a different negotiating situation: that of Abraham and God concerning the righteous people of Sodom (Gen. 18:23–32). In that situation, Abraham stood as a determined human attorney before the Judge of all the world. Perhaps we might invoke Carol Gilligan's insights in order to draw a comparison between Abraham's stand before God, in the matter of Sodom, and the midwives' stand in the matter of giving life to the infants. Gilligan asserts that the moral judgment of men and women is based on different worldviews concerning the relationship between the self and the environment. Unlike scholars of the development of morality who had preceded her, Gilligan does not view women's morality as less developed than that of men. To her view, they are two complementary outlooks, each important in its own right. The moral judgment of women, she argues, is based on a sense of responsibility to lessen suffering in the world—real, tangible suffering. This is a morality based on caring for others, on a personal touch. The morality of men, on the other hand, is based on principles of justice and rights. Men define the moral imperative as a demand to respect the rights of others and to protect every person's right to life and to self-fulfillment.[22]

Abraham's action consists of a dialogue with God in which he attempts to dissuade God from imposing collective punishment on the inhabitants of Sodom. It is easy to identify the sense of justice underlying his arguments: "Will You then destroy the righteous together with the wicked?" (Gen. 18:23); "Far be it from You; shall the Judge of all the earth, not do justly?" (verse 25); "Will You then destroy the entire city for lack of five?" (verse 28). The midwives, on the other hand, are guided by a feminine ethic of helping those in distress, healing, and caring. They perform acts of kindness and charity; their aid to the birthing mothers goes beyond the requirements of their job. Gilligan bases her explanation on Chodorow's developmental theory, according to which feminine being is based largely on connection, tangibility, and healing; this finds expression in the all-encompassing contact of the midwives with the mothers and their living conditions. In contrast to Abraham, who confronts God directly and whose arguments are based on abstract principles and on boundaries and distance between himself and God ("Behold now, I have taken upon me to speak to the Lord, I—who am dust and ashes" [verse 27]), the midwives choose a more indirect route in appealing to God. They fear—or so they claim—for their own safety, and they seek refuge; their defiance is hinted at only between the lines. Responsibility and caring among the parties (the midwives, the mothers, Israel, God) are a dominant element in the system of dialogue that they create. Clearly, the expositor seeks to cast the midwives, including their rhetoric, in a distinctly positive light.

> A different interpretation: "The midwives feared God" (1:17): They adorned themselves with the example set by their ancestor. This refers to our patriarch, Abraham, as the Holy One, blessed be He, testifies concerning him (Gen. 22:12), "For now I know that you fear God . . ."[23] He opened an inn, and would feed those who passed to and fro, uncircumcised people. [The midwives] said, "Those whom we are unable to feed—shall we then kill them?"
>
> —Exodus Rabba 1:15, 4, Shinan, p. 62

This unit continues to heap praise upon the midwives—this time by creating an explicit analogy, not a mere allusion, between them and the founding father of the nation, Abraham. Like him, the midwives, too, fear God. The expression "adorned themselves" means that they adopted for themselves the same orientation.[24] Abraham's fear of God was manifest, according to the midrash, in his opening of an inn and provision of food to all who were in need. This teaching is based on the image of Abraham as a practitioner of hospitality.[25] According to the midrash, Abraham performed kindness toward human beings in general, paying no attention to the fact that they were uncircumcised. The midwives, following his life-giving example, refuse to kill the infants. The parallel that is drawn between the midwives and Abraham places them on the elevated pedestal of righteous pioneers—individuals who changed the world through their actions and their faith.

In this sense, the parallel crosses gender boundaries, declaring that women may achieve a status of fear of God that is equal to that of men. On the other hand, the midrash may be seen as an act of masculine appropriation of the midwives' righteous action, whereby the model that they follow is the act of a man—the father of the nation.

However, there is more to the matter. Orly Lubin, in her reading of this midrash, reminds us that, in order to follow a political, critical reading, it is necessary to forgo a homogeneous reading that assumes a unified subject.[26] In fact, this is a proposal to read from changing reading positions, or a movement over a network of different reading positions; to rove over the text instead of piercing it.[27] A movement of this kind, to my mind, provides us here with an outstanding opportunity to clarify the meaning of "feminine" fear of God as opposed to "masculine" fear of God, on the basis of the accumulated images in these midrashim.

A look at the texts upon which the midrash under discussion is based, reveals a most interesting fact. It turns out that, in symmetrical contrast to the midwives' fear of God, apparent in their giving life to the infants, the fear of God that the text attributes to Abraham pertains specifically to his readiness to sacrifice his son at God's command: "For now I know that *you fear God*, seeing that you have not withheld your son, your only one, from Me" (Gen. 22:12). The surface of the midrash, as we have said, presents Abraham as a hospitable figure, a generous giver of life. This is the basis for the comparison of the midwives to him: he feeds and gives life to people, and the midwives, too, give life. The image of the midwives procuring food for the birthing mothers and their infants, as mentioned in the previous unit, likewise strengthens this comparison. At the same time, the evidence that is cited to prove Abraham's fear of God creates an ironic contrast between him and the women who are praised for giving life to the children. The verse selected from the context of the Binding of Isaac creates a contrasting parallel of gender difference: it seems that the masculine act that is presented through the accumulated midrashic depiction is characterized by a wish or readiness to kill the sons. The feminine act is presented as a stubborn, brazen, defiant resistance to this murderous power.

Freud attached formative personal and cultural significance to the Oedipal complex.[28] Much has been written on a reading of the Binding of Isaac from a psychoanalytic perspective, but for the purposes of the present discussion, suffice it to mention the psychological infrastructure of the competitive relations and mutual threat between son and father, as expressed specifically in this biblical narrative.[29]

The accumulated homiletic materials presenting Pharaoh, Amram, God, and Abraham as representatives of the male project of killing male children, is unique to midrash Exodus Rabba. In the more ancient parallels, as well as the broader and more organized elaboration in the Babylonian Talmud, this theme is not featured in the same prominent and disturbing manner in which we encounter it here.

The units from Exodus Rabba depict a troubling picture of a life-and-death struggle. This is a universal intergender struggle, crossing cultural boundaries. The case of the midwives in the midrashic view points to a broad principle of gender relations as set down by the Sages. The midrashim create a significant reinforcement of the voices that are opposed to conventions that are taken for granted. In contrast to Exum's reading mentioned above, which views the "episode" of the biblical story of the midwives as a feminist outcrop that proceeds from and returns to a patriarchal hegemony that continues into infinity, it would seem that the homiletic reading of the Sages expressed here describes a profound difference between men and women. It illuminates a fundamental situation in which women represent valued qualities, elevated above men. In the composite picture that arises here, men have a tendency toward control and killing, while women rebel against death, in favor of life. The positive depiction of the midwives in the text serves the Sages as the platform for some trenchant moral and theological messages, including grave reservations about the "existing situation." From what we understand from their words about Pharaoh, who is unquestionably an extreme example, we are invited to examine a broader male-cultural foundation that is, from a moral point of view, most problematic.

The ideal system that is set forth here seems to find an echo in Sara Ruddick's "maternal thinking."[30] Ruddick, who addressed the dialectic of the institution of motherhood and the experience of motherhood, emphasized its philosophical, moral aspects.[31] She argues that motherhood generates in the mother a special type of awareness of others and of herself. Maternal self-awareness is characterized by treating others as subjects who are essentially free and worthy of recognition, and as needing care and nurturing, not necessarily supervision and control. "Maternal thinking" refers to intellectual abilities that the mother develops, decisions that she makes, metaphysical approaches that she adopts, and values that she establishes. Motherhood, to Ruddick's way of thinking, is a discipline. Moreover, the mother is a moral subject whose self-awareness contains an awareness of the needs of others, and whose nurturing work may serve to inspire political values and consideration. Ruddick brings the mother's voice into political discourse and draws a connection between maternal thinking, pacifism, and the defense of life, on one hand, and between masculine power and militarism, destruction, and death, on the other. Motherhood entails the nurturing of unique human beings and protecting them for their own sake, while masculine militarism requires the destruction of the objects of maternal nurturing, for abstract reasons. She presents masculinity versus motherhood as the kingdom of death versus the kingdom of life, and demands that the government of masculine politics adopt the sane and life-preserving form of power that is expressed in motherhood.

Of course, it is possible to criticize the thinking of Gilligan and of Ruddick as painting the feminine and maternal voice in overly rosy colors in their attempt to transform it into a moral code of concern for the other: one might counter this picture with instances of feminine and maternal violence,[32] or broaden the "maternal" function (as Ruddick indeed does) to include anyone who raises and cares for offspring. Nevertheless, it appears to me that the midwives—at least according to the manner in which they are presented in the midrash—are women who operate on the sociopolitical level, bringing to it the moral feminine voice. They enlist varied and sophisticated strategies in order to further their worldview.

How are we to understand the manner in which the Sages read the story of the midwives? Why do they amplify the rhetorical, moral, and political power of these women to such a degree, in relation to the textual narrative? The feminine powers of childbirth receive no comparable praise anywhere else, in either the Bible or the midrash. Unquestionably, the key to understanding this question lies in the national context of the narrative. The admiration for childbearing femininity, fighting for life and its continuation—as described in the midrash—is the result of the need to imagine the birth of a nation, a metaphorical birth.[33]

The metaphor of birth is, it seems, the most dominant metaphor in the national biography. As noted, the Book of Exodus offers a complex and fascinating representation of the birth of the Jewish nation. The metaphor of the symbolic birth, in all its details—the suffering of servitude (birth pangs); the splitting of the sea and the passing through (the birth process itself), and so forth—creates a close bond with the gender identity of nationalism in general and of Jewish nationalism in particular. As Hamutal Tzamir notes, in her discussion of the modern context,[34] national desire—even in the Bible and in the midrash—is masculine desire by definition and by structure, and it is formulated within the framework of a gender power struggle for the possibility of giving birth, and for the ways of birth.

Anthropologist Nancy Jay has addressed the ceremonies of sacrifice in ancient religions from a gender perspective, and argues that these are fundamentally ceremonies of pseudo-birth by means of which men, born of women, create male fraternity and generate a masculine collective. She presents this mechanism as a strategy by means of which men contend with three challenges: they are born from women, they are dependent on women in order to procreate, and their fatherhood is not visible and therefore requires proof. In order to compensate for these three "problems," men appropriate from women the power of childbirth and transform it from something concrete and physical into something abstract and symbolic; from something individual into something collective—that is, from the birth of a single, mortal, transient human being into the birth of an eternal collective (nation/state); from a birth by woman into a birth without women; and from individual birth as giving life to birth of the collective by taking life. In this manner, men give birth to society and establish it as a masculine dynasty that transcends the fate of individual death.

This masculine fraternity regulates social relations and ensures control of the means of production and of the positions of power, by leaving them in the hands of the men of the family—that is, handing them from generation to generation, from father to son.[35] Jay argues, inter alia on the basis of an analysis of ancient Hebrew culture, that there is a structural contrast between sexual reproduction and social replication, reflected in a struggle between nature and culture.[36] Death violates the internal order of the sacrificial body, the product of the sexual mechanism of reproduction, only to be reorganized on a different, external level—that of social order.

The destruction of the organic, living body turns it—according to her theory—into an effective mark of social order.[37]

It is fascinating to consider the overlap of the conflict between men and women, and the values of life and death that surround the event of birth in the midrashic unit discussed above, in light of Jay's theory. If we go back to Exum's discussion, to which we referred at the outset, it must be acknowledged that what we have here is glorification of the power of the midwives, which may be interpreted as recognition of women's power of childbirth and life, and its empowerment—specifically within the political and national context. Indeed, this is a process of appropriating birth for procreation that functions as part of a patriarchal symbolism. In other words, the empowerment of women serves as an element of a procreation project that is fundamentally masculine. At the same time, we cannot ignore the fact that the midrashim cited above express a unique and powerful flash of recognition of feminine power and of the moral position that gives rise to it. Jay's model describes the distancing of women from the collective spheres generating social order in different cultures. The Sages not only refrain from distancing women from the metaphorical birth of the nation; they applaud the power and role of femininity that acts on behalf of the establishment of the nation, all the while exposing its political and moral struggle against the ethos of sacrifice.

≋ 4 ≋

JUDITH, WIFE OF R. HIYYA

A Story of Women's Pain

IN THIS CHAPTER we propose a gender-based reading of the story of a certain woman who features in the world of the Sages—Judith, wife of R. Hiyya the Great. What first caught my attention about her was the fact that she is mentioned by name, which is fairly uncommon in talmudic sources.[1] Like the stories of women in the Bible, it would seem that Judith's story, too, is a suppressed narrative that survives in the textual reality of the Talmud in the form of fragmented remnants.[2] A most problematic characteristic—from a feminist perspective—of talmudic narratives is the silence of women: the muting of their voices and experiences, their invisibility, in fact, their erasure from the text. The story of Judith, despite its fragmentary nature, awards the woman at its center a name and a voice, thereby undermining some patriarchal norms and assumptions and raising unsettling questions about them. The Talmud relates two extremely brief stories about Judith, each consisting of a dialogue between her and her husband. Since both dialogues share the same background—her great suffering in childbirth—there is room to discuss both within the same framework. We will examine these brief narratives with special attention to the gender perceptions that they embody.

The story of Judith must be approached against the backdrop of the genre it exemplifies and within the context in which it appears. Two cultural-literary trends converge here, and this confluence explains some of the difficulty entailed in identifying authentic feminine voices in the rabbinic corpus: one is the diminished, fragmentary presence of women's voices in this literature; the other pertains to the minimalist character of the legends of the Sages in general.

The literary genre of "legends of the Sages" is widely dispersed, with examples to be found throughout the tannaic and amoraic literature, in the Mishna, the Tosefta, the midrashim, and the Talmuds. These narratives are guided and molded by three interconnecting interests: didactics, idealism, and aesthetics.

The didactic interest speaks to the fact that these literary texts were created in order to educate their audience. It should be noted that the legends of the Sages generally do not offer a "lesson" or "moral" in the simple sense of the word. They do not always educate toward defined values; they sometimes even construct contradictory value systems that are not resolved within the world of the narrative. The attitude toward the characters is often ambivalent, and the action takes place in a dialectical, equivocal mood. At the same time, the act of reading, and its invitation to the reader to participate in an especially intensive process of imbuing significance, serve an important didactic purpose: education toward dialogic thinking and dynamic study that seeks to understand the different horizons of the text and of its readers.

The interest in the realm of ideals relates to the set of beliefs and opinions that form the backdrop to these narratives. Thus, through these literary expressions we are able to learn much about what the Sages thought and believed. To the extent that these narratives have a historical aspect to them, they are located within the history of ideas.

The third interest underlying this genre is the realm of aesthetics. The legends of the Sages, at their best, are sophisticated, dramatic narratives full of inspiration. They incorporate various elements of literary style, including dialogues, analogies, motifs, wordplays, and more. Fundamentally they rest on a vision of aesthetic unity in which every component serves a function within the overall literary framework.[3]

The reading proposed here addresses the diverse functionality of the narrative devices and gives meaning to the story of an unusual woman who does not submit to her husband's will, who deviates from social conventions and rebels against the "women's fate" that condemns her to suffering. Our reading will attempt to reconstruct and draw out what is concealed behind the recorded dialogue.

"ONE WHO IS WISE WILL ACQUIRE CONTRIVANCES" (PROV. 1:5)

Let us begin with the story that appears in the Babylonian Talmud, Tractate Yebamot 65b, which stands out in its fine literary quality and the complexity of its relations with the context. The legends of the Sages have reached us in diverse halakhic or exegetical contexts. In their original forms, they were meant to serve functions related to the worldview of the Sages of the generation in which they were written. Some of the stories are meant to illustrate and demonstrate religious and moral principles. The story we will examine here appears in the context of an exploration of the command, "Be fruitful and multiply" (Gen. 1:28), and it seemingly also provides an answer to the question of who is commanded in this regard (answer: the man). The complexity of the story's relationship to its context—the halakhic discussion within which it is set—will be addressed after we examine the anecdote itself.

> "Judith, wife of Rabbi Hiyya, suffered in childbirth. She changed her costume [disguised herself] and came before Rabbi Hiyya. She said to him, 'Is a woman commanded concerning the command to "be fruitful and multiply," or not?' He told her: '[She is] not.' She went and drank a sterilizing potion. When [the matter] eventually became known to him, he said to her: 'If only you had borne me one [more issue of the] womb.'"[4]

This is the bleak story of a woman whose pain in childbirth leads her to adopt extreme measures. How is the story to be understood? How can the wealth compressed in this minimalist anecdote be unpacked and appreciated? It seems that we must undertake a close reading that addresses the narrative's diverse dialogic aspects.

As noted, although the legends of the Sages are literary texts that were created to educate their listeners, they do not point to a clear moral lesson in the simple sense. The brevity of this anecdote, like other stories of the same genre, invites intensive efforts on the part of the listener to fill in the gaps and derive meaning.[5]

The efficacy of the strategy of dialogistic reading, which co-opts the reader into conducting a charged dialogue with the text, reveals itself at the outset, from the moment we are introduced to the main character and the situation: "Judith, wife of Rabbi Hiyya, suffered in childbirth." This may be viewed as a fairly standard introduction: characters in rabbinic literature are regularly identified by conventional identities via their relationship to a recognized Sage. Characterizing someone by means of family connections helps to frame the character's identity, locating her, first and foremost, within a certain social and family system. However, a gender perspective imbues this exposition with narrative value, too. The first word, *Judith,* represents a woman with a first name and signifies the distinct nucleus of an identity that stands alone.[6] Immediately thereafter, the character is identified as "wife of Rabbi Hiyya"—in other words, at a certain stage she became Rabbi Hiyya's spouse, and the result of this pseudo-natural union, in which a man cleaves to his wife and they become "one flesh," is that she experiences "suffering in childbirth."

The next scene places a disguised Judith in front of her husband, the rabbi and religious authority. Three questions arise at this point: (1) What is the purpose of Judith's appearance before a rabbi? (2) Why does she consult specifically with her own husband? (3) How, and for what purpose, does she disguise herself?

The purpose of Judith's appearance before a rabbi is related to her attempt to relieve herself of the pain of childbirth. She attempts to clarify her status with regard to the commandment to "Be fruitful and multiply," and to look into the possibility of avoiding another pregnancy. Judith's choice to address her question specifically to her husband may be explained in terms of the fundamental concepts of feminine ethics, as described by Carol Gilligan.[7] From Judith's point of view, the issue of fertility pertains to the relationship between herself and her husband, and it is in this context that she presents her question specifically to him.

At the same time, it is clear that her appeal is caught up in a tangle of familiar gender- and culture-based power struggles. Does Judith's behavior indeed conform to the idea of feminine morality as Gilligan describes it? Why does she disguise herself? Why does she hide her identity from her husband? This act, echoing the biblical motif of women's masquerade, presents Judith as a woman occupying a position of weakness and inferiority with respect to the man she faces.[8] As in the biblical precedent, here too the disguise provides the woman with the opportunity to be otherwise, free, to sidestep her inferiority and the system of laws that harms her.

Like the biblical women, Judith is driven by distress to confront a powerful man in an indirect manner. This is a type of manipulation, which makes it clear that Judith and her husband are not on the same side; they are adversaries.

Attention should be paid to the information gap here. How and why does Judith disguise herself? Seemingly, the textual description—literally, "changed herself with her clothes"—is meant to emphasize the act of disguise, rather than to persuade the reader that her change of apparel was enough to keep her husband from recognizing her. Is the purpose of the disguise merely to prevent her from being recognized? If so, it is possible that she disguises herself as some other woman. A different possibility is that Judith dresses herself as a man. Such an act, as in the cultural practice of drag (wearing clothing of the other sex, and specifically garments signifying a particular social role), expresses the critical and subversive intent that is at the foundation of our narrative situation.[9] In *Gender Trouble,* one of the central texts of queer theory, Judith Butler questions the binary distinction between culture and nature and between sex and gender, arguing that the categories of "man" and "woman" themselves are political categories from the outset, rather than "natural" ones.[10] Drag is the ultimate metaphor for gender, because it exposes its imitative character. Butler suggests that its "subversive possibilities should be played and re-played to make the 'sex' of gender into a site of insistent political play."[11]

I believe that a more fruitful reading of the text understands Judith's situation as one of gender disguise, in view of the formal, legal question that she addresses to him: "Is a woman commanded concerning being fruitful and multiplying, or is she not?" Judith does not tell her personal story and request a ruling on her situation. The appeal to halakha, ignoring the individual, private aspect of suffering, sits well with her disguise as a man. It seems that Judith adopts her unusual approach out of a belief that Rabbi Hiyya will allow no room for consideration of personal suffering, so that a request for empathy and identification would be pointless. According to this interpretation Judith is a sophisticated woman who knows what she is up against. She approaches him with the intention of playing in her husband's court—the halakhic court—and beating him there.

This possible reading illuminates Judith's specific success as dialectically related to the general gender predicament: it is by means of borrowing a male identity that she obtains what she wants as a woman seeking to liberate herself from patriarchal structural modes that imprison her in her body and cause her great suffering. Hiding her true identity means, inter alia, setting aside feminine morality (to use Gilligan's term) in favor of a mechanism of male morality that permits her to achieve a defined goal. At the same time it must be emphasized that, from Judith's point of view, the system of male morality as maintained by Rabbi Hiyya is problematic in its own right, because it seems to entail a double standard: a direct question, asked by his wife, will receive one sort of answer (tainted with his own interests), while an approach by an uninvolved party will receive a different answer. We discuss this complexity below.

Why does Judith not ask an open question, such as: "Who is commanded to be fruitful and multiply?" Is her formulation itself also part of the strategy aimed at obtaining the answer she seeks? We cannot determine with any certainty whether she knows the answer to the question or not. Perhaps she does not know. However, her masterful manipulation raises the possibility that perhaps, like a good lawyer, Judith is posing a rhetorical question with the intention of receiving a ruling that will release her from further childbearing. Rabbi Hiyya responds, innocently, that a woman is not obligated with regard to the commandment to "Be fruitful and multiply"—thereby, with his own words, decreeing extinction for his future progeny. The sophisticated ruse allows Judith to exploit and interpret the patriarchal law to her own advantage, so that it is specifically by means of the law that she is able to exempt herself. In addition to framing her as a subversive interpreter of the law, her act says something more general and very important about the complicated manner in which the patriarchy sometimes protects women from itself.[12]

However, we must also consider the meaning of Rabbi Hiyya's view, and how it sounds to his wife. Does Judith need a halakhic ruling simply as a legal rubber stamp for her actions? Does the fact that she is a woman—who is not obligated—serve as a real loophole that offers her salvation, demonstrating a pro-women understanding of the non-obligation? Or does she perhaps hear in it the summary of an entire patriarchal approach to women's status in general, and its bearing on the process of reproduction in particular? Should this be understood as the moment when Judith realizes that she is not prepared to bear suffering in order to be nothing more than a vessel, a device, whereby her husband fulfills *his* commandment? Is it here that she understands the full depth of the perspective that views her as a means rather than as a partner?

The next stage in the narrative is her act: Judith drinks a sterilizing potion.[13] The Sages discuss such potions and their use by both sexes, mainly to cause sterility and to prevent pregnancy.[14] The measure of freedom that Judith assumes here in carrying out this act must be emphasized. The relationship between the ruling that she is not obligated to "be fruitful and multiply" and the drinking of the sterilizing potion is not simple and self-evident. In any event, although she has presented a general question to a formal arbiter of legal authority, her view of morality and the law are altogether private and context-related, as we learn from her actions, rather than from her query to her husband.

The final scene once again leaves gaps with its minimalist style: "When it eventually became known to him . . ."—what became known to him? Does he become aware of the whole story (including the disguise), or only the fact that his wife has become sterile? How does it become known to him? What takes place in the psyches and the consciousness of the characters with this discovery? And what is the meaning of Rabbi Hiyya's concluding words, "If only you had borne me one [more issue of the] womb [*keres*]?" In what tone were these words uttered? Should we be focusing on the synecdoche,[15] *womb*, which uses the vessel that contains the pregnancy to refer to its product—the infant, thereby exposing the instrumental view of the feminine entity in Rabbi Hiyya's perception? Or should we perhaps be focusing our reading on the expression *if only*, with its emotional charge, suggesting Rabbi Hiyya's profound emotional bond with his wife and the children she has borne him? Either way, it would seem that empathy is not what Rabbi Hiyya is expressing here: either he is unaware of the extent of his wife's suffering or he chooses to ignore it. In this reading, the story highlights the problematic marital relationship between Rabbi Hiyya and Judith, raising pointed questions about its qualities of sharing and honesty.

Does this story have a clear moral lesson? Perhaps, in shifting our emphasis from the intention of the text to a description of the act of reading, we open up diverse interpretive possibilities. The lacunae illuminated above would seem to allow for more than one possible reading. The gender interest that has directed our reading allows us to discern the story of the great anguish of a woman whose pain in childbirth leads her to a place of rebellion against her suffering. It presents Judith as a woman who will not simply accept her fate, and who does what she can to free herself from the patriarchal interests that force her body upon her against her will. We might read this as the story of a woman who performs an act of *tikkun* (repair) for herself and reassumes her independent, individual identity, not completely conditioned by the social norms that define her; simply—Judith.

I believe that Gilligan's theory concerning the stages of a woman's development may illuminate another aspect of Judith's act. According to Gilligan, women define their identity primarily through relationships, intimacy, and caring for others. It is only at a mature stage of their development that they come to grips with the significant power of individuation and stand up for their right to include themselves and their own needs within the framework of their interpersonal involvements.[16] Perhaps a "midlife" Judith is a woman who insists on her right to avoid pregnancy without being pursued from within with the accusation of selfishness for the rest of her life.

At the same time, it is clear that the story can only be understood in the context of gender power relations within which it is even possible to ask whether a woman may decide to avoid a process that causes her immense physical pain. The story in fact describes a reality in which the woman is clearly dependent on a rabbi or a man, and on his ruling: her action would apparently not have been taken had she not received his confirmation that she was exempt from the obligation of pregnancy. Judith reminds us that authority is based on power, and that power has existential significance. Her story is one of a woman who maneuvers authority in order to achieve what she wants.

"YOU HAVE BESET ME BEHIND AND BEFORE" (PS. 139:5): THE STORY IN CONTEXT

Mishnah: A man is commanded to be fruitful and multiply, but a woman is not. [However,] R. Johanan b. Baroka said: "[It is with regard] to both of them that the text says, 'And God blessed them, and God said to them: Be fruitful and multiply and replenish the earth' (Gen. 1:28)" (Mishna Yebamot 6,6).

Gemara: Whence is this deduced? R. Ile'a replied in the name of R. Eleazar son of R. Simeon: The Bible states, "And replenish the earth, and subdue it." It is the nature of a man to subdue but it is not the nature of a woman to subdue. [But one might argue,] on the contrary—"and subdue [in the plural] it" implies two! R. Nahman b. Isaac replied: [The expression] "And you subdue it" [*kivshuha*] is written without the letter *vav,* such that it alludes to the singular form (although it is pronounced as the plural verb). R. Joseph said: Hence, the proper proof-text is in fact, "I am God Almighty, be fruitful and multiply" (Gen. 35:11)—where the command is written in the singular, rather than in the plural. R. Ile'a further stated in the name of R. Eleazar son of R. Simeon: Just as one is commanded to say that which will be obeyed, so is one commanded not to say that which will not be obeyed. R. Abba stated: It is a duty; for the text teaches, "Reprove not a scorner, lest he hate you; reprove a wise man and he will love you" (Prov. 9:8).

R. Ile'a further stated in the name of R. Eleazar son of R. Simeon: One may modify a statement in the interests of peace; for it is written, "So shall you say to Joseph: Forgive, I pray you now, your brothers' iniquity" (Gen. 50:17). . . . At the school of R. Ishmael it was taught: Great is the cause of peace. For its sake even the Holy One, blessed be He, modified a statement; for at first it is written, "My lord being old" (Gen. 18:12), while afterwards it is written, "And I am old" . . . (ibid., 13)[17]

Judith, the wife of R. Hiyya, suffered in childbirth. She disguised herself and appeared before R. Hiyya. She said to him, "Is a woman commanded to be fruitful and multiply, or is she not?" "No," he replied. His wife then went and drank a sterilizing potion.

When the matter became known to him, he exclaimed, "If only you had borne me one more [issue of the] womb!" For a Master stated: Judah and Hezekiah were twin brothers, and Pazi and Tavi—twin sisters [all having been born from Judith]."

—Babylonian Talmud, Yebamot 65b
(MS Vatican 141)

In the literary research on legends of the Sages, insufficient emphasis has been placed on the manner in which the relations between the text and the context may change the meanings of a given narrative, or open it up to different exegetical possibilities. In order to address this issue in relation to the text above, we must look at the broader context in which the narrative appears. The comments of the Gemara surrounding the story relate to information that implies the unusual extent of Judith's suffering: the statement that follows the story seems to indicate that she actually bore two sets of twins—twin boys and twin girls. Thus, she has experienced two unusually difficult pregnancies and two complicated births. If childbirth is painful where there is just one fetus, then Judith's experience was surely exceptionally excruciating, and her desire to spare herself a recurrence of this pain and suffering is understandable. From her point of view, only the absolute removal of the possibility of future pregnancy can relieve her distress.

Parenthetically, attention should be paid to the play on the concept of doubling that underlies the concept of disguise and the related motif of twins. In Genesis Rabba 60, we find: "There were two women who covered themselves with a veil, and gave birth to twins—Rebecca and Tamar. Concerning Rebecca, it is written, 'And she took the veil and covered herself' (Gen. 24:65). Concerning Tamar, it is written, 'And she covered and wrapped herself with a veil'" (Gen. 38:14). The act of veiling, creating a double identity, reverberates in the midrash with the birth of twins. Every disguise entails a duality, for even though the persona is seemingly concealed, in many instances concealment actually reveals a great deal. Perhaps in the case of Judith, too, there is this sort of thematic connection between disguise (duality of identity) and the bearing of twins—in fact, two sets of twins.

The assumption that a clear distinction may be drawn between that which is included in the text and that which is outside of it reflects both exegetical and historical naiveté. Nevertheless, it is worth noting that the actual narrative is introduced with the words, "Judith, wife of R. Hiyya . . . ," and the information as to pain is conveyed in a laconic manner that requires no explanation: "suffered in childbirth." To my mind, there is room to suspect that the interpretation based on historio-biographical facts that follows, is intended to somehow moderate the radicalism of the story. The context in which it appears may be viewed as a metaphorical embodiment of a pincer movement by means of which the Gemara silences the story's outcry and its critical elements. The redactor is telling us, as it were, "Judith was an extreme case, which doesn't teach us anything." But is this in fact the case?

Another point that arises from the juxtaposition of historio-biographical facts to the narrative is that the context illuminates the story not as addressing the practical obligation entailed in the commandment to reproduce, but rather as dramatizing the power relations between the sexes in the context of childbirth and reproduction. When the Sages discuss the question of how many children one is commanded to bear in order to fulfill the obligation to "be fruitful and multiply," opinions are divided as to whether the minimum requirement is a son and a daughter or two sons. In a different version, the options under debate are either a son *and* a daughter, or a son *or* a daughter.[18] According to the biographical context provided for the story, it is clear that R. Hiyya and Judith have fulfilled their obligation. Thus, what is at stake here is not an existential, religious issue, but rather a political, gender one.

The general discussion of which our story is a part, concerns the Mishna: "'A man is commanded to be fruitful and multiply, but a woman is not.' [However,] R. Johanan b. Baroka said: '[It is with regard] to both of them that the text says, "And God blessed them, and God said to them: Be fruitful and multiply and replenish the earth" (Gen. 1:28).'" The Sages award tremendous importance to this commandment, which they regard as the first commandment in the Torah.[19] They regard abstaining from this commandment as tantamount to bloodshed and the diminishing of the Divine image in the world.[20]

The central place of women in the processes of fertility would cause us to expect them to be viewed as partners. Underlying the talmudic discussion as to whether women can be obligated with regard to this commandment or whether they are exempt, stands the moral question as to the logic of an exemption for women in a realm so fundamental to their gender identity—that of pregnancy and childbirth.[21] From this perspective, the splendid argumentation of the Gemara, with its attempt to evade the plain meaning of the commandment that is given to man and women equally, is thought provoking.

Esther Fisher discusses the debate in the Gemara and presents it as background to her understanding of the two main approaches surrounding the woman's exemption from certain commandments. One views the exemption as a sign of inferiority, which is the result or the cause of the social hierarchy. This orientation creates the ideal of equalizing the obligations incumbent upon women with those incumbent upon men, in order to rebalance the hierarchy. Naturally, it will tend to expose the rabbinic positions that maintain that women are indeed obligated with regard to the commandments in question. The other approach does not view the women's exemption as a sign of inferiority, but rather as a "differentness" indicating that men and women have different essences and purposes. This approach does not seek to "repair" the situation by imposing the same obligation on women, but rather justifies and glorifies their state of exemption. This approach views the rabbinic orientation and the consequent halakhic position as arising from consideration for women and concern for their welfare.[22]

Let us now consider what meanings may be derived from the redaction work. Viewing the matter simply, we might regard the inclusion of the story of Judith in its context as evidence of the recognition that pregnancy and childbirth sometimes entail great physical and psychological suffering for women (in the ancient world, death in childbirth was a common phenomenon). This recognition would highlight the unfairness of obligating women with regard to this commandment.[23] According to this approach, the story might offer support for the initial (majority) opinion in the Mishna, maintaining that women are exempt. Were it not for their exemption, Judith would be condemned to continued suffering.

However, a closer look at the texture of the discussion allows for a different view, which rejects, or at least weakens, the majority opinion of the Mishna.[24] It would seem that the story of Judith, appearing at the end of the discussion, plays an important role in this sort of reading. The opening statement of the story seeks to fill in the gap created between the two tannaic views presented in the Mishna—the majority view, maintaining that women are exempt, and the view of R. Johanan ben Baroka, who maintains that they are obligated. The next part of the discussion seems unrelated to the main topic: there are two more teachings by R. Ile'a in the name of R. Eleazar b. Simeon, but it is specifically here that we find a significant echo of Judith's story and an understanding of its function.[25]

The conceptual common denominator linking the teachings cited here is the idea that sometimes peace and human sensitivity are more important than speaking the truth—that is, in some instances it is better to "modify [a statement] for the sake of peace." Elsewhere in rabbinic literature we find references to falsehood employed as a means to achieve peace. It is interesting that the sphere of gender, and—more specifically—the relations between husband and wife, is a specific area in which, according to certain sources, it is permissible to lie in order to bring peace.[26]

If we wish to recognize this as an important principle, then we must ask ourselves: What is this truth that is better not to utter? On the face of it, one might argue—as Fisher does—that the question concerns the debate between the majority opinion and R. Johanan ben Baroka. This being the case, there are two exegetical possibilities: one is that the words of the majority opinion are the truth that must be concealed because exposing it would allow women freedom of choice in the matter. The other is that it is the opinion of R. Johanan ben Baroka that is the truth, and this must be concealed because exposing it would allow women to feel important—or, alternatively, would remove their freedom of choice in this matter.[27]

The connection between the idea of "modifying [a statement] for the sake of peace" and the story of Judith is both substantial and linguistic. The teachings deal with non-utterance of the truth in the context of avoiding conflict within a given relationship, and the concealment of Judith's identity may be interpreted in this way. The linguistic connection that is woven between the texts centers around the verb *le-shanot* (to change). We find that it is permissible to *change* the truth for the sake of peace; we also find that Judith *changes* her appearance. In other words, she modifies the truth for the sake of peace in order to avoid entering into a direct conflict with her husband. Moreover, we might suggest that the story supports two different moral options, both of which limit or reject the majority position. One option is that even though the majority opinion is the truth, the fact that R. Hiyya does not hide it from Judith is problematic, because it causes her to drink the sterilizing potion. If this truth is not hidden, the story seems to be saying, women will exploit the situation, and some will refrain from bearing children. The second option is that Judith's story is testimony to both the profound morality and the practicality of R. Johanan ben Baroka's opinion. It is problematic to enlist women for the difficult task of pregnancy and childbirth without granting them the merit of fulfilling a commandment. They cannot be left with the curse, "In pain shall you bear children," while at the same time being divested of the right to full partnership in the commandment to "be fruitful and multiply." In this sense, the story might be viewed as criticism of the majority opinion and indirect support for the minority view in the Mishna.

From a different, somewhat meta-poetic perspective, one might view this part of the discussion as an almost declarative expression of a feminine moral position influenced by the contexts of events and by relationships, as Gilligan describes it. The perception that "a person may modify the truth for the sake of peace" is understood here as a benevolent outlook maintaining that in the event of a conflict between peace and truth, peace should prevail. As the Sages recount elsewhere, this dilemma was implanted in the world at the time of Creation:

> Rabbi Simon said, "At the moment the Holy One chose to create Adam, the ministering angels broke up into factions. Some said, 'Create him,' while others said, 'Do not create him.' Thus it is written, 'Loving-kindness and truth will meet, righteousness and peace will kiss.'" (Ps. 85:11):
>
>> Loving-kindness said, "Create him, for he will do acts of loving-kindness."
>>
>> Truth said, "Do not create him, for he is full of falsehood."
>>
>> Righteousness said, "Create him, for he will perform much righteousness."

Peace said, "Do not create him, for he is essentially quarrelsome."

What did the Holy One do? He took Truth and cast it down to the earth. Thus it is written, "And truth will be cast to the earth" (Dan. 8:12). The ministering angels said: Sovereign of the Universe, Why do You shame Your very seal? Let truth rise from the earth. Thus it is written, "Truth will sprout from the earth." (Ps. 85:12)

It would seem that Judith may be identified with the statement, "Just as one is commanded to say that which will be obeyed, so is one commanded not to say that which will not be obeyed." In other words, there must be some correlation between the content of a statement and the listener to whom it is addressed. The disguise may be read as a sophisticated expression of this view: Judith manages to change the situation by changing the "identity" of the addressee. Ironically, her untruth exposes his truth—and thus the road is paved for the loving-kindness that she performs toward herself.

Thus, beneath the dominant patriarchal voices in this discussion we hear other voices that are vital and redemptive. Jewish feminists in our times who focus on areas of halakha related to childbearing may benefit from a closer look at the story of Judith within its context. There is no doubt that on one hand the story reflects masculine considerations with no direct input of feminine insights.[28] On the other hand, the fact that the woman's role in childbearing is defined as her facilitating the fulfillment of her husband's commandment to "be fruitful and multiply," is illuminated in this discussion in a multifaceted manner, and it may indicate the antipatriarchal criticism rustling beneath the surface of the text. From this perspective, my reading responds to Boyarin's challenge to view rabbinic texts as "[necessarily failed] attempts to propose utopian solutions to cultural tensions."[29]

"IT IS NOT IN YOUR MOTHER'S POWER"

Before addressing the second story about Judith, let us consider the literary issue arising from the juxtaposition of narratives dealing with the same character and reading them in the same context. The legends of the Sages are almost always brief literary units describing a concise episode in the life of their characters. Usually, such units do not fall on the historical time line—that is, they do not relate the date or period of the event described to other events or periods in the life of the same character. The story does not build a narrative that follows a character from birth to death. While we may assume that the scholars for whom these legends were written were more broadly familiar with these characters and the events of their lives, the biographical details conveyed in the stories are usually subservient to the particular circumstances of the narrative framework. Their purpose is not to enrich our knowledge about the character—his/her environment, family and social ties, education, and so on—but rather to contribute to the specific point of the story and its distinctive situation. Alon Goshen-Gottstein rejects the historic value of the details recounted in these legends, arguing that rabbinic sources do not necessarily convey historical facts about their characters, but they do illustrate the cultural spheres of interest that find expression in the stories told about them.[30] In other words, the conceptual themes reflected in a certain character in a story may teach us more about the world of the creators of the story than they do about the characters themselves.

The legends of the Sages create a general tension between the centrality of the character, whose biography (as a relatively lengthy narrative) forms the background to the story, and the aesthetic norm of a brief text.[31] It would seem that, more than any other poetic trait, it is the minimalism of the legends of the Sages that will not permit the containment of a full biographical format; at most it contains some stage of it.[32] As in biblical narratives, the legends of the Sages are devoid of free motifs—that is, the narrator never conveys details that are not necessary for the molding of the story. The focus on the essential point, and the exclusive use of bound motifs,[33] are the guidelines shaping the aesthetic ideal of this minimalist poetics.

Discussion of biography in rabbinic literature is therefore characterized by these two central characteristics of these texts: on one hand, the minimalism of the legends of the Sages, which describe only a certain segment of the life of the character (whether that character is fictional or historical); on the other hand, the existence of a number of stories about a given character within the same literary world. In some instances these stories contradict one another; in other instances they do not seem to connect with one another and it is impossible to decide on their location on the historio-chronological time line.

Despite the above consideration, it would seem that awareness of the cultural information stores among a community concerning a certain character, transcending the framework of a single narrative, is often important for an understanding of the dynamic of the process of its reading. In our instance, as noted, we have two stories that not only focus on the same characters, but also share the same expositional background. In a certain sense they may be read as two variations on the same theme.

> "...Judith, R. Hiyya's wife, suffered travail in childbirth. She said to him: My mother told me: 'Your father received [a token of] betrothal [*kiddushin*] on your behalf from another man when you were a child.' He replied: '[The testimony of] your mother does not have the power to forbid you to me.'"
>
> —Babylonian Talmud, Kiddushin 12b
> (MS Vatican 111)

The story appears within the framework of a discussion about the validity of a first or subsequent betrothal in light of various claims, and this incident is cited as an example of the rejection of a claim that seeks to undermine the validity of a current marriage on the basis of testimony as to a previous betrothal. R. Hisda cites the story of Judith as a precedent for rejecting annulment of a second marriage on the basis of unsubstantiated testimony as to a previous betrothal. The story, which took place decades before the time of the narrator, serves as proof that if no tangible evidence is produced, a marriage is not annulled on the basis of partial testimony or rumors.

The strategy that the main character, Judith, employs in this story to achieve her aim may be even more extreme than in the first story, and is focused directly on her marriage to R. Hiyya. It appears that her suffering in childbirth is so great that she is prepared to pay the heavy economic and social price of divorce if that will save her from further childbearing.

To justify the divorce, Judith claims that she has become aware that while she was still a child, her father betrothed her to another man, and she therefore cannot continue living with R. Hiyya (for this effectively makes her an adulteress, and her children *mamzerim*). She claims that this information comes from her mother. Attention should be paid to the fact that the elements of cunning that we encountered in the first story are intensified here to the point of what may be an outright lie: Judith invents this story in order to free herself from her husband.

As in the previous story, the character of R. Hiyya appears in his professional context, as a judge, but here he addresses the case fully aware that it is his wife who stands before him, and that the matter at hand pertains to the continuation of their marriage. R. Hiyya responds, in accordance with the discussion in which the story is integrated, that Judith's mother and her testimony do not have the power to annul the validity of their marriage. He thus rejects the claim, and the marriage remains valid.

In order to grasp the more profound gender significance of the story, it is necessary to read it as a story that establishes a feminine voice and subject within the reproductive context. Judith lies, but the materials of the lie should be examined with a view to understanding the consciousness that gives rise to it, as well as the consciousness that responds to it. The main character brings a certain type of claim that rests upon a "maternal legacy." In a certain sense, she may be viewed as trying to clarify something about the continuity of her own self, before she became the "wife of R. Hiyya," and the possibility of bringing that self to the fore. She speaks about herself in the first person, making a statement about her childhood that is cited as testimony given by her mother. Judith is claiming a different sort of knowledge and argument from those of R. Hiyya, but in the context of the gender power relations upon which the story is based, this attempt is doomed to failure. R. Hiyya responds to his wife in the language of the legal arena: he nullifies the mother's power, severing Judith from the preceding link in the feminine chain, and tells her, "[The testimony of] *your mother* does not have the power to forbid you to me." A close analysis of his response shows it to be an *argumentum ad hominem*: it attacks not the claim itself, but rather its source. It would therefore seem that what is being rejected here is something broader and more fundamental than the halakhic question at hand.

The Achilles' heel of this patriarchal text is the point where it acts against itself. The same voice of the feminine subject that it tries to annul

91

is brought to the fore in the story and exposes the radical option that may, perhaps, in a different time and in different circumstances, undermine the "father's order" and direct some difficult questions at it. Out of her suffering in childbirth Judith seeks to undermine the masculine heritage that proclaims, "In pain shall you bear children, and your desire shall be for your husband."

Unlike the previous story, in which Judith emerges victorious, having achieved her aim (no further pregnancies), she emerges from this story in an inferior position. Is there a connection between her direct submission to R. Hiyya and her failure in this instance, in contrast to the cunning strategy that she employed in the previous story, leading to success? Is her failure connected to the fact that she speaks to him in the language of a specific, personal "case" rather than in the language of the "law" and the "general rule," as in the previous story?

R. Hisda, as noted, uses Judith's story as a precedent in support of his position that a second marriage is not to be forbidden on the basis of partial testimony or rumors concerning an earlier marriage. In relating this incident, he intends to show that stories about past events that are known only from hearsay are not to be relied upon. It is for this reason that he chooses a story relating to a rumor that there is considerable room to regard as a fabrication. He removes the story from its particularity and turns it into a model example, imbuing it with new meaning in the context that interests him: nullification of the undermining element that may be brought as a claim to a previous marriage.

The theoretical possibility of locating the stories on some time line of biographical continuity in Judith's life allows us to imagine that the event recounted in tractate Kiddushin preceded the event described in Yebamot. The disguise episode represents a drawing of conclusions from the failure in the first story. In other words, having failed in her attempt to break up her marriage, as a way of ending the suffering of childbirth, Judith draws the obvious conclusions and adopts a more sophisticated strategy. This allows her, finally, to achieve what she wants.

≋ 5 ≋

THE VOICE OF DOUBT

The Wife of R. Simeon ben Halafta
and the Uncanny

For Rotem, on doubts and loves

"To be or not to be," Shakespeare's immortal formulation of uncertainty, echoes in the consciousness of each of us. Meaningful thought and life processes entail complex relations between fundamental certainties and the existence of doubt. Each of these spheres possesses its own special qualities.[1] Philosophy and science are heavily weighted in the direction of skepticism, with the aim of balancing the human psychological tendency to create false certainty. In literature, uncertainty may be a central quality of particular characters or serve as a literary device to create tension, a dilemma, or ambiguity.

In this chapter we address a legend of the Sages whose contribution to our understanding of the dimensions and potency of the self-criticism embedded in this literary genre has not, in my view, been awarded the attention it deserves.[2] On the face of it, uncertainty arises from lack of knowledge, but, as we shall see, the possibility of casting doubt assumes that much is known, and every skeptic professes many certainties. It is through a woman that our story voices doubt, and our inquiry will seek to discover the sort of certainty or knowledge that is assumed by this feminine questioning.

> Once R. Hiyya the Great and R. Simeon b. Halafta were sitting studying the law in the great study hall of Tiberias on the eve of Passover [some say on the eve of Yom Kippur], and they heard the sound of people talking.

R. Simeon asked him, "What are these people doing?"

He answered: "He who has [money] is purchasing [his needs for the festival], and he who has not is going to his master [employer], that he may give it to him."

He said: "If so, I will also go to my Master, that He may give me." He went out and prayed in the arena of Tiberias,[3] and he saw a hand holding out a pearl to him. He went and took it to our teacher [R. Judah the Prince].

[R. Judah] said to him: "From where did you obtain this? It is priceless [literally, *stardust*]. Take these three dinars and go and make preparations in honor of the day, and after the festival we shall advertise it, and whatever price we obtain for it, you shall have."

He took the three dinars, made his purchases, and went home. His wife said to him, "Simeon! Have you turned to theft? You earn no more than a hundred coins; what, then, is [the meaning of] these purchases?"

He immediately told her what had happened. She said: "Do you then desire that your canopy should contain one pearl less than that of your fellow in the world to come?"

He said to her: "What shall we do?"

She said to him, "Go and return your purchases to their owners, and the dinars to their owner, and the pearl to its owner."

When our teacher heard of it, he was grieved; he sent and had her brought to him. He said to her, "How much anguish you have caused this righteous man."

She answered him, "Do you then desire that his canopy should contain one less pearl on your account in the world to come?"

He said to her, "Even if it contains less, can we not make it up?"

She answered him, "Rabbi, in this world we have merited to see your face, but did Resh Lakish not teach that [in the world to come] every righteous man has his own chamber?"

And he acknowledged her [lesson]. Moreover, it is the way of supernal beings to give but not to take. [Thus,] this latter miracle was [even] greater than the former: When [R. Simeon] accepted [the pearl], his hand was below, but when he returned it his hand was above, as a man who lends to his fellow.

—Ruth Rabba 3, 4[4]

The plot of the story is built on the tension between the poverty characterizing the present and the faith in great reward in the world to come; between the human desire to escape destitution and the ability to reconcile oneself to it, trusting in the Master of the world. At the center of this conflict we find R. Simeon ben Halafta, a contemporary of R. Judah the Prince, who is presented as a wonder-worker and as possessing supernatural powers. Seemingly, this story glorifies the acceptance of deprivation in this world through a description of the double miracle performed for R. Simeon.

The story opens with R. Simeon b. Halafta and R. Hiyya engaged in Torah study on the eve of Passover (or of Yom Kippur). R. Simeon is distracted by the sound of people outside who are going about their purchases for the festival. He thinks about his own poverty and is disturbed by his inability to celebrate the festival properly. His colleague's explanation about the custom of workers going to their employers to collect payment leads R. Simeon to turn to his Master—God—and he is immediately answered.

R. Simeon's motives in proceeding to consult R. Judah the Prince—a great Sage and a wealthy man—are open to different interpretations, but it is clear that R. Judah immediately perceives the jewel to be of Divine origin, and worth a great deal of money. He proposes to wait until after the festival to have it appraised, in the meantime giving R. Simeon three dinars to cover his household festival expenses.

R. Simeon returns home with his purchases, seemingly pleased with his success and unprepared for his wife's reaction to the miracle. She argues that a person dare not receive anything in this world that will detract from the reward awaiting him in the world to come. R. Simeon's wife is depicted as a forceful character with a clear idea of what belongs where, and she insists that every asset be returned to its source.

R. Simeon's distress over this turn of events arouses the pity of R. Judah, but his attempts to change her position are ineffectual. A simple reading of the story conveys the impression of a woman who is "more Catholic than the pope"; a sort of scholarly extremist who cites Resh Lakish's teaching that every righteous person has his own reward awaiting him in the world to come, and leads those around her to recognize the importance of reconciling oneself with one's financial situation—or, in other words, with the "existing order."[5]

A critical gender reading of the story may overturn the conclusions of this simple reading and illuminate the power of the social and theological questioning embodied in the feminine voice. Carol Gilligan focuses on the uniqueness of the woman's voice and the importance of listening to it: "By voice I mean something like what people mean when they speak of the core of the self. Voice is natural and also cultural. It is composed of breath and sound, words, rhythm, and language. And voice is a powerful psychological instrument and channel, connecting inner and outer worlds."[6] The conceptualization of the feminine voice in Gilligan's theory will help us to clarify the role of the woman's speech in this story.

The way in which R. Simeon's wife confronts her husband—and, later, also R. Judah the Prince—shows the power of this character, who is a contrast to the usual feminine stereotypes. She is not a passive figure, nor one whose interests extend only as far as the home and its material needs. One might say that this woman is almost a symmetrical inverse of the fisherman's wife in the popular folktale, who dreams of ever more grandiose living conditions. In response to R. Judah's attempts at persuasion, the wife of R. Simeon voices the "absolute truth" of the society of the Sages—the idea that righteousness is an individual matter not subject to partnership—in a tone of doubt and irony.[7] This nameless woman confronts the representatives of the society of Sages defiantly and fearlessly.

For the purpose of developing a plot whose subject is the tension between poverty in the present and faith in reward in the time to come, it would suffice for the story to feature only R. Simeon and his wife. Indeed, this possibility finds expression in the parallel text in Tanhuma,[8] which omits R. Hiyya and R. Judah, as well as in the similar (and in many ways opposite) story of R. Hanina b. Dosa and his wife.[9] Our narrative, by contrast, shifts the attention given to the financial situation away from the narrow family context, and endows the wife of R. Simeon with a voice of supreme irony. The manifestly social orientation of the story locates the marital dialogue within the context of the society of Sages in its broader sense.[10]

In the reading proposed here, we question why R. Judah the Prince, who knows R. Simeon b. Halafta and is familiar with his financial situation, does not trouble himself prior to the appearance of the pearl to contribute a portion of his own tremendous wealth, so that his colleague can properly fulfill the requirements of the festival.[11] The chasm separating the wealth of the president of the Sanhedrin from the destitution of the scholar who lacks the means to purchase his basic necessities, cries out to the heavens. "Rabbi, in this world we have merited to see your face," declares the wife of R. Simeon. Is this in fact so? It seems to me that her words express protest against an antisocial social reality in which each righteous man has his own, private, self-contained realm—in *this* world. The woman's voice unmasks a society that lacks the most elementary degree of solidarity. The inability of a person to make his festival purchases testifies to the absence of a basic social infrastructure that would allow the members of society to maintain themselves and fulfill their religious requirements. In confronting R. Judah, the woman is in fact declaring, "God may have His reasons for creating and maintaining poverty in this world, but that in no way exempts you from seeking and pursuing justice."[12]

As to the obvious question of why R. Judah gives R. Simeon the three dinars only after the pearl materializes and not before, when he was in need, it would seem that, in some way, R. Judah needs this poverty-stricken righteous man and his righteous wife, and the lesson that they come to teach. R. Judah somehow knows that R. Simeon b. Halafta (and not he himself) will experience a miracle—that is, Divine intervention in the perverted social order. More broadly, this is the whole point of the story: this righteous couple teaches him—and the readers—that while the righteous may have a direct connection with the upper worlds, this in no way excuses or repairs the social distortions of this world.

The intention of the narrator in noting that "he acknowledged her [lesson]" is obscure: the victory of R. Simeon's wife is absolute, for not only do R. Judah and her husband "obey" her, but the very heavens do, too. At the same time, the conclusion of the story—"It is the way of supernal beings to give but not to take. [Thus,] this latter miracle was

[even] greater than the former: When [R. Simeon] accepted [the pearl] his hand was below, but when he returned it his hand was above, as a man who lends to his fellow"—makes this a bitter, shameful victory. The latter miracle—the taking back of the pearl by the heavenly hand—makes a greater impression and has greater impact than the first miracle of the pearl descending from heaven.[13] The impact of the miracle can be understood in different ways. As I understand it, the movement of returning the pearl to heaven creates a dramatic picture of a man stretching out his hand, palm down, toward heaven as though extending a gift or loan to his fellow. This inversion of the "natural" state of affairs, in which the heavens are in the position of giving, drives the theological irony of the story to a shocking extreme: God is compared, as it were, to a beggar gathering alms from the lower worlds.

If our understanding of the conclusion of the story in its social and theological context is correct, we conclude that the lesson that R. Judah—as well as the heavens themselves—is supposed to learn from the woman, has not been learned. In fact, what the story describes is a conversation of the deaf.[14] Whether the narrator of the story is hostile toward R. Judah and his household or whether it is meant as criticism of the "upper" classes, wherever they may be, at any time or place, the voice of R. Simeon's wife is like a message in a bottle cast upon the sea of culture. It is the voice of doubt, asking penetrating questions about the existing social order: Does every righteous person indeed have a place of his own in the world to come? In what way does this imagined reality impact our conduct in this world? What sort of relations of give-and-take exist between living human beings and the upper worlds?

The voice that the story lends to a woman, in this instance, has great persuasive power specifically because it echoes powerful inner voices. In his article titled "The Uncanny," Freud discusses a certain emotional effect in which something that is known, familiar, and friendly is at the same time foreign, unfamiliar, and anxiety-provoking.[15] The "uncanny" is produced in the seams of the relationship between knowledge (that which I know and recognize) and the casting of doubt on that knowledge. In other words, even though the woman is presented in many talmudic texts as foreign and external—the "other" that must be silenced—she is in fact closer than she seems. She is threatening precisely because she is at one and the same time both familiar and foreign, the same and different. She provokes anxiety because she causes the talmudic man—the subject—to question the certainty with which he supposedly knows and is familiar with himself. In the same way, femininity as otherness is "uncanny" because it is not the *opposite* of masculinity, but rather that which *questions* the oppositeness of male and female. Femininity resides within masculinity; it resides there as "otherness," as deconstruction of it, as a questioning of its homogeneity.[16]

We find that a study of the sources through a reading "from the margins"[17] may reveal many subversive foundations embedded in talmudic texts. The heterogeneity of rabbinic culture includes opposing and suppressed positions that challenge hegemonic assumptions and values. The exposure of this heterogeneity opens the door to renewed thinking about the patriarchal nature of the rabbinic corpus.

6

OPEN TO CONQUEST

Prostitution—Temptations and Responses

EVERYONE, IT SEEMS, knows the answer to the question: Which is the oldest profession in the world? The difficulty in defining *prostitution* arises in no small measure from the need to distinguish between this realm and other sorts of relationships that involve sexual relations outside of the marriage framework, such as adultery and concubinage. Prostitution is a timeless, universal phenomenon that expresses very clearly the unequal power relations between men and women in society, and it seems reasonable to assume that it will continue to exist as long as this inequality remains. From a feminist perspective it is clear that the ideological purpose of the cliché about the "oldest profession in the world" is to perpetuate prostitution as a timeless phenomenon, an immutable natural law.

Most of the definitions of this social institution in the ancient world are functional in nature and include three main components: indiscriminateness (the absence of any framework governing the choice of partner for the sexual act); the absence of emotional involvement; and payment. Prostitutes in the ancient world were mostly women; the clientele was always male. Ancient patriarchal societies sanctified the masculine sexual drive, which was considered uncontrollable, and asserted its need for release. Obviously, the element of "indiscriminateness" is problematic by definition, since it implies some degree of freedom of choice and ignores the coercion and duress that are inherent to this phenomenon. Most prostitutes in the ancient world were not free, but rather maidservants who were forced by their masters to engage in this activity. The free women who turned to whoredom (mostly former maidservants who had been freed) sold their bodies for money out of necessity, mostly against a background of poverty and need. In other words, they were victims of the system.[1]

The Bible adopts a negative religious and moral attitude toward prostitution. A prostitute is someone who receives payment for the sexual services that she offers, as evidenced in the prohibition, "You shall not bring the hire of a prostitute . . . into the house of the Lord your God for any vow" (Deut. 23:19). Additional explicit prohibitions and severe sanctions apply in situations involving a certain status on the part of the woman—such as adultery (where the question of payment is irrelevant; the essence of the prohibition relates to the fact that the woman is married) or a prostitute who is the daughter of a kohen.[2] The Sages debated how the phenomenon should be defined, and although one view maintains that any woman who engages in sexual relations outside of marriage (even if she is single, and even without payment) falls into this category, this opinion was rejected. The majority ruled that a prostitute is defined as a woman who engages in relations with a man whom she is forbidden to marry, by reason of one of the various categories of prohibited relations.[3] In rabbinic literature we find no distinctly halakhic definition pertaining to prostitution as an occupation.[4] Nevertheless, it was a common phenomenon in the urban Roman environment in which the Sages were active, as indicated in many different sources.[5]

One might say that the attitude of the ancient Jewish world toward prostitution was a dualistic one: on one hand, the phenomenon was denounced and relegated to the functional and moral margins; on the other hand, it was acknowledged as an integral part of political, social, and cultural life. A double standard in these moral matters seems to have existed even then. In a world in which the most common form of contraception consisted of abortion or abandonment of unwanted babies, men availed themselves of the bodies of their legal wives only occasionally. Their remaining libido was spent among thousands of submissive, destitute, defenseless prostitutes living on the fringes of society. The men exempted themselves from responsibility for the fate of these women by means of payment, usually a paltry sum.[6]

The practice of prostitution relates to the differentiation between the erotic body and the reproductive one. At the foundation of the patriarchal structuring of the sexes is the idea that there is a moral distinction between a woman's fertility and her sexuality, finding expression in the Madonna/whore duality. A woman's "natural" destiny, according to this world of concepts, is self-actualization through her reproductive ability. The "good girl," from the moral perspective, is the loyal wife and devoted mother who radiates asexuality. The "bad girl" is the prostitute who gives independent expression to her sexuality. This figure is cast out and relegated to a miserable existence outside the bounds of polite society.[7] This distinction will occupy us as we come to examine the way in which the Sages read the story of Rahab.

Rahab is the harlot who hides the spies dispatched by Joshua to survey Jericho in anticipation of the conquest of the city (Josh. 2). She takes them into her home and conceals them among stalks of flax arranged on her roof. Inter alia she tells them that all the inhabitants of the land are fearful of the children of Israel, and makes them promise that in return for her aid, they will save her family when the city is conquered. Rahab then deceives the king's soldiers, helping the spies to escape and saving their lives. The promise is fulfilled: the same spies return in person to Rahab's house to save her and her whole household.

This is unquestionably a strange story. The spies go no farther than the harlot's home in the wall of the city, and then escape back to Joshua. Later we read of the miraculous crossing of the Jordan by the entire nation, and the walls of Jericho, too, fall in a miraculous way. Clearly, the spying mission is superfluous for the purposes of military preparation. So what were the spies actually doing in Jericho?

The biblical story interweaves different registers.[8] On the overt level, it describes a secret military mission relating to a certain politico-national state of affairs. On a deeper level, the story arouses many sexual associations and touches on intergender relations.[9] The linking of the act of military conquest and the idea of "coitus" with (penetration of) the land is expressed through the language, metaphor, and imagery that the text uses to describe spying. This is not a purely linguistic matter; it reflects deeply rooted customs and mechanisms of ancient social and legal thinking. Anthropologists have shown, for example, that in various cultures the conquest of territory was not considered complete until the women of the conquered nation had been raped by the conquerors.[10] The analogies between the "land" and "woman" in many biblical texts are unquestionably part of the background to the story.[11]

The rhetorical aim of the story has been discussed in various contexts. Zakowitz maintains that it ridicules Joshua and the spies, with the aim of amplifying God's greatness.[12] Newman proposes that the story began as an oral legend retold by Rahab's tribe, which lived in Jericho, with a view to reminding the Israelites of their debt to the Rahabites.[13] Whatever the case may be, the image of the woman arising from the story is an equivocal one. On one hand, she is a foreign element who belongs to the "enemy camp," and is also a prostitute. On the other hand, Rahab is portrayed in the story as a positive character who saves the "good guys" and aids the conquest of the city that represents the gateway to the promised land.

This stereotyped dualism in the description of the woman character conforms to the insights and conclusions arrived at by Sandra Gilbert and Susan Gubar.[14] Following a study of Victorian literary texts, they sketch the system of feminine stereotypes as being based on a formative image of woman who is both angel and monster, with an emphasis on the simultaneous coexistence of both poles. The social culture is critical of this duality, for two reasons: first, because it always, necessarily, includes the negative aspect; and second, because duality implies a lack of cohesion, and this in itself is perceived as a negative characteristic of the feminine figure. For Gilbert and Gubar, this stereotype represents the most extreme mechanism in the structuring of the attitude toward the "other."

Rahab, who is depicted by the Sages as oscillating between the two poles—positive and negative—simultaneously attracts and repels. Unquestionably, she serves as a national, social, and gender "other." It is interesting to examine the different ways in which the Sages present this unique character.

> Rahab the harlot would cohabit with her compatriots from inside [the walls] and with bandits from the outside, as it is written, "For her house was on the town wall, and she dwelled upon the wall" (Josh. 2:15).
>
> —Sifri Zuta 10, 29 (Horowitz, p. 263)

The harlot, the liminal figure whose house is on the town wall[15]—the border separating the town from what is outside of it—is essentially loyal to no one. The word *homa* (wall), which appears twice in the verse, is interpreted as an allusion to the two spheres in which Rahab offers her services: she is available both to the people of the city, who are within the walls, and to the bandits who roam outside of it. The prostitute who gives herself to many men does not belong to any of them. She provides sex services to anyone who serves her interests. This sort of opportunistic character is a prime source of information as to the fighting capacity of a certain group of people, or the dispirited fear of another. Indeed, the prostitute, who is familiar with the most intimate masculine secrets (on the physical and symbolic levels alike) makes vital gossip available to the conquerors:

> Rahab the harlot, too, told Joshua's spies: "For we have heard how the Lord dried up the water of the Reed Sea before you, when you came out of Egypt" (Josh. 2:10). What do we deduce from the fact that elsewhere it is written, "neither was there spirit in them any more" (Josh. 5:10), while here we find the verse, "nor did the spirit of any man rise any more"? [This means that] they even lost their virility. And how did she know this? Because, as one of the Sages taught: "There was no prince or ruler who had not visited Rahab the harlot."
>
> —Babylonian Talmud, Zebahim 116 a–b
> (according to MS Munich 95)

This teaching rests on the hermeneutical law known as the *gezera shava*—an argument from analogous expression. The identical word—*spirit*—appears both in the story of Rahab and in the story of the conquest of the land. It connects two texts that are seemingly far removed from one another, imbuing the connection between them with meaning: the narrator who describes the psychological state of the enemies of the Israelites "echoes" and confirms, as it were, what Rahab had told the spies.[16] It turns out that the political situation is hurting business. According to this tongue-in-cheek midrash, Rahab complains to the Israelite men about the fear that plagues the leaders of Jericho, causing sexual impotence. The connection between their psychological and physical state is something she is qualified to testify to. Perhaps the author of the midrash is hinting that Rahab's contacts with politicians, and perhaps also senior military personnel, award the information that she offers added importance. In any event, it seems that in assessing the opposition he is likely to encounter in Jericho, Joshua can rely on the information provided by the harlot and take it into account in planning his strategy.

It must be acknowledged that Rahab, as depicted in the biblical story, does not share the life of most prostitutes who are downtrodden victims beholden to pimps and subjected to violence and exploitation. She is not described as weak in any way. On the contrary, her power and competence are most impressive. Rahab is the active character; she sets the tone; it is she who advances the views of the narrator concerning the historical ramifications of the story (as we shall see). She is even referred to by her own name, in contrast to most women in the Bible and even the spies themselves, who are referred to as the "two men." She hides them, leads the king's messengers astray and frustrates their efforts, overcomes the challenge presented by the closing of the city gates, plans and executes a rescue operation, giving the spies detailed instructions for escape (in contrast to the minimal guidance provided by their own leader, Joshua), and eventually comes to an agreement with them.[17] In other words, she is very knowledgeable about the political and social situation, she is active and manipulates all the males around her, and all this while managing to take care of her own interests with impressive success.

Rahab's power and her influence on the masculine world are manifest in the teachings of the Sages. Not only the "princes and rulers" of Jericho are affected by her; she makes no less of an impact on the imagination of the talmudic Sages:

> Our Sages taught: There have been four exquisitely beautiful women in the world: Sarah, Rahab, Abigail, and Esther. And those who say [according to a known tradition] that Esther had a greenish hue, replace Esther (in the list) with Vashti. Our Sages taught: Rahab led [men] astray with her name; Jael—with her voice; Abigail—by her memory; Michal, daughter of Saul, by her appearance. Rabbi Isaac taught: Anyone who said, "Rahab, Rahab" would immediately experience a seminal emission. To which Rabbi Nahman responses, "I can say, Rahab Rahab, many times over, and it has no effect on

me." He replied, "What I said applies to one who knew and was familiar with her."

—Babylonian Talmud, Megilla 15a
(according to MS New York)

Rahab is counted as one of the most beautiful women in the world. On one hand, her beauty may explain her power of attraction, which is the power of temptation. On the other hand, beauty is a special feminine quality that is bound up with the positive light in which her character is viewed. According to Rabbi Isaac, the suggestive name of the harlot of Jericho (*rahav* = wide), as the text states—"a harlot woman whose name was Rahab" (Josh. 2:1), suggesting a wide and unselective opening (which, as noted, is part of the definition of prostitution)—was itself sufficient to arouse a man who heard it to a sexual climax. The "argument" between R. Isaac and Rabbi Nahman as to the validity of this depiction brings a smile to the face of the female reader, who imagines the respected Sages entertaining sexual fantasies and competing over their sexual self-control (the basic assumption being that men's control over their sexual drive is limited). Characteristically for those who deal in words, there is a sort of "philosophical" debate here as to the suggestive power of words to arouse desire in men. The motif of control, the question of who controls whom—the man controlling the woman or vice versa; the man controlling his desire or vice versa—is one of the deeper questions addressed by the Sages' reading of the story.

The sources that we shall now examine focus on the main direction of the rabbinic reading of the character of Rahab. As we shall see, they convert her and transform her into the mother of priests (*kohanim*) and prophets. The early centuries of the Common Era were a formative period for a new collective Jewish identity. Internal and external events, including the destruction of the Temple, cultural assimilation, and the growth and spread of Christianity, exerted heavy pressure on the rabbinic establishment, forcing it to consolidate more clearly the parameters of its imagined community.[18]

In Second Temple period literature, as well as in later rabbinic literature, we find narratives whose main theme is proselytism.[19] We find stories of characters who arrived at a recognition of the power of God—such as

Jethro (Ex. 18:10), Hiram (II Chron. 2:11), Nebuchadnezzar (Dan. 2:47), Ahiur (Judith 14:10), Heliodorus (II Maccabees 3:35–39), and others. In many instances, a cultural fantasy arises in a situation where a nation under foreign domination imagines an inverse state of affairs, in which the rulers become subjugated. These fantasies generally concern high-profile characters such as kings and ministers.[20] In our instance, the character is of lower status—a woman prostitute, who is given an important role at a key point in the national narrative. The question, then, is how Rahab comes to be honored in this way.

In order to lay the foundation for an understanding of the Sages' tremendous act of appropriation, we must first consider the gender "workings" of Rahab, who does not easily respond to the binary categories of "man" and "woman." Rahab—and perhaps the prostitute in general—offers us an opportunity to examine the elusive nature of gender concepts and their permanence. To this end we will take a brief detour into theory.

One of the common questions—if not the most common—in discourse about the differences between the sexes, concerns the origins of these differences. The discourse turns on three central concepts, which have traditionally been viewed as being interlinked: sex, gender, and sexuality. The concept of "sex" refers to physical and biological differences; as such, it is generally perceived as something "natural." The concept of "sexuality" pertains to the object of a person's sexual desire, and generally speaking, heterosexuality—certainly in Jewish culture—is considered the natural and desirable norm. "Gender" refers to the sociocultural differences between the sexes, and pertains to what makes us masculine or feminine; thus, the focus here is behavioral rather than physiological, with the emphasis on socially and culturally structured qualities or behaviors in relation to the question of what is a man or what is a woman. For example, gentleness, softness, and solicitude are generally attributed to women, while valor, courage, and toughness are generally attributed to men. The gender category highlights and sharpens the historical, social, and cultural context in which the differences between the sexes should be understood.

Until the advent of feminism, these three concepts were regarded as being perfectly aligned. In other words, if someone possessed a certain (female) set of sexual organs, she would develop feminine qualities and abilities, would engage in roles that society defined as feminine, and would feel a sexual attraction to the opposite sex (men). Hence Freud's famous conclusion that "anatomy is destiny": that is, our sexual organs determine our personal qualities, our behavior, and the object of our desire. The interconnection of these three areas was perceived as something "natural," fixed, and unchangeable. Any behavior or quality that violated this order was perceived as a deviation from the norm, as a pathological manifestation that needed to be restored to the "natural," normative path.

One of the first effects of feminism was a severing of the connection among these three concepts. This is the significance of Simone de Beauvoir's assertion that "one is not born, but rather becomes, a woman." In other words, women and men do not have inherently different natures, and anatomy is not destiny; rather, society and culture define what is considered feminine or masculine, and it is these factors that try to fix these definitions as something "natural."[21]

Judith Butler is a feminist theoretician whose questioning of the concept of gender may help us to understand the case of Rahab. Butler argues that we should speak of a gender continuum, rather than fixed and clear gender forms, such as "men" and "women." In *Gender Troubles* she questions the binary distinction between culture and nature, and between sex and gender, arguing that the categories of "woman" and "man" are political from the outset, rather than "natural." All bodies are genderized from the start of their social existence, and this indicates that there is no "natural body" that precedes culture. Butler maintains that our concept of two separate sexes—and our resulting perception of the male and female bodies as fundamentally different—is likewise the product of language, culture, and regimentation. The structuring of this regimentation serves the interest of presenting the two sexes as different from one another, so that they will be attracted to one another.

Butler asserts that gender is an act, action, or performance that is constantly taking place, because it is impossible to exist as a social being outside of gender norms. It is the perpetual performance of gender that lends it meaning. If gender is action, doing, then gender may in fact be "done" differently, in such a way as to *demonstrate* its performative nature, instead of *concealing* it. This is how one creates "gender troubles," or uses the law against itself. The subversive act that is available to us is not to live beyond gender categories, but to act in such a way as to demonstrate their unnaturalness.

In the midrashim, the Sages portray Rahab as a "top prostitute," the sort described by Beauvoir: "[T]those women who exploit their sexuality to the extreme create a situation for themselves nearly equal to that of a man; beginning with that sex which gives them over to the males as objects, they come to be subjects. Not only do they make their own living like men, but they exist in a circle that is almost exclusively masculine; free in behavior and conversation . . ."[22]

Accordingly, we might regard Rahab as someone who "performs" the gender of a "feminine woman" through her very functioning as a harlot. She plays a feminine game (of a tempting, pleasuring, beautiful woman), but her identity should not be confused with the role that she plays. This is merely her "work." It is easy to understand, on the basis of the concepts presented above, why Rahab's behavior in the story follows several masculine norms. While courage is generally perceived as a "masculine" trait, Rahab's courage finds expression in her hiding of the spies, as well as the lie that she brazenly tells the king's soldiers. This involves considerable personal risk, for she may be exposed as a traitor to her city. Her intense activism is certainly a "masculine" trait. Foreign women are described in several places in the Bible as independent women who are not subservient to fathers, husbands, or brothers. Rahab is presented as having her own home, as supporting herself, and also as taking care of her family's safety. As such she is powerful enough to maintain a code of hospitality that can be upheld only by a citizen who is the head of the family. According to ancient Israelite norms, from this perspective, too, she is more like a man than like a woman.[23]

Against the backdrop of this gender duality of Rahab's character, let us try to analyze the central idea behind the Sages' teaching regarding her conversion. The plot of this interpretation rests upon the biblical narrative, which notes that she recognizes the God of Israel, and that Joshua leaves her alive after the conquest of the city. The critical element providing the platform for the exegetical direction taken by the Sages is the fact that Rahab recognizes God's power.[24] Incidentally, the conclusions of Bible research suggest that the theological unit presenting Rahab as being courageously loyal to the Israelite nation and the God of Israel (Josh. 2:9–11) is not part of the original narrative.[25] The midrashim do not address this possibility; for the midrashic author we are dealing with, Rahab's declaration of faith is a heartfelt expression of truth. It is not a game, a temporary disguise, that Rahab dons for reasons of expediency. Her declaration is an illumination, a revelation of the proper path, a gateway to sincere conversion.[26]

> They said: Rahab the harlot was ten years old when Israel left Egypt, and she was a prostitute throughout the forty years that they were in the wilderness. At the age of fifty she was converted, and she said: "Master of the universe, I have sinned concerning three things; forgive me by virtue of three things: the cord, the window, and the wall—as it is written, 'She let them down by *the cord, through the window,* for her house was in the *town wall,* and in the wall she dwelled'" (Josh. 2:15).
>
> —Mekhilta de-R. Ishmael

During the period of the Mishna and the Talmud, the process of conversion involved three main components: observance of the commandments, faith in the God of Israel, and joining the Jewish community. As we shall see, the midrashim concerning Rahab's conversion touch on all three of these aspects. The biblical account does not address the question of whether, following the Israelite conquest, Rahab continued to engage in prostitution. The rabbinic legend relies on Rahab's acknowledgment that "the Lord your God is God in the heaven above and upon the earth below" (Josh. 2:11), presenting a far-reaching development of her belief in the power of the Israelite nation and its God, leading to her repentance.[27]

The above midrash connects the biography of the harlot from Jericho to the biography of the nation of Israel. She is a professional, veteran harlot, with forty years of experience: years of shame, disgrace, social censure. With the arrival of the nation of Israel in the land, the midrash tells us, a new Rahab is born—as a proselyte. This woman, who has lived most of her life in the heterotopic sphere of prostitution[28]—at the same time contained within and excluded from society—now leaves it and assumes a stable and respectable social and national identity. The story of Rahab's conversion confirms the view of prostitution as a form of performance rather than as an immanent, defined, fixed identity as a certain kind of woman.[29] The Sages' ambivalence toward the "other" is expressed here in the desire to control it by assimilating it.

Rahab seeks God's forgiveness, by virtue of having helped and saved the spies, for the three commandments that she violated before joining the Israelite nation. The "three commandments" that she alludes to have a clear gender orientation; they are the three commandments specific to women: *nidda* (ritual purity surrounding the menstrual cycle), *halla* (separating a portion of dough for the priests), and lighting candles (to usher in the Sabbath).[30] Her atonement is symbolized here through three objects: the cord (*hevel*), the window (*halon*), and the wall (*homa*), corresponding to the three commandments. As in other rabbinic legends relating to prostitutes, the crux of the message conveyed here concerns the power of repentance to bring reward even to great sinners.[31]

Ahuva Ashman, who addresses the story in its context, notes that this is the first narrative in (deuteronomist) biblical historiography whose subject is the execution of the command to conquer the land, but which in fact describes its non-execution, owing to the failure to fulfill the command to destroy the city entirely.[32] The allusion to the Exodus from Egypt assumes a sarcastic tone here. The scarlet thread, corresponding to the blood on the doorposts by virtue of which the Israelite houses were "passed over" during the plague on the firstborn,[33] now allows for a "passing over" of a Canaanite household that the Israelites are commanded to destroy. A Canaanite harlot succeeds in outsmarting the Israelite decree of complete annihilation of the Canaanites. The biblical historian chooses to begin the story of the conquest of the land specifically with a story of heresy, which—from his perspective—is the early seed that will flower in the eventual destruction of Israel and Judea. The story seeks to allude to a repeated pattern in biblical historiography: relations with other nations, and especially the Canaanites, will lead Israel astray to idolatry and a violation of the covenant between God and His people. The earliest steps of the Israelites upon the land of Canaan seal their fate, because they fall into the trap: they forge a covenant with the Canaanites, and will therefore later be destroyed. The remnants of the nations who survive the Israelite law of annihilation, such as Rahab and her family, are a trap that will lead the heart of the people astray and bring about their downfall. According to this reading, the foreign harlot is the link connecting the nation of Israel with its own destruction, embodying the stereotype of the woman who tempts the man and so leads to his own demise.[34]

From this perspective, the direction adopted by the Sages as arising from the following source is especially interesting, for Rahab is not just another proselyte; the midrash teaches that she became none other than the wife of the nation's leader, and one of the ancestors of Hulda, the prophetess. Her integration into respectable Jewish society is beyond question.[35] It is interesting to note that in a different tradition, too, a "positive" foreign woman like Rahab may become part of a respected dynasty: in the New Testament, Rahab is mentioned as part of the lineage of Jesus.[36] Likewise, in the Epistle to the Hebrews (11:31), in the chapter devoted to biblical characters who are role models owing to the power of their faith, Rahab appears as part of a venerable pantheon that includes, inter alia, the three patriarchs.

R. Nahman's teaching that Hulda the prophetess was a descendant of Joshua, raises a question, since we learn elsewhere that she was among the descendants of Rahab:

> R. 'Ena Saba cited the following in objection to R. Nahman: Eight prophets who were also priests were descended from Rahab the harlot . . . R. Judah says: Hulda the prophetess was also one of the descendants of Rahab the harlot. [We know this] because it is written here "the son of Tikvah" and it is written elsewhere [in connection with Rahab] "the line of [*tikvat*] scarlet thread." [R. Nahman] replied: . . . Through a merging of my teaching and yours we arrive at the truth that she became a proselyte and Joshua married her.
>
> —Babylonian Talmud, Megilla 14b
> (according to MS New York)

Here, too, the midrash links two seemingly unrelated verses on the basis of the common word—*tikva*—that appears in both. Attention should be paid to the fact that the midrash does not hesitate to connect a personal name with the name of an object, and on this basis to conclude that there is a connection between the spies' promise of Rahab's reward, and the reward that she actually receives from God. It may be that through this hermeneutical teaching the Sages seek to cleanse Joshua of his deviation from the command of annihilation and from the critical position that the story appears to adopt concerning the failure to fulfill it. To counter the story of heresy against the covenant, the Sages present a story of joining the covenant, a wondrous story of ascent "from the lowest depths to the loftiest heights." The Israelites are proceeding to the next significant stage of their national cultural consolidation: the conquest of the land and its settlement. Their passing "via" the harlot who is destined to convert becomes, in rabbinic literature, a symbol of their domination of the space of the "heterotopic" other, taming it and civilizing it.

According to this reading, Rahab plays a key role in the civilizing of the nation of Israel in its land. As Pardes notes, she is the vital gateway through which those seeking to enter the land must pass (perhaps this, too, is hinted at in her name).[37] Incidentally, it is not only here that sexual relations with a harlot play a role in shaping a conformative masculine identity. One of the most ancient narratives presenting the harlot as a civilizing element in society appears in the Sumerian *Epic of Gilgamesh*.[38] In this sense, the harlot as a liminal character who crosses over to the "right side" confirms the victory of the Israelite cultural identity.

Rabbinic literature includes many stories based on the homology between gender identity and group identity—that is, the Sages use the gender other to speak about the ethnic other. This homology is based on the fact that, for the most part, both of these identities are built on a system of contrasts in which each defines itself by means of its negative. The use of this homology is effective for two reasons: it works to anchor cultural, fluid meanings in "natural" categories which are seemingly fixed and firm; at the same time it creates a hierarchy of preferred identities and serves as a tool for controlling differentness and discouraging deviation. It is therefore not surprising to find so many stories about identity involving feminine characters in general, and questionable women in particular.[39]

In sum, we might say that the Sages solve the problem of the simultaneous duality of the feminine character by sorting out Rahab's angelic/monstrous biography over a chronological time line: at first she is a monster, but after she sees the light she becomes an angel, converts, marries Joshua, and becomes a loyal wife and dedicated bearer of progeny.

The next text we shall look at testifies to the exegetical effort demanded of the Sages in order to introduce Rahab into the ranks of the Israelite elite.

> "And they turned and went up to the mountain" (Deut. 1:24). This tells us that it is the way of spies to go up the mountain. Accordingly, we find concerning Rahab and Joshua's emissaries: "She said to them, Go to the mountains, lest the pursuers harm you, and hide there for three days, until the pursuers return, and afterwards you shall go on your way" (Josh. 2:16). This tells us that the Divine spirit rested upon her, for had the Divine spirit not visited her, how could she know that they were destined to return in three days? Hence, this must be telling us that the Divine spirit rested upon her.
>
> —Sifri Deuternomy 22

Rahab is not only depicted here as a shrewd woman who is able to size up the political situation and use others for her own needs, but she is also awarded extraordinary honor: she is inspired by nothing less than the Divine spirit. As part of the tradition that there were prophets and leaders who emerged from Rahab, the midrash finds a basis upon which to propose the signs of prophecy that sprouted within her early on: the fact that she knew in advance that the spies must hide in the mountains for three days, until the pursuers would return—which is what indeed happens, as recorded in verse 22.

The story of a Canaanite harlot who converts and marries an Israelite leader is unquestionably the reflection of a patriarchal fantasy. It is an ethnic fantasy illuminating the consolidation of an imagined community that is chosen, as well as a sexual fantasy in which the beautiful and desirable harlot becomes an individual's wife. The rabbinic narrative takes to an extreme the patriarchal trends that are to be found in the biblical narrative and that exist there in tension with other themes. The woman who does not obey the laws of the establishment and the loyalties that it demands of her, except to herself and her family, is disturbing. In response, the establishment tames her, slotting her into the box that is meant for women.

The elements of identity that Rahab is willing to shed and to don in accordance with the changing conditions of her life and her private needs are set within the "proper order."

From this perspective the rabbinic "narrative" may be viewed as one that educates women to identify completely with the man who offers them protection, support, and patronage, for a woman who does so is praised and rewarded. Rahab's sophisticated and independent feminine character—a complex character that operates in a consistent manner, faithful to herself—is transformed by the Sages into a "developing" character; one who comes to "see the light."[40] In this sense they fall into a typical masculine trap that identifies strength and power with conquest and appropriation. In my mind's eye I picture this wise woman reading the Sages' teachings about her and smiling to herself: they still have much to learn before they discover "what women want."

7

THE MYTH IN THE ATTIC
The Call of the Deep

A MYTH IS traditionally defined as a story about the history of the gods or their powers. Theories of myth from the nineteenth century assumed that myths dealt only with the physical world. Myth was understood as belonging to religion, regarded as the primitive parallel of science—which was considered altogether modern.[1] In the twentieth century, the claim that the ascent of science nullified myth was rejected. New theories sought to preserve myth by redefining it. Despite some points of contact between myth and scientific inquiry or philosophy, we draw a distinction between them, and this distinction pertains to the method and manner of discourse. Myths are formative stories that reflect psychological, religious, social, and national elements. They never happened, and they are happening all the time.[2]

Many twentieth-century scholars of Jewish studies expressed, in offhand comments, their nonmythical view of rabbinic literature.[3] Gershom Scholem had the following to say about the rejection of myth by "classical Judaism" (that is, the Bible and talmudic literature):

> The original religious impulse in Judaism . . . has always been characterized as a reaction to mythology. In opposition to the pantheistic unity of God, cosmos, and man in myth, in opposition to the nature myths of the Near-Eastern religions, Judaism aimed at a radical separation of the three realms; and, above all, the gulf between the Creator and His creature was regarded as fundamentally unbridgeable. . . . Judaism strove to open up a region, that of monotheistic revelation, from which mythology would be excluded. Those

vestiges of myth that were preserved here and there were shorn of their original symbolic power and taken in a purely metaphorical sense. Here there is no need to expatiate on a matter that has been amply discussed by students of Biblical literature, theologians, and anthropologists. In any case, the tendency of the classical Jewish tradition to liquidate myth as a central spiritual power is not diminished by such quasi-mythical vestiges transformed into metaphors.[4]

In commenting on the unavoidable presence of myth in religion and, more generally, in culture, Itamar Greenwald criticizes the basic premise of Jewish studies, according to which the substance of myth is regarded as a mental disturbance or a form of cultural primitivism. In his view, the study of myth in Jewish contexts must occur in an environment where there is maximum openness to the existence of forms of thought and expression that deviate from the accepted norms: "Where rationalist realism reigns, there is no real survival of myth and its study."[5]

Myth, which has been identified with nonrational elements—and hence supposedly also with premonotheism or amonotheism—was, until recently, excluded from the realms of research in talmudic literature.[6] However, some contemporary scholars of midrash now agree that a significant number of aggadic rabbinic teachings belong to the realm of myth.[7]

Obviously, the aim of our discussion here is not to assert the mythical nature of rabbinic literature in general, although attention its mythical elements may stimulate a rethinking of the place of myth within this literature. I emphasize, to be perfectly clear, that the view that enlightened religion must be "clean" of any mythical "dross" seems to me problematic in its own right, and of extremely questionable validity.[8]

As to questions of gender in the study of myth, I believe that if we were to try to award gender characteristics to different genres, it might be argued that myth is one of the most "feminine" categories, based on its connection with "nature," the "world of emotions," the "nonrational," and multiplicity.

There is no question that moral monotheism, which made use of polytheistic mythological traditions for its own purposes, also repressed mythical forces that remain alive and active in Jewish literature throughout the generations. Rabbinic literature invokes many such mythical elements and forces and tells their story. God's oneness and His masculine depiction naturally direct the search for the feminine aspects of the world and of society into the realms of myth. As Pardes explains, monotheism had much to offer, but its benefits came along with a new set of challenges. The ability of a masculine God to fulfill feminine and maternal roles when necessary, was not always convincing.[9]

On the overt level, the myth of the abyss that we will discuss here deals with the nature of the world and the physical elements comprising it. As I understand it, it relates inter alia to the structuring of "femaleness" and "femininity," and as such it plays a role in molding gender knowledge in talmudic literature. My symbolic reading of the myth understands it as a story not about the world, but rather about the human experience of the world. I regard with due seriousness the fact that mythological stories have the power to convince people to accept a certain social hierarchy and to award validity to the idea that social strata have always existed.[10]

AN UNOFFICIAL GODDESS

The "deep" (*tehom*), the primeval water of Creation, is a feminine element that plays a role in the cosmogenic biblical myth. It must be stated that many creation myths describe primal water—symbol of the source of everything in the world—as preceding primal matter. As we know, amniotic fluid is the first environment experienced by the human fetus; it is the space within which the embryo takes form and develops. This may explain the central place occupied by water in mythological thought. The only teaching that is explicitly defined in the talmudic sources as a teaching about the act of Creation is to be found in the Palestinian Talmud, Hagiga, chapter 2, law 1. It teaches that the original state of the cosmos is defined as "water in (or *with*) water," and the act of Creation is a process of transition from this watery state to a state in which land can come into existence.[11]

Mircea Eliade, one of the greatest twentieth-century scholars of religion, examined the symbolism of water in different cultures and noted the centrality of water-related motifs. He regarded the characteristic formlessness of water as the key to understanding its role in the processes of Creation:

MYTH IN THE ATTIC

> Principle of what is formless and potential, basis of every cosmic manifestation, container of all seeds, water symbolizes the primal substance from which all forms come and to which they will return either by their own regression or in a cataclysm. It existed at the beginning and returns at the end of every cosmic or historic cycle; ... In cosmogony, in myth, ritual and iconography, water fills the same function in whatever type of cultural pattern we find it; it *precedes* all forms and *upholds* all creation. Immersion in water symbolizes a return to the pre-formal, a total regeneration, a new birth, for immersion means a dissolution of forms, a reintegration into the formlessness of pre-existence; and emerging from the water is a repetition of the act of creation in which form was first expressed.[12]

In the story recounted in the first chapter of Genesis, the deep already exists when God begins to create the world: "The land was chaos and void, with darkness upon the face of the deep, and a spirit of God hovered over the surface of the water" (Gen. 1:2). In other words, before God came to create order and bring the world into existence, the deep covered the face of the earth. The Hebrew Creation story parallels other ancient works, first and foremost the *Enŭma Eliš*, the Babylonian creation myth. Shifra and Klein summarize the exposition as follows:[13]

> Before the heavens are created with all their host, and the earth and all that is upon it, the universe is full of Tiămat alone—the primal sea (salt water) and her partner, Apsu—sweet water, and their waters mingled. Apsu and Tiămat produce four generations of gods. The games of the young gods disturb Tiămat and Apsu at rest. In order to be able to sleep in peace, Apsu suggests—at the advice of Mummu, the steward of his house—that the young gods be annihilated. But Tiămat, the mother who gave birth to them, will not agree. When Apsu's plan becomes known to the young gods, the god Ea kills Apsu with magical incantations, establishes his temple upon him, settles in it with Damkina, his wife, and bears Marduk, the wisest and mightiest of the gods. The young Marduk disturbs the rest of the gods with his games with stormy winds. The gods, allies of Tiămat, call upon her to wage war against the rebellious gods, to avenge the death of Apsu, her husband, and to put an end

to the noise that disturbs their rest. Tiămat accedes to their pleas, retracts her refusal to annihilate her children, and prepares for war. She creates eleven battle monsters, and appoints Kingu as king and captain of the army.[14]

The gods are frightened by the power of Tiămat and are at a loss as to how they might prevail. Marduk volunteers to fight Tiămat on condition that he will be made king of the gods. This is agreed, and Marduk proceeds, armed with weapons that he has fashioned, to wage war against Tiămat:

> Then advanced Tiâmat and Marduk, the counsellor of the gods;
> To the fight they came on, to the battle they drew nigh.
> The lord spread out his net and caught her,
> And the evil wind that was behind (him) he let loose in her face.
> As Tiămat opened her mouth to its full extent,
> He drove in the evil wind, while as yet she had not shut her lips.
> The terrible winds filled her belly,
> And her courage was taken from her, and her mouth she opened wide.
> He seized the spear and burst her belly,
> He severed her inward parts, he pierced [her] heart.
> He overcame her and cut off her life;
> He cast down her body and stood upon it.[15]

The killing of Tiămat is the beginning of the story of creation, for Marduk, the victor, forms the world out of her split corpse: he sets down one half as the heavens, and the other half as the earth.

According to this myth, Marduk brings order to the world specifically through his lack of compassion and scruples. Before he seizes power, everything is fluid and undefined, as in the "formlessness and void" that exists before God separates the upper waters from the lower waters.[16] Afterwards, everything is distinct.

Hermann Gunkel, a prominent nineteenth-century biblical scholar, understood the word *tehom* (the deep) as being etymologically related to the name of the Mesopotamian goddess Tiămat, and viewed her as the draconic feminine representation of the powers of the sea and of destruction, an echo of the Babylonian myth within the biblical one.[17] The uniqueness of the Hebrew Creation story lies in its presentation of God, the Creator, as the only God; there are no other divinities involved in the story. The monotheistic biblical narrative offers no accounts of wars between gods.[18]

Folklore scholar Raphael Patai describes the status of the deep in the mythical hydrography of the Bible. From the time of the Creation of the world, the deep occupied an important place in the emerging world order, and to this day it lurks beneath the earth (Gen. 49:25; Deut. 33:13). The deep is not one; there are many "deeps" (*tehomot*), connected to and communicating with one another (Ps. 42:8). The blessings of the deep are the springs that water the earth (Gen. 49:25; Deut. 33:13; Ps. 78:15; cf. Deut. 8:7 and Prov. 8:28). However, the fountains of the great deep may also bring destruction, as, for example, at the time of the Flood (Gen. 7:11; 8:2), and in the time to come (Ez. 26:19; 31:15). Thus, the deep also serves as a symbol of catastrophe and suffering (Jonah 2:6). God's fire may consume the great deep (Amos 7:4), and in general God does as He wishes with the deep (135:6). The deep trembles at the sight of God (Ps. 77:17), but is also able to praise Him (Ps. 148:7).[19]

The identification of the deep as a powerful primal feminine force that was defeated by and made subservient to the One God offers a basis for understanding the development of the myth in talmudic literature. The discussion below is a sort of gender monograph of the deep in rabbinic culture.

Sherry Ortner addresses the issue of female subordination and seeks an explanation for this universal phenomenon. She finds that there is something in the generalized structure and conditions of existence that leads every culture to perceive women as less valuable and as subservient to the dominion of men:

> [M]y thesis is that woman is being identified with, or, if you will, seems to be a symbol of, something that every culture devalues, something that every culture defines as being at a lower order of existence than itself ... and that is "nature" in the most generalized sense. Every culture, or, generically, "culture," is engaged in the process of generating and sustaining systems of meaningful forms

(symbols, artifacts, etc.) by means of which humanity transcends the givens of natural existence, bends them to its purposes, controls them in its interest. We may thus broadly equate culture with the notion of human consciousness ... by means of which humanity attempts to assert control over nature.[20]

Since culture comes to rule over nature, and since women are perceived as closer to or part of nature, it is only "natural" that they be made subservient, ruled over, and suppressed. Clearly, this identification of women with nature is the product of culture, and the surrounding myths are intended to establish and support this view of femininity. This sort of perspective sheds light on the unique cultural texture of the subjugation of the feminine to the masculine when it comes garbed in mythical-symbolic attire, and creates a critical view of it.

The femininity of the deep is related to its inherent multiplicity. Tiâmat is split in half, and the waters in chapter 1 of Genesis are separated, becoming the "upper waters" and the "lower waters." In Hebrew, the word for water—*mayim*—is a paired plural word, and this serves to mold its status as feminine in rabbinic literature. This structured multiplicity goes against the Divine sexual order, which is based on "the One," one single existence, signifying masculinity. The primordial separation "between water and water" (Gen. 1:7) underlies the water's craving to return to its original state, to unite with itself—a situation depicted in rabbinic sources as the copulation of the upper and lower waters. Water is a split essence in the world as we know it, and this essence assumes secondary gender qualities in rabbinic literature. The gender division between the different types of water is expressed in the separation into gathered water and running water—the former being perceived as feminine; the latter as masculine. An examination of a range of texts characterizing the deep, its tendencies and its roles, allows us to trace the assumptions and values molding the cultural description of the feminine:

> What is the meaning of the verse, "Deep calls to deep, at the call of Your deluges ..." (Ps. 42:8)? R. Levi said: The upper waters are male, while the lower [waters] are female. The former cry out to the latter, "Receive us! You are creatures of the Holy One, blessed be He, and we are His messengers!" They immediately receive

them, as it is written, "Let the earth open up" (Is. 45:8)—as a female opens to a male, "and bring forth salvation" (ibid.)—being fruitful and multiplying; "let it cause righteousness to spring up also" (ibid.)—this is the descent of rain; "I, the Lord, have created it" (ibid.)—[meaning,] *therefore* I have created it, for the perfection of the world and for its habitation.

—Genesis Rabba, parsha 13
(Theodor-Albeck p. 122)[21]

The waters of the deep are perceived in this midrash as a vital element facilitating the irrigation of the earth. Through cooperation with the upper waters—the rain—and through their agreement to the act of "copulation," they ensure the fertility of the land.[22] In other words, the feminine element is presented as possessing qualities of passivity and a "lower" position (both in the physical sense and, perhaps, an inferior value or status), with the potential of being "closed" or "open." It is the feminine that facilitates fertility. Indeed, in Moses's parting blessings prior to his death, mention is made of the fountains crouching in the deep as a source of abundant blessing for the earth:

"And to Joseph he said, Blessed of the Lord be his land . . ." (Deut. 33: 13)—This teaches that Joseph's land is blessed more than any other land; "From the precious things of heaven, from the dew" (ibid.)—that dew falls there all year round; "and from the deep that couches beneath" (ibid.)—indicating that this area has abundant springs.

—Sifri Deut. 353

However, while water in general, and the deep in particular, are perceived as vital for the existence of the world, they are also a threat, with the potential to destroy. In the story of the Flood, in addition to the great quantity of rain that falls, the fountains of the deep open up, flooding the earth and destroying it (Gen. 7:11). The midrash describes this copulation of the male and female waters in its destructive context:

R. Zadok says: On the 10th of Mar-Heshvan he entered the Ark, and on the 17th the floodwaters came down from heaven—these being the masculine waters, and the waters of the deep rose up—these being the feminine waters. They joined one another and rose up to destroy the world, as it is written, "and the waters prevailed exceedingly" (Gen. 7:19).

—Yalkut Shimoni, Noach 56

The destruction of the world, as described here, results from the fateful unification of the upper and lower waters. The mingling of these waters thus possesses both positive potential for fertility and reproduction, and negative potential for annihilation. The split essence of water entails contrasts, both blessing and curse. This stereotypical duality of the feminine entity (water as a primal element) reflects the literary picture analyzed by Gilbert and Gubar in their work, *The Madwoman in the Attic*.[23]

In the Bible, the waters of the deep themselves are often identified with evil—inter alia, owing to the sea monsters that dwell there: "Praise the Lord from the earth, O monsters and all deeps" (Ps. 148:7). Elsewhere, Israel's enemies are compared to waters surging over them: "Then the waters would have overwhelmed us; the stream would have gone over our soul. Then the waters would have gone over our soul" (Ps. 124:4–5). It must be noted that the identification of evil with the feminine is an ancient patriarchal concept, as formulated, for example, by Pythagoras:[24] "There is a good principle which created order, light, and man, and an evil principle which created chaos, darkness, and woman." The moral or value-related aspect of the myth assumes disturbing significance in the following source:

> In the beginning, God sought to establish the world, but found no one [worthy] until the forefathers appeared. This may be compared to a king who wanted to build a city. He issued a decree and [his servants] searched for a place where the city could be built. When he came to lay the foundations, the waters rose up from the deep and would not allow the foundations to rest. Once again he tried to lay foundations, in a different place, but the water overturned them. Eventually he arrived at a place where he found a great boulder; he said, "Here I shall establish the city, upon these boulders." Thus, in the beginning the universe was water [mixed] with water, and God

sought to establish worlds, but the wicked would not allow it. Concerning the generation of Enosh it is written, "Then they began to call in God's Name" (Gen. 4:26)—but the waters arose and flooded them ... Likewise, the generation of the Flood was wicked, as the text testifies in their regard: "...Who said to God, Depart from us ..." (Job 22:17)—the waters arose and did not allow the foundations to be laid upon them, as it is written, "Whose foundation was overflown with a flood" (ibid. 16), and it is written, "All the fountains of the great deep were broken open" (Gen. 7:11). Once the forefathers appeared and were [found] worthy, the Holy One, blessed be He, said: "Upon these I shall establish the world"—"For the pillars of the world are the Lord's, and He has set the world upon them" (I Sam. 2:8).

—Exodus Rabba 15

The history of humankind, as described here, reflects the mythological struggle between water and stone, between fluid and solid, between the many and the one, between chaos and cosmos, between nature and culture. The wicked are the surging water, while the forefathers are the solid rock upon which the world can be established. Irigaray's theory may shed some interesting light on this series of dichotomies.[25]

In the chapter on "The 'Mechanics' of Fluids" in her essay *This Sex Which Is Not One,* she exposes the interconnectedness of the fundamental assumptions underlying three types of knowledge: science, philosophy, and psychoanalysis. Science, she argues, tries to understand reality as the relations between entities that are structured in terms of the basic characteristics of a solid—clear boundaries, cohesion, permanence in space—while ignoring the fluid element, which represents a different physical dynamic based on change and impermanence. Psychoanalysis tries to base its explanation of the human psyche and sexuality on an ideal of masculinity, and therefore erases feminine otherness, turning it into "the opposite of masculinity." Philosophy, too, identifies itself as dealing with fixed categories and the relations between them, viewing anything that cannot be set down and defined as a threat to man's very existence as a free and thinking species. The links between these preferences in science, philosophy, and psychoanalysis is proof, according to Irigaray, that the symbolic order in

Western culture awards the same qualities to man and to nature—"nature" insofar as it is subjugated to the human perspective and to the centrality of masculinity.

The myth, of course, sets aside any notion of chronology in arguing that the possibility of establishing the world on a stable foundation is related to human conduct. Its ideological bias is clear. The feminine aspect of the deep is related here to the forces of nature, evil, and wickedness. Fluid water, lacking any fixed form, "overturns" the foundations that God seeks to lay for the world; this is the wickedness of the morally corrupt early generations. The waters, the deep, are—according to this tradition—part of nature that disrupts and undermines the foundation of culture; they are an element that must be made subservient and ruled over in order for culture to exist. The foundation is one, and the boulder that is ultimately located and found worthy is likewise one (in the metaphor), even though it actually represents a plurality (the forefathers). This will be the foundation of the world.

The following midrashim likewise address the story of the destruction of the world in the Flood. They cast the contrast between the mountains and the deep as an essentially moral dichotomy:

> "And God remembered Noah and every living thing and all the beasts" (Gen. 8:1): It is also written, "Your righteousness is like the great mountains, Your judgments are a great deep; Lord, You preserve man and beast" (Ps. 36:7). R. Ishmael said: [In dealing with] the righteous ones who accepted the Torah, which was given from the great mountains—You perform righteousness with them up to the great mountains. However, the wicked, who did not accept the Torah given from the great mountains—You are exacting with them down to the great deep. R. Akiba said: He is exacting both with these and with those. God is exacting with them down to the great deep—He is exacting with the righteous, punishing them for the few evil deeds that they committed in this world, in order to bestow tranquility upon them, granting them a good reward in the world to come. And He bestows tranquility upon the wicked, giving them reward for the simple good deeds that they performed in this world, in order to punish them in the world to come.

R. Levi said: One might imagine this as [a scene in which] the righteous dwell in their abode, and the wicked in theirs. The righteous in their abode—"I will feed them in a good pasture, and upon the high mountains of Israel shall their fold be" (Ez. 34:14). The wicked in their abode—"On the day when he went down to Sheol I caused the deep to mourn (*he'evalti*), to cover itself for him ..." (Ez. 31:15).

R. Judah said: The word [as it is written in the text] is, "I led (*hovalti*)."—One does not make a covering for a vat out of gold or silver; rather, one uses the same material of which it is made—clay.[26] Likewise the wicked are darkness, Gehennom is darkness, the deep is darkness. *I led* the wicked to Gehennom, and I have covered them over with the deep; darkness covers over darkness.

R. Jonathan taught in the name of R. Josiah: The verse should be transposed and read as follows: "Your kindness transcends Your judgments as the mountains transcend the great deep. Just as these mountains have no end, so the [reward of the] righteous has no end. Just as these mountains press upon the deep, so that it will not rise up and flood the earth, so the righteous suppress [Divine] punishments, so that they will not emerge and consume the world. Just as these mountains are sown and they produce fruit, so the actions of the righteous produce fruit, as it is written, 'Say of the righteous that it shall be well with them, for they shall eat the fruit of their doings' (Is. 3:10). And just as the deep cannot be fathomed, so there is no fathoming the punishment of the wicked. And just as the deep is not sown and does not bear fruit, so the deeds of the wicked do not produce fruit—for if they were to produce fruit, they would destroy the world."

—Genesis Rabba 33, 1 (Theodor Albeck pp. 298–300)[27]

The midrash addresses the parallel dichotomies (mountains-deep, and righteous-wicked) through a gathering and linking of verses from throughout the Bible.[28] In the various teachings, the deep is described as Gehennom, as a lowly place, the dwelling place of the wicked, an infinite space covered with darkness in which nothing grows or bears fruit. This image echoes Simone de Beauvoir's description of a certain aspect of myths about women:

> Thus, Mother Earth has a face of darkness: she is chaos, where everything comes from and must return to one day; she is Nothingness. The many aspects of the world that the day uncovers commingle in the night: night of spirit locked up in the generality and opacity of matter, night of sleep and nothing. At the heart of the sea, it is night: woman is the *Mare tenebarum* dreaded by ancient navigators; it is night in the bowels of the earth. Man is threatened with being engulfed in this night, the reverse of fertility, and it horrifies him. He aspires to the sky, to light, to sunny heights, to the pure and crystal clear cold of blue; and underfoot is a moist, hot, and dark gulf ready to swallow him; many legends have the hero falling and forever lost in a maternal darkness: a cave, an abyss, hell.[29]

A later midrash describes the cruel conduct of the generation of the Flood as an expression of moral corruption, and this may enhance our understanding of the feminine image of the deep. The midrash suggests that when the people of this wicked generation saw the deeps rising to flood the world, they drowned their newly born infants:

> "The mercies of the wicked are cruel" (Prov. 12:10)—This refers to the [people of the] generation of the Flood, who were cruel. Our Sages of blessed memory taught, When the Holy One, blessed be He, brought the waters of the deep upon them and they saw the fountains rising up to surge over them, what did they do? They had many children, as it is written, "Their seed is established [*nakhon*] in their sight with them" (Job 21:8)—for a woman would conceive and then give birth [the very next morning], as it is written, "And be ready [*nakhon*] in the morning" (Ex. 34:2). "And their offspring before their eyes" (Job 21:8)—indicating that they lived to see their great-grandchildren. Some of them took their offspring and placed them over the deep, pressing them down with no mercy. Therefore it is written, "The mercies of the wicked are cruel" (Prov. 12:10).
>
> —Midrash Tanhuma (Warsaw) Noah 7

The killing of the infants by drowning them—returning them, as it were, to the amniotic fluid, the place from whence they emerged—symbolically heralds the destruction of the world, the return to a state of "water in water." Water as the primal source of life becomes here a place of death. The midrashic text creates a framework within which the despicable act (drowning children) is matched with the punishment meted out to the perpetrators: with a sort of poetic justice, they themselves drown in the Flood.

This midrash alludes to the etymological connection between the word for "mercy" (*rahamim*) and the word for "womb" (*rehem*). It describes cruelty in the sense of an absence of mercy (*rahamim*)—the feeling of identification with the pain and suffering of someone else—and connects it indirectly with the womb (*rehem*) as an organ within which the fetus develops (and as a place that is perceived as the seat of mercy). The reason for the drowning of the children is not made explicit in the text, but a parallel text indicates the possibility that this was a pagan act of sacrificing children to the deep in order to quiet it: "Each took his child and placed it over the deep and held him down, so that the water would not rise up over them."[30] It seems that the deep is perceived by the evil generation of the Flood as a sort of wild, hungry goddess that must be appeased with sacrifices in order to minimize the damage that she inflicts.

It should be remembered that human sacrifice in general, and child sacrifice in particular, are documented in ancient sources extending over the area from Carthage to the Land of Israel. More than 20,000 burial caskets containing the remains of children and fetuses were discovered at the Tophet of Carthage, a site of child sacrifice to the Phoenician gods. The pathological findings from these remains do not indicate a natural death. Researchers have found a correlation between the number of caskets placed in the Tophet and the general situation of the city: during times of crisis, caskets were laid there at an accelerated pace—perhaps with a view to appeasing the gods, or to regulate population growth in keeping with the city's resources. Explicit declarations denouncing the offering of human sacrifices and expressing absolute opposition to this phenomenon are found throughout biblical literature.[31]

The story of the Flood describes the deep in a universal context. It is interesting to note how the same idea is molded in the particular Israelite context. In the song uttered after the splitting of the Reed Sea, the waters of the deep are said to have covered over the Egyptians: "The depths [*tehomot*] have covered them, they have descended to the bottom like stone" (Ex. 15:4), and to have frozen still at a puff of the Divine spirit: "the depths were congealed in the heart of the sea" (ibid. 8). These verses express God's control over the mighty waters that symbolize mythical forces. The identification of the deep with evil is removed here from its literal sense, becoming a tool in God's hands for punishing wickedness. God's control over the deep allows Him to make use of it in order to perform goodness:

> "The deeps have covered them" (Ex. 15:5)—[If so, then] what is the meaning of the words, "they sank to the depths"? This teaches that the great sea broke through and the water fought with them [the Egyptians], inflicting all manner of punishments. Therefore it is written, "They sank to the depths, *like stone.*" In the same way that a person treats others, so he is treated. They [the Egyptians] had said, "When you look upon the birthstones ..." (Ex. 1:16); therefore You made the water like stones for them, and the water pummeled them because of [their decree concerning] the birthstones, therefore it is written, "like stone" (Ex. 15:5).
>
> —Mekhilta de-Rabbi Ishmael Beshalah

This teaching, too, connects the retribution meted out to the wicked with their sin, in keeping with the principle of "measure for measure." The teaching is based on the *gezera shava*—the appearance of the same word (*birthstones/stone*) in two seemingly unrelated sources.[32] Pharaoh had issued a decree to the Hebrew midwives: "And he said: When you deliver the Hebrew women, you shall look upon the birthstones: if it is a boy, you shall kill him, but if it is a daughter, she shall live" (Ex. 1:15). Various ancient sources attest to the fact that women would give birth kneeling upon two smooth stones that were placed at a certain distance from one another. The space between the stones, and the distance from the floor, gave the midwife, who sat opposite the birthing woman, some room for her work. This would seem to explain the significance of the birthstones in the verse cited above.[33] Once again we encounter the motif of infanticide—but this time it involves national and gender discrimination, since Pharaoh's decree pertains exclusively to male Hebrew infants. The punishment, "measure for measure," is a display of Divine Providence; it demonstrates clearly the Divine system of justice—as well as showing off the author of the midrash and his virtuoso performance in connecting different parts of the Bible.[34]

Pharaoh issues his directive to women—the Hebrew midwives—who evade it. Whether their disobedience reflects their fear of God, as attested to in the text, or arises from a system of values that will not countenance such murder, it is clear that the story of this national conflict is molded through gender discourse.[35] Shadowing and corresponding to the hand of the Divine warrior, waging war against the Egyptians, we identify a feminine hand: the powerful hand of a Divine Mother or Midwife. In a certain sense, God continues the work of the midwives from Chapter 1 of the Book of Exodus: while they save the children of Israel from the depths of the Nile, God saves them from the mighty waters of the Reed Sea.[36]

The deep, identified as a feminine power, drowns Pharaoh and his army in the sea in a revenge of sorts for the decree that the Hebrew babies should be drowned. As punishment for this murderousness, the enemy sinks in the mighty water like a stone. A parallel text states the analogy more explicitly: "Because [the Egyptians] hardened their hearts like stone."[37] The cruel masculine essence is symbolized here by the "stones," while the feminine essence is symbolized by the deep, which swallows them. The symbolism of the stone and the water, solid and fluid, are clearly very central to the structuring of the gender aspects of this myth.

Birth as a liminal event in which life comes into contact with death (in the ancient world, it was not unusual for women and/or newborns to die in childbirth), in Egypt as in the generation of the Flood, casts the deep as a chaotic force lacking boundaries and form, which threatens to ruin the order. The sources cited above also reveal a perception of the power of the feminine, and the fear that it arouses in males: the fear of death, of drowning, of being consumed by it.

CHAOS AND COSMOS: THE DEEP AND THE TEMPLE

One of the most fascinating aspects of the characterization of the deep in rabbinic literature is the relationship between it and the Temple. In his book *The Myth of the Eternal Return,* Mircea Eliade addresses the importance of the geographic center, the importance of origin in time, and myths and rituals that facilitate the overcoming of the "terror of history" by breaking through it and returning to the mythical starting point of reality.

Eliade describes the act of Creation as an event that took place through a suppression of disorder, a suppression of the chaos that preceded it (and in the beliefs of certain cultures, as we have seen, this suppression was accompanied by a war against the powers of evil, demons, and so forth). The transcendental entity—God, the gods, the primordial ancestors, and so on—bestowed order on the world, in some ancient past, and gave it direction. It is only after the establishment of order and the suppression of chaos that the world is actually created. The imaginary vertical line connecting the three layers of the cosmos—the transcendental, the actual, and the subterranean—is the "gateway to heaven," like Jacob's ladder, or the "center of the world," the *axis mundi*. At this point there is a "breakthrough of sanctity," the boundaries between the different planes of existence become blurred and dissolve, and man is able to communicate with the upper world. This sacred vertical axis takes different forms: a mountain, a city, or a Temple, or sometimes simply a staff, a pillar of fire, or a pillar of cloud. Eliade compares the "breakthrough of sanctity" via the *axis mundi* each time anew to a mini-Creation: the war of the Supreme Entity against the chaos and void. This being so, the colonizing or civilizing of any new area requires a search for the crack, the opening, the place of the "breakthrough of sanctity," and it is from this point that the new territory can begin to be built. Each culture has its own special ways of perceiving the location of this point; it is never arbitrary.[38]

The feminine deep is an essence devoid of any defined form, while at the same time symbolizing containment and inclusion. As we have seen, it is one of the symbols of chaos and nature, which threaten to seize control of the social order symbolized by the Temple. In rabbinic literature, following Creation the deep is situated below the earth, imprisoned and sealed with a special stopper. The Temple is built precisely on that most dangerous site—the mouth of the deep—as an additional means of protection, to stop it from erupting outward.

With regard to the discussion about the deep in the Temple context, it should be noted that water is vitally important for the Temple ritual.

Washing with water is the main preparation that the priests (*kohanim*) must undertake before entering the Temple and approaching the altar. Water was supplied to Jerusalem, a city with scarce water sources, from nearby springs, especially the Shiloah. It is interesting that the longing for closeness to God is expressed by the psalmists specifically as they sit at natural sources of water. It is the quenching of thirst with this water that arouses in them a great thirst for God, for His Temple, and for His closeness like the water.[39]

Eliade contends that cosmological traditions express the symbolism of the center using concepts borrowed from the sphere of embryology. God created the world as a fetus. Just as the fetus starts growing from the navel, so God started the Creation of the world from its "navel." The Temple, according to this approach, sits at the very center of the world—the place from which the world was created. This place maintains contact with the deep, with the primal water of pre-Creation. This contact, by its very nature, has a dual potential—for nourishment and life, on one hand, and for destruction and death, on the other.

In spatial terms, the connection between the Temple and the deep passes through the *shittin*—the openings of the shafts at the bottom southwestern corner of the altar through which the fluids (wine, water) poured onto the altar, drained down. These shafts are described in many different traditions, some of which feature cosmological elements while others do not.[40] The following midrash offers an idea of the mythical geography of the *axis mundi*, these shafts that lead down to the deep:

> R. Johanan stated: The shafts have existed since the six days of Creation, for it is said, "Your rounded thighs are like the links of a chain (*halaim*), the handiwork of a skilled artist" (Song of Songs 7:2). "Like the *halaim*" implies that their cavity descends to the deep; "the handiwork of a skilled artist" means that they are the skillful handiwork of the Holy One, blessed be He.
>
> The school of R. Ishmael taught: *"Bereshit"*—read not *"bereshit"* ("In the beginning" [Gen. 1:1]) but rather "He created the shaft(s)."
>
> It has been taught: R. Jose says, The cavity of the shafts descended to the deep, and David dug sixteen thousand cubits over them, as it is written, "Let me then sing to my Beloved a song of

my Beloved concerning His vineyard. My Beloved had a vineyard, on a very fruitful hill. And He dug it, and cleared it of stones, and planted it with the choicest vine, and built a tower in the midst of it" (Is. 5:1–2)—this refers to the Temple, "And also hewed out a vat therein" (ibid.)—this refers to the altar. And some say, "And also hewed out a vat therein"—these are the shafts.

—Babylonian Talmud, Sukka 49a
(MS Munich 140)

Attention should be paid to the erotic semantic field from which the images used here are taken. The shafts of the Temple, leading from the altar down to the deep, were formed during the six days of Creation, and they are the skilled work of God's hands. These are the hidden parts of the feminine body of the maiden from the Song of Songs, and are compared in the verse to items of jewelry. Rashi explains the word *halaim* as follows: "A cluster of golden jewelry is called a *hali ketem, el-hali* in Arabic, and our Sages taught concerning the shafts for [draining of] the libations, that they were formed from the six days of Creation in a rounded shape, like a thigh, as *halaim*—a term alluding to openings, as in 'the openings [*huliot*] [in the stone covering] over the water cistern.'" Here, the name *hali* is understood as being derived from the word *halal* [cavity].[41]

The "vineyard," the image employed by Isaiah as quoted by R. Jose, is likewise a symbol frequently used to signify the female sex organ in the language of love imagery in Song of Songs.[42] The Temple in all its minute detail is depicted as the embodiment of cosmic order and its beauty. The deep is therefore located beneath the altar, the cultic center of the Temple, and maintains spatial contact with it via the shafts. These are described in the midrash in terms evoking beauty and artistry.

Moreover, the shafts are the vessels through which fluids from the libations offered upon the altar in the actual world are carried to the subterranean world—the deep. The ritual act of the water libation, which pertains specifically to these shafts, may be seen as a refined form of sacrifice to the deep—a sort of tax to be paid to an entity that is not "officially" a goddess, but should most certainly be kept happy.

The shafts are related to another concept derived from the same root—*sh-y-t*—which is likewise at the center of the world: the *even ha-shetiya*, the "foundation stone," from which the world was formed. One of the explanations offered by the midrash is that this was a stone that God cast into the sea—that is, into the primordial deep.[43]

> And it was called *shetiya* [foundation]:... R. Isaac said: The Holy One, blessed be He, cast a stone into the ocean, from which the world then was founded as it is said: "Whereupon were the foundations thereof fastened, or who cast [laid] its cornerstone?" (Job 38:6).
>
> —Babylonian Talmud, Yoma 54b
> (MS Munich 6)

The "foundation stone," according to the various teachings, is the place from which the world was formed; a sort of cosmic stem cell from which the universe developed. On one hand, its name—*shetiya,* meaning "drinking," indicates its watery aspect, the element of the deep, of chaos. On the other hand this stone is a solid object that blocks the mouth of the abyss, the opening of the deep, holding back its water from bursting forth and destroying the world—as happened, for instance, at the time of the Flood.

> As the navel is set in the center of a person, so the Land of Israel is set in the center of the world, as it is written, "... that dwell at the center of the earth" (Ez. 38:12). And from it there emerges the foundation of the world, as it is written, "A psalm unto Asaf: The Mighty One, God, the Lord, has spoken and called the earth from the rising of the sun to its setting" (Ps. 50:10.) From whence? "Out of Zion, the perfection of beauty, God has shone forth" (ibid. 2). The land of Israel is located at the center of the world, and Jerusalem is at the center of the Land of Israel, and the Temple is at the center of Jerusalem, and the Sanctuary is at the center of the Temple, and the Ark is at the center of the Sanctuary, and the foundation stone is before the Ark; from it the world is formed. And Solomon the wise located the roots spreading from it to the entire world, and planted all kinds of trees on them, and produced fruit; therefore he says, "I have made for myself gardens and orchards" (Eccl. 2:5).
>
> —Midrash Tanhuma (Warsaw)
> Kedoshim 10

The concentric pattern set forth here assumes the concept of the deep within it, even though it is not mentioned explicitly—perhaps because it is hidden and is not part of the exposed surface. Solomon, the wisest of men, knows the secret of the water that is beneath the stone, and he plants a variety of trees there. Thus, the deep is present as a crucial basis of the *axis mundi*, for it is the source of vitality and life in the world. The tannaic traditions concerning the shafts and the foundation stone reflect differences of opinion among the Sages concerning the place of the Temple as the axis of the universe.[44] To summarize thus far, we might say that the Sages acknowledged the importance of the deep and its contribution to the world, but its proximity to the surface of civilized existence was a constant threat. The way to preserve the life-giving function of the deep while avoiding the danger of annihilation was to keep it subservient and under control. The spatial proximity of the deep to the site of the "breaking through of sanctity" therefore has a dual and ambivalent significance—an idea especially developed in the following teaching:

> R. Hisda said to a certain Sage who was arranging his teachings before him, "Do you know what David's fifteen Songs of Ascent corresponded to?" The other replied, "Thus said R. Johanan: When David dug the shafts, the deep rose up and threatened to submerge the world, and David thereupon uttered the fifteen Songs of Ascent and caused its waves to subside." He answered him, "But if so, should they not be called Songs of Descent, instead of Ascent?" He said, "Since you have reminded me, it was stated thus: When David dug the shafts, the deep arose and threatened to submerge the world. David inquired, 'Is there anyone who knows whether it is permitted to inscribe the [Ineffable] Name upon a shard, and cast it into the deep so that its waves should subside?' No one answered a word. David declared, "Whoever knows the answer and does not speak, may he suffocate." Whereupon Ahitophel adduced the following a fortiori argument: "If, for the purpose of establishing harmony between man and wife, the Torah said, Let My Name that was written in sanctity be blotted out by the water—then surely the same may be done in order to establish peace for the entire world!" He therefore said to him, "It is permitted." [David]

then inscribed the [Ineffable] Name upon a shard and cast it into the deep, and it receded sixteen thousand cubits. When he saw that it had receded too far, he said, "The closer it is, the better is will be for the world." He uttered the fifteen Songs of Ascent, raising it fifteen thousand cubits, and stationing it one thousand cubits [below the surface].

—Babylonian Talmud, Sukka 53a
(MS Munich 95)

The subject of the story is the bursting forth of the waters of the deep when David dug the shafts of the Temple. The narrative has a brief exposition: in the study hall of R. Hisda there sits a Sage whose role is to recount legends to him. R. Hisda asks him if he is aware of a reliable tradition as to the significance of David's "fifteen Songs of Ascent." Apparently, R. Hisda recalls some sort of explanation, but he is unsure of himself. A summarized version of the story succeeds in recalling to mind the explanation as recounted by R. Johanan: When David digs the foundations for the Temple, he reaches the deep, which overflows and threatens to drown the world.[45] David knows that if he takes a clay shard, inscribes God's Ineffable Name upon it, and casts it into the deep, the waters will be calmed, but it is clear that the Name of God inscribed on the clay shard will thereby be erased in the water. At first, no one dares rule whether he is permitted to do so. In view of the immediate danger, he "threatens" that anyone who knows the answer but refrains from uttering it, will suffocate. The threat is a rhetorical one: if the world is submerged by the waters of the deep, all of humanity will drown—and this is death by suffocation.[46] Ahitophel is David's advisor and a Sage; he knows the law.[47] In the ceremony held for a *sotah,* a married woman suspected of adultery, a parchment inscribed with the biblical unit discussing this situation is dipped into the bitter waters, and the text—including the Name of God that it contains—is dissolved and erased. Ahitophel reasons that if it is permissible for the Name of God to be obliterated from a parchment for the sake of restoring peace between a husband and wife, then surely the same principle must apply if the welfare of the entire world is at stake.[48] Ahitophel therefore permits the act, and David carries it out. The deep is so terrified by the shard bearing the Name of God that it recedes sixteen thousand cubits—so that the land now becomes parched. In other words, there is a balance between proximity and distance that must be maintained by the deep and the land in order for the ground to be watered without danger. In order to achieve the desired result, David recites the Songs of Ascent, and with each of them, the deep rises a thousand cubits.

This complex story may be interpreted in different ways and through different methodological contexts.[49] Our focus here is on the gender system of signs and symbols embedded in it. As background to our understanding of the story we must keep in mind a dialogue between David and Solomon concerning the building of the Temple:

> David said to Solomon: My son, it was my intention to build a House for the Name of the Lord my God. But the word of the Lord came to me, saying: You have shed much blood, and have waged great wars; you will not build a House for My Name, for you have shed much blood upon the earth before Me. Behold, a son will be born to you, who will be a man of tranquility, and I will give him rest from all his enemies round about, for his name will be Solomon (*Shelomo*), and I will give peace (*shalom*) and quiet to Israel in his days. He will build a House for My Name, and He will be My son, and I will be His father, and I will establish the throne of his kingdom over Israel forever. (I Chron. 23:7–10)

David is a man of war and bloodshed, and he is therefore disqualified from building the Temple, which should arise in a spirit of serenity and peace. Nevertheless, the desire to build the Temple continues to burn in him, and this explains the digging of the shafts in our story. This point, which is the basis for understanding the story, complicates matters for the author of the midrash, who must contend with the question of whether this digging of the foundations of the Temple is a legitimate expression of religious devotion, or an act that reflects some degree of rebellion against God's will.

As we have seen, the deep is the deepest primal force that existed prior to Creation. The foundations that King David seeks to lay for the Temple go all the way down to this root—symbolizing the fact that the cosmos, the orderly, rational, sacred, and masculine Creation, encounters at its foundation chaos—the undefined, undifferentiated element of existence; the feminine. The digging of the foundations entails drilling holes in the ground, the digging of shafts, contact with the deep. The very digging of the foundations for the Temple entails an inherent tension between the desire to keep the future edifice stable and anchored in the ground, and a drawing closer to the undefined and therefore destabilizing and subversive realm symbolized by the deep. David is required, in fact, to maintain a dialogue with the deep and to restrain it. The danger is real and significant, since the balance set down by God during the six days of Creation may easily be upset. Indeed, the deep realizes its potential to swell and rise, and threatens to destroy the world.

In the sources examined above, we saw different expressions of the relationship between stone and water, between the solid masculine element from which the world is created, and water as the formless feminine realm into which it is cast. The solid shard with God's Name inscribed on it, intended as a metaphorical stopper, is a cultural variation of the stone. A pottery shard is a quintessential symbol of human civilization. For the foundation of the future Temple to proceed properly, it is necessary to regulate the relations between the cosmos and chaos, and to fix them in such a way as to preserve the fertility of the world on one hand, while protecting it from annihilation, on the other.

David knows the strategy to quiet the deep, but it is not clear to him whether he is permitted to apply it. This expresses the extreme nature of the magical act of erasing God's Name in water. David is frightened: perhaps as someone who is accustomed to trespassing and invading the sphere of others, he is able to sense the dangerous boundary before him, and therefore he seeks approval for an act whose magical nature is clear. From this perspective we detect something of an analogy between David and the deep: both are liable to subvert and break through their boundaries. Perhaps this is the reason for the depth of the hostility between them. Standing poised on a boundary is always a powerful experience of friction, fear, curiosity, concentration of energy, eruption, explosion.[50]

At this point Ahitophel enters the story. The Bible presents Ahitophel as an advisor known for his good counsel—to the point that consulting with him is comparable to seeking God's word (II Sam. 16:23). Nevertheless, the biblical author, who supports David, notes that Ahitophel—in his official advisory capacity—ends up betraying the king (II Sam. 15:12; I Chron. 27:33).

Ahitophel's presence serves our story on many levels, since through him there develops a parallel between "peace between husband and wife" and "peace for [or *the welfare of*] the entire world." Ahitophel hints at David's sin with a married woman (both through his mention of the *sotah* ceremony, alluding to adultery, and through his own family connection to Bathsheba), creating a metaphorical connection between it and the fact that David is a man of war.

Despite Ahitophel's approval, it soon becomes clear that David's solution has produced unexpected results: the deep does recede, but too far. The balance has not been restored. The act of casting the shard with God's Name into the deep is an act that is too "strong," too aggressive; it is the language of war (perhaps echoing the subjugation of the sea monsters in the war against Tiâmat).

In order to achieve a balance in the relations with the deep, David needs a different approach: one of language; that is, nonviolent, lyrical speech. This quality is available to David since he, too, is a man of contrasts: he is a man of war, but at the same time also a man of poetry and love. His transition to song expresses his understanding that the "trick" that allows the world to exist in peace and goodness is to recognize its contrasts and find the proper balance between them. Subjugation of one side by the other will lead the world to destruction.

In this regard it must be remembered that a border is also a seam, a join. The Songs of Ascent is the general name given to chapters 120–134 of Psalms, all attributed to David. This collection of fifteen psalms is conventionally regarded as a distinct unit, whose special character is manifest in both its conceptual content and its formal and artistic aspects. In terms of content, the unit as a whole awards a place of honor to Jerusalem, the Temple, and the Temple service. For the most part these psalms also express a supplication for Divine aid and salvation. Especially interesting are the associations with water, gushing and flooding (122:4; 124:4–6). These psalms were apparently meant to be sung by the Levites standing on the steps ("ascents") leading up from the women's courtyard to the general courtyard of the Temple. In other words, these psalms are uttered within an area that is in between the congregation of women and the congregation of men, at the place that is the navel of the world. The Songs of Ascent uttered by David maintain the boundary, prevent a widening of the chasm, and heal and join the sides.

The story may be read as being critical of David, and as coming to teach him that the dialogue maintained among the three layers of existence—the heavenly, the real, and the subterranean—comes from the realm of the marital relationship, between husband and wife. This is speech that recognizes boundaries and respects them; it is speech of process, of song, of peace.

The invasion of borders, and of boundaries in general, is a major theme in the story and in the understanding of the gender relations that it expresses. The act of Creation is an act of placing a boundary and defining the places and roles of the different elements. At the same time, the border itself is a place; it is a meeting point. Formally, the border establishes two poles of some sort of value dichotomy. The most powerful encounters are always on the border, at the edge, at the limit, where one moves to a new place. The behavioral, experiential expression of being "on the border" is an expression of self-restraint, the need not to cross the border, the border as a final barrier before eruption or deviation.[51]

The concept of "the place"—the site of the Temple, the place of God—is determined in relation to the "other." The Temple is located on the border, a place that contains and embodies undoing and liberation, a deviation from the usual, the self, the familiar. The symbol of this "other" here is the deep; the feminine "other." The individual who builds the Temple will be a man of peace; someone who knows and recognizes the importance of boundaries and respects them.

In a different sense, we might read the story as being about identity and about dialogue between different inner qualities. The transition from otherness as "someone who is not me," to otherness as "someone who I am not," is the beginning of the shift from the thick border of identity to its thinner one.[52]

David is presented in the story as a round, developing character. In order to understand the change that he undergoes over the course of the story, in gender terms, we must introduce the concept of the *anima*. *Anima* and *animus* are terms coined by Carl Jung to describe the archetypal images underlying our experience of members of the opposite sex. The animus is the image of man in the eyes of woman, as well as the masculine side of herself, while the anima is the image of woman in the eyes of man, and the inner feminine aspect of his own self. While the influence of the anima and animus may become consciously known, they themselves remain beyond consciousness and direct perception. The anima is the softer element in a man's psyche, and where the anima is dominant, the man is more sensitive, spiritual, and tends toward changes of moods.[53]

Of course, the drama of identity and otherness does not take place only around such thick boundaries as those distinguishing between women and men. In a broader context, too, it is clear that the "other" is also the great hope, the key to exiting the closed world of "I" or "we." Revelation of the other "on the outside" is also, at the same time, a revelation of the other "within." David is a man of war, and his bloodied hands prevent him from building the Temple. The transformation that David undergoes in the story may be viewed as a therapeutic process whereby the strong, aggressive, masculine character within him gives way to another aspect of him—the psalmist. It is interesting that Jung viewed the anima/animus as one of the sources of our creative ability. According to the story, David discovers within himself his creative, feminine powers, in order to bring peace to the world.

As long as the Temple stood, the waters of the deep were trapped beneath it, and only the water and wine libations would run down to it, via the shafts. However, the Sages paint a picture of the future messianic times, when a great fertility will spread to the entire world, with a swelling of the deep that will turn into a flowing, purifying river:

> R. Phineas in the name of R. Huna of Sepphoris said: The spring that will issue from the Holy of Holies in its beginning resembles the antennae of locusts; as it reaches the entrance to the Sanctuary it becomes as the thread of the warp; as it reaches the doorway to the entry hall it becomes as the thread of the woof; as it reaches the entrance to the [Temple] Court, it becomes as large as the mouth of a small flask . . . From there onwards ". . . he measured a thousand cubits and he made me pass through the water; the water

was up to [my] ankles. Again he measured a thousand, and made me pass through the water; the water was up to [my] knees. Again he measured a thousand, and made me pass through water up to [my] loins" (Ez. 47:3–4), [rising higher and higher] until it reaches the entrance to the House of David. Once it reaches the entrance to the house of David, it becomes a great stream, in which men and women afflicted with gonorrhea, menstruating women, and women after childbirth bathe, as it is said: "In that day there shall be a fountain opened for the house of David and for the inhabitants of Jerusalem, for purification and for sprinkling." (Zach. 13:1)

—Babylonian Talmud, Yoma 77b
(MS Munich 6)

The mythical description of the stream emerging from the Holy of Holies at the End of Days illustrates the swelling of the spring as it rises from the *axis mundi* and flows eastward. The encounter with these "living waters" connected to their source is an encounter with the purifying force that transforms one from a state of ritual impurity to a state of ritual purity. As we saw in the previous sources, the Temple is not only the source of sanctity, but also a source of life. The same water that is vital for fertility and life in nature—in its absence everything wilts and dies—is also the water that purifies man from a state of impurity related to cyclical fertility and physical life. This stream, with its sweet water that restores the salty, desolate eastern region of the Land of Israel to life, has its source in the deep that lies beneath the Temple.[54]

At the building of the Temple, relations are such that the sanctified, artistic building that is the work of human hands suppresses and restrains chaos by concealing it and compressing it, but at the End of Days nature in all its vitality will once again burst forth from the heart of that which is fashioned and constructed. From the altar, upon which a fire usually burns, water will flow. The place associated with sacrifice and death will become a source of life. The idyllic picture painted here is one in which the water does not destroy the Temple, nor does the Temple imprison the water.[55] Is such a relationship between the feminine and masculine indeed possible? Is subjugation and control of one element by the other the only way to achieve harmony? A culture that structures a complex myth like that of the deep possesses some understanding of the relationship between gender relations as they are and as they should ideally be.

The very description of the End of Days as a state in which harmonious relations, without subjugation and control, prevail between nature and culture, shows that even these categories lack meanings that are constant and consistent at all times. The deep—and nature in general—can be viewed as an obstacle, as a destructive element, or as an element symbolizing peace, flow, fertility, and purity. In rabbinic sources the metaphors of "nature" and "culture" are highly relevant for an understanding of gender, and the more closely we examine how this culture uses this symbolic, structural system, the more accurate our understanding will be of its internalized gender mechanism.

8

THE CREATION OF WOMAN

Men Are from Babylon; Women Are from
the Land of Israel

THE PERCEPTION OF finality and completion requires that there first exist a model that defines the whole. I confess that I find the formulation of conclusions to be one of the more distressing norms entailed in writing. This, too, I believe, is a function of gender identity. The difficulty in concluding with some sort of theoretical generalization, summing up one's arguments in a concise, analytical way, and committing to conclusions with the validity of truth is a symptom of the discomfort shared by many women scholars who join the philosophical, academic discourse whose rules were set down by men.

In this final chapter I would like to address two parallel versions of a story addressing the theme of gender. I will attempt to give an accounting of the reading process with a view to illuminating the methodological benefits that each variation offers, and its potential contribution to the study of talmudic literature.

The core of the story that will be discussed here should be understood against the background of the rather widespread phenomenon of encounters and conversations between non-Jews and Jewish Sages, as recorded in rabbinic literature.[1] The particular situation concerns a debate between a man and woman about the myth of the creation of woman in the Book of Genesis:

> And the Lord God caused a deep sleep to fall upon the man, and he slept; and He took one of his sides, and closed up the flesh in its place. And the Lord God fashioned the side which He had taken from the man into a woman, and brought her to the man. And the

man said, This is now bone of my bones, and flesh of my flesh; she shall be called Woman, for she was taken from man.

—Genesis 2:21–23

Let us begin with a midrashic text from Genesis Rabba, originating in the Land of Israel, which depicts an encounter between a female character referred to as *matrona* (a Roman noblewoman) and R. Jose ben Halafta, one of the greatest fourth-generation tannaic Sages.[2] The noblewoman is the subject of considerable academic interest.[3] Some scholars have attempted to reconstruct an actual historical character, while others have focused on her literary characterization. It is not clear that this woman ever actually existed—especially since the appellation *matrona* is a general term used to refer to upper-class married Roman women.[4]

> A Roman noblewoman questioned R. Jose, saying: Why [did God create Eve] through theft [of Adam's side]?
>
> He said to her, "If someone were to deposit a single ounce of silver with you, in secret, and then you returned him a pound of silver, in public, would this be considered stealing?"
>
> She said to him, "Why, then, in secret?"
>
> He answered her: "At first, [God] created her for him, but he saw her full of mucus and blood, and he distanced her from himself. [God] created her over again [this time, out of Adam's sight]."
>
> She said to him, "I can even add to what you have said: I was supposed to marry my mother's brother, but because I grew up in the same house as him, he found me unattractive—and he went and married another woman, less beautiful than I."
>
> —Genesis Rabba 17:7 (Theodor Albeck edition, 158)

The dialogue between R. Jose and the noblewoman proceeds from this foreign woman's familiarity with the biblical narrative.[5] She addresses the Sage with a provocative question: "Why did God steal?" challenging the morality of casting a deep sleep on Adam in order to "steal" part of him.

R. Jose responds with a parable formulated as a rhetorical question: Is this really theft? His choice of this genre assumes the woman's intelligence and ability to understand the parable's meaning. His message is that the small deposit that Adam entrusts to God (the "ounce of silver") is more than amply repaid by the complete woman he receives in return (the "pound of silver").

The terms "in secret" and "in public" do not sit altogether comfortably within the semantic field of the parable—the world of commerce—and this draws our attention to the materials from which it is created. On the face of it, the semantic field continues the noblewoman's original question, which pertains to theft. What is stolen, if not property? However, upon deeper reflection it becomes clear that the concept of commerce is also related to the ancient idea that woman is the property of man.[6] Another possibility points to the symbolic element of the parable, signifying the act of copulation between man and woman: the man deposits his seed "in secret" in the woman's womb, and after some time he receives the payback—the newborn—"in public." (It is interesting to note the linguistic connection between the "deposit" (*hafkada*) mentioned in R. Jose's parable and the term *pekida* which is used in rabbinic literature in reference to the moment of conception.)[7]

R. Jose does not hesitate to use a parable that compares God to a woman. God receives, in secret, a side; the woman receives seed. Obviously, the parable works in both directions: it bestows upon women—including this Roman noblewoman—a Divine aspect at the same time that it awards God a feminine aspect. The birth (creation) of woman from man through the hand of God is described in a manner reminiscent of the process of women's childbirth, since this is the only model of birth that we are familiar with.

In any event, after Eve is created from Adam's side, we read: "This is now bone of my bones, and flesh of my flesh; she shall be called woman, for she was taken from man" (Gen. 2:23). In other words, Adam is satisfied with the "pound of silver" with which God repays him, and is somehow aware, after the fact, that she was taken from his own flesh, although no one tells him this. R. Jose's rhetorical question therefore leads to the conclusion that no theft took place here, since Adam receives in return more than what was taken from him, and he is satisfied with the transaction.

To summarize the manner in which R. Jose responds to the noblewoman's provocative question, he "wraps" his insight into the story in a parable that, on one hand, illustrates his interpretation of the text, while on the other hand demanding a hermeneutic effort on the part of his listener. He achieves all this while at the same time alluding to intimate relations between a man and woman. This last aspect is a not insignificant matter, and we might suggest that it infuses the dramatic dialogue between this Jewish man and non-Jewish woman with an intimacy all of its own.

It seems that the woman's second question comes from a different place emotionally. It is no longer "monologic" in nature, to borrow Bakhtin's term, but rather "dialogic," and uttered with the purpose of learning and understanding. "Why then in secret?" Why does God need to cast a deep sleep on Adam while He creates woman? Although in a certain sense this question takes up the inquiry where the previous one left off, the level of moral outrage seems lower.

R. Jose responds with a brief homiletic story that expands on the gap signified by the words, "This is now . . ." (or, more literally, *this time*) (verse 23). Woman was created through a process of trial and error. The first attempt failed, but the second, improved project was a success. R. Jose's response to this question can be read in different ways. It may be read as an expression of complicity, formulated in a patronizing way and accompanied by an intimate wink by the teacher to his student. God is the ally of the man; He creates a woman for him in order to alleviate his loneliness, and goes to some trouble to please him.[8] Woman is created for man, and in accordance with his taste. God is presented here not as a Divine Power who forces His inscrutable will on His creation, but rather as an agreeable, accommodating Being. Perhaps there is even an expression here of willingness on God's part to include man in the act of Creation, considering that man provides the "raw material," and when the finished product does not find favor in his eyes, God creates a new one for him.

Alternatively, R. Jose's response may be read in a confessional tone, such that the Sage offers intimate testimony as to the nature of every man, himself included. The reason for the second attempt at creating woman is aesthetic.[9] The man is "turned off" by the birth process that brings him face-to-face with his flesh-and-blood physicality. Exposure to the creation/birth process causes him to reject this feminine creature as a partner.[10] The deep sleep is therefore God's way of sparing the man this unpleasant experience, so that he will not be disgusted by the woman.[11] From a feminist perspective, it is clear that the attitude of the story toward birth is one of appropriation, childbirth-envy, fear of childbirth, aversion toward birth and the body, and all the other difficult feelings that men must contend with.

R. Jose talks with the woman about mucus and blood—which are the natural continuation of the conception that he had hinted at in his original parable. His educational approach is one that allows for the sexual human body to exert its powerful presence. In this intimate teaching moment, where R. Jose expresses something of his understanding of the world of men, the noblewoman takes a step toward him, too, agreeing with his words, augmenting them, and awarding them additional validity.

A traditional hegemonic reading would interpret the noblewoman's offering of her own story as confirmation of her renewed recognition that God is not a thief. Moreover, not only is He morally upright, but He even demonstrates sensitivity—both psychological and aesthetic—toward man's weaknesses.

However, if we examine the text from a feminist perspective, it seems that the "teaching moment" experienced by the noblewoman leads her to an intimate identification with Eve. In feminine style she complements the learning with a personal story, revealing a painful experience of rejection taken from her own personal life. Her uncle, whom she had been meant to marry, is not attracted to her despite her beauty (of which she herself is well aware), simply because he was close by while she was growing up. The woman he chose instead was less beautiful. A man's desire for a woman, according to this account, requires a certain measure of distance; it is the aesthetic mystery that fans masculine erotic attraction. Thus, the noblewoman imbues the drama of the creation of woman with a personal voice and perspective. She illuminates the creation of woman, with its purpose of pleasing man, as an act that can also be hurtful. This is not just an expression of agreement with R. Jose's view, but also an expression of criticism and protest over the pain of the feminine subject.

It is difficult not to view the position of the noblewoman within the story as being conveyed in a sympathetic manner that also conveys esteem, as befitting her elevated social status. This feminine model is certainly exceptional in relation to the status and characterization of women in rabbinic literature. The noblewoman is a round, developing character. Initially, she is defiant and speaks from a position of strength, knowledge, and self-confidence; she is ready to learn Torah in partnership with a man, a Jewish Sage; and her personal knowledge, born of experience, is unquestionably granted recognition and status. It is her words that open and conclude the story. Her sphere of subjective, emotional knowledge complements and reinforces what R. Jose understands with the help of the world of creative imagination.

In a certain sense, the story concludes with the recognition that gender differences are more profound and significant than cultural differences: the "foreign" noblewoman discovers that her personal experience confirms and echoes the "Jewish" insight into the nature of men as a factor that shapes the fate of women. Gender experiences contain a universal element that transcends culture.

A parallel narrative appears in the Babylonian Talmud, and while it is similar in many respects, it is entirely different in spirit. Without addressing the issue of which came first, let us consider its literary qualities on their own merits, and in comparison with the parallel originating in the Land of Israel:

> The Emperor once said to Rabban Gamliel: Your God is a thief, for it is written, "And the Lord God caused a deep sleep to fall upon the man, Adam and he slept; [and He took one of his sides, etc.]" Thereupon his daughter said to him: "Let me reply to him." [Turning to the Emperor,] she said: "Give me a commander." "Why do you need him?" he asked. She replied, "Thieves visited us last night and robbed us of an earthen pitcher, leaving a golden one in its place." He exclaimed, "If only such [thefts] would occur every day!" She explained: "Was it not to Adam's gain that he was deprived of a side and given a handmaid like myself to serve him?" He replied: "This is what I mean: he should have taken it from him openly." Said she to him: "Were that the case, she would be loathsome to him." She then ordered, "Bring me a piece of raw meat," and placed it in a ladle.[12] Then she offered it to them: "Eat!" They

replied, "We find it loathsome." To which she replied, "So it was with Adam: Had she been taken from him in the open, she would have been loathsome to him."

—Babylonian Talmud, Sanhedrin 39a
(according to the Yemenite MS)

The similarity between the two accounts is clear. Here, too, we have the story of a debate that starts off with a challenge—more brazen than in the version originating in the Land of Israel—concerning God's immoral act in the process of creating woman. The response to the claim is similar: God took little and repaid much. The continuation of the story is also familiar: the next question is why this had to be done without Adam's knowledge, and the message is once again that when the man is exposed to the process of creation, or preparation, the finished product turns him off.

Nevertheless, this literary brew—seemingly concocted from the same ingredients—has a different flavor. The story of R. Jose and the noblewoman has at its center an intercultural tension upon which there "rides" a gender tension. The Babylonian version quickly abandons the intercultural issue, concentrating on the gender realm. How does this happen? Concerning the identity of the heroine of the story, traditional and modern scholars alike are divided as to whether she is the daughter of Rabban Gamliel or the daughter of the Emperor.[13] As I see it, the fact that the text is not clear as to which "side" she belongs to is an important literary datum. This artistic trick renders national identity secondary—not to say irrelevant—in relation to gender identity.

Deutsch argues that "a Roman noblewoman maintaining dialogue with a Jewish Sage on theological questions exists in the Babylonian Talmud, too, but there she is not referred to as *matrona* or *matronita*; rather, she is usually called a 'daughter of the Emperor,' and sometimes by another name such as Cleopatra, or others."[14] It seems to me that, in any event, the understanding that she is the daughter of the Emperor seems the more reasonable and the more useful to the story. This exegetical position then locates the debate and the drama of the confrontation as taking place between the Emperor and his daughter. While it is triggered by the Emperor's provocation toward Rabban Gamliel, it is the Emperor's daughter who engages in debate with her father concerning the biblical story of the creation of woman.

This version of the story is simpler than the first one. It is less dense, there are almost no gaps, and the parable is more plainly suited to the lesson it teaches: the accusation concerns theft, and the parable illustrates, as it were, the report of a theft. In contrast to the noblewoman in the previous version, who—as noted—is a round and developing character whose own painful personal story is revealed in the text, the Emperor's daughter is a flat character who remains static over the course of the story. She adopts the same imperious manner, reflecting her noble status, from beginning to end ("Let me reply to him," "Give me a commander," "Bring me a piece of meat").

The dialogue between the daughter and the Emperor entails a dramatic "showing," whereas the dialogue between the noblewoman and R. Jose involves only "telling." The woman here dramatizes the report of a theft in order to poke fun at the claim that taking Adam's side could be viewed as an offense. Likewise, the argument as to a man's nature is dramatized through the parable of grilling meat on a fire, which is not far removed, materially, from the process of creating a woman out of mucus, meat, and blood. The daughter's actions are a sort of performance that she stages before the astonished eyes of the Emperor, Rabban Gamliel, and the servants of the palace.

In a traditional hegemonic reading of the story, the role of the Emperor's daughter is to defend the prevailing order. She advocates for the God of the Jews, as though telling her father, "Perhaps what God did seems to you like an act of theft, but in fact it was not only a moral act, but also a wise and benevolent one: God took a side from Adam, but gave him a handmaiden to serve him. Moreover, God was considerate of Adam's emotional responses, and therefore anesthetized him so he would not be exposed to the process of the creation of woman." Of course, the fact that a woman—and a non-Jewish woman, at that—defends the God of the Jews, constitutes "incontrovertible proof" that the existing order is just and proper. The male point of view—that of the Emperor, Adam, and perhaps also the narrator—is presented as the only point of view in the world. This is reality; there is no other.

A feminist rereading reveals another subject—woman. It emphasizes the hierarchical relations and characters in the story: God, the Emperor, Rabban Gamliel, the Emperor's daughter, a commander, slaves, Adam, Eve... ultimately, at the very bottom, the animal whose flesh is burned. This reading is sensitive to the fact that story specifically places the defense of women's servitude and inferior status in the mouth of a woman, and suggests that this chauvinist text thereby exploits women all over again.

However, we might propose another feminist reading that is more amused than bitter. It must be emphasized that in this version it is not a wise man who offers answers to difficult questions, but rather a woman, with status and presence. She engages in no prior consultation, but "expounds" with no hesitation, speaking out fearlessly before the two distinguished men in front of her. I choose to read her performance as a satire on the entire rabbinic discourse about woman, in which she represents nature, the physical, flesh. Woman is "food" for the man; he is the predator, she is the prey.[15] The proffering of raw meat is an audacious act; it is a far cry from the pained recollection of the noblewoman in the previous version. It adopts the semantic field of the kitchen—demonstrating along the way one of the main services that women perform as handmaidens to their husbands.

I understand the daughter's protest against the existing gender relations as an ironic argument directed at her father, the Emperor, concerning his double standard: Why is stealing forbidden, while oppressing a woman as a handmaid is acceptable? "You see yourself as enlightened," she tells her father, "but in fact you exploit; your comfort comes at someone else's expense. Moreover, you deny and dismiss the injustice involved. You do not wish to know that those whom you exploit are living subjects." The raw meat indirectly hints at the fact that comfort at the expense of others does not begin and end in the human realm; it also applies to animals. The hegemonic worldview is illuminated here as a consciousness that is in denial, preferring not to see the injustice that it perpetrates, while enjoying its results.

Despite the discomforting picture aroused by a feminist reading of the story, it must also be recognized that, in contrast with the parallel dialogue written in the Land of Israel, which conveys intimacy and a well-developed dialogic element, there is something entertaining in the dialogue between the Emperor's daughter and her father; the debate is almost a game. There is certainly some protest here concerning man's nature and the inferior status of the woman, but it is a satirical protest, essentially monologic. Some of the elements of the satire pertain to the fact that the very voicing of protest or criticism over the woman's subjugation is amusing when it emanates from the Emperor's daughter. It is a polemical debate, and my feeling is that the Babylonian version of the midrash emits a masculine feeling, while the parallel source originating in the Land of Israel is fundamentally more feminine, softer, and more afflicted.

This prompts us to ponder the reason for cultural differences between Babylon and the Land of Israel, and their possible influence on the spirit of the two parallel versions of our story. Boyarin points to a close connection between (national) oppression and damage to the male self-image. He emphasizes the self-feminization of Sages as a positive, sensitizing element of their collective identity: the nation's longing for liberation from the chains of exile, in his view, is inextricably bound up with the Sages' desire to rehabilitate their masculinity out of a belief that life in exile was womanly, pathological, humiliating, and undignified.[16]

Historians of the period of the Mishna and Talmud might address the question of whether there is any connection between the political crisis in which the Jewish community in the Land of Israel found itself in the early centuries of the Common Era, and the fact that the story is told from a "feminine" point of view that is sensitive to the suppressed, authentic voice emanating from a heavy heart. Correspondingly, they might address the possibility of a connection between the relatively stronger political situation of the Jewish community in Babylon, and the polemical, masculine, almost arrogant tone of the Babylonian version of the story. Arriving at answers to these questions would require a comprehensive comparative study pertaining to gender orientations in the Land of Israel and in Babylon. I believe that this example points to a fascinating field for further study and investigation.

As I have shown throughout the book, a feminist reading of the representations of women and femininity in the classic corpus of rabbinic literature offers an opportunity to note the early worldviews of women by Jewish men. In fact, it reveals much about men: their attraction to members of the opposite sex; their enchantment with women, sometimes bordering on admiration; their dependence on women for the shaping of their personal and collective identity; the anxiety arising from this dependence; and its suppression, displacement, and translation into various forms of control, supervision, and exclusion.

All of this is seemingly self-evident. Nevertheless, in an expression such as "Women are a nation unto themselves" (Shabbat 62a) I detect—along with distance, wonderment, misunderstanding, and exclusion of the "other" closed in upon herself—a profound identification, encouraging in its own right, of femininity as essence. *Essence,* as I see it, is not a dirty word or concept that must remain outside of the feminist lexicon. *Essence* is close in meaning to *entity*—something with an objective rather than a functional existence. Women are a "nation," says Ula, a fourth-century talmudic Sage living in the Land of Israel. They have their own unique culture, traditions, language, unwritten laws, and social conduct.

I acknowledge that this statement, coming from outside the feminine world, sits well with a significant chunk of my own experience as a feminist woman. Without committing myself as to the source of the differences between women and men, I believe deeply in the need to recognize feminine culture and to give expression to women's uniqueness in all social institutions: language, family and educational system, religion, law, and administration.

This book contains different attempts to examine aggadic literature from an unprejudiced feminist perspective. I have set aside apologetics and have taken no detours around sensitive areas; the reading that I propose adopts a wary approach toward the sources. At the same time, I have not denied myself—nor, I hope, my readers—the pleasure of a renewed encounter with the dynamic resources of rabbinic culture. The quest for an encounter with texts addressed to others, and with a world inhabited by others, requires a special type of listening. A true encounter takes place only where there is trust and respect. I believe that this is the only platform that can facilitate a clarification of the profound questions bound up with the imagination of gender concepts and the relationship between them and reality. The participation of women of our generation in critical scholarly discourse of the sources of our culture serves to broaden them, to engage them in lively debate, to interpret and reinterpret them, and to demand that they play a role in modern spiritual life—a vision encapsulated in the words, "Like a hammer shattering the rock" (Jer. 23:29).

NOTES

INTRODUCTION

1. For a clear and concise presentation of feminist theory, see Ross, *Armon ha-Torah,* pp. 33–46.
2. Cixous and Clément, *Newly Born.*
3. De Lauretis, *Technologies,* xi.
4. "Creative transformation" is a concept that Moi uses to describe the political influence that may be brought about through the appropriation of the cultural materials at our disposal. Moi, *Sexual/Textual Politics,* p. 101.
5. Leibowitz, *Emuna,* pp. 71–75.
6. Gadamer, *Truth and Method.* For a synopsis of his view, see Ross, *Armon ha-Torah,* pp. 300–301.
7. Showalter, *New Feminist Criticism,* pp. 7–13.
8. Gilbert, "What Do Feminist Critics Want?" pp. 29–45.
9. Lubin, "Isha Koret Isha."
10. Moi, *Sexual/Textual Politics.*
11. Lubin, *Isha Koret Isha,* pp. 100, 219–220.
12. Morrison, *Playing in the Dark,* pp. x–xii.
13. Moi, *Sexual/Textual Politics,* p. 120
14. See, for example, Winkler, *Constraints of Desire;* Brenner, *Intercourse of Knowledge;* and Konstan, *Sexual Symmetry.*
15. Boyarin, *Carnal Israel,* p. 10. See also his more general exposition in the introduction.
16. The first studies in this area began in the 1970s and 1980s. For a discussion of the reasons for the late appearance and relatively slow development of this sphere of research, see Satlow, *Tasting the Dish,* p. 2.
17. Boyarin, *Carnal Israel;* Biale, *Eros ve-ha-Yehudim;* Eilberg-Schwartz, *God's Phallus;* Eilberg-Schwartz, "The Problem of the Body"; Satlow, *Tasting the Dish.*
18. For example, Cohen, *Rereading Talmud;* Rosen-Zvi, *Ha-Tekkes;* and others.
19. For example, Satlow, *Tasting the Dish;* Peskowitz, *Spinning Fantasies;* Schremer, *Zakhar u-Nekeva Beraam.*
20. Zunz, *Die Gottesdienstlichen* (Sermons).
21. For a comprehensive and fairly up-to-date review of the literature pertaining to the relationship between halakha and aggada in rabbinical literature, as well as the history of this ancient distinction, see Lorberbaum, *Tzelem Elohim,* pp. 105–123.

NOTES

22. Rosen-Zvi, "Mysogyny and Its Discontents," pp. 217–227. The references are to Rosen-Zvi's definitions of the fundamental formulations of the historical philological approach, *Ha-Tekkes,* pp. 11–12, nn. 41–43, and his critical view of them. For another review of the different directions in this area of research, see Alexander, "The Impact of Feminism."

23. See also his reservations concerning this approach; Rosen-Zvi, *Ha-Tekkes,* p. 11.

24. For an accounting of the representations of the relations between expositor and text within the context of the discussion of rabbinical literature, see Halbertal, *Mahapekhot Parshaniyot,* p. 197.

25. Lorand, *Al Parshanut,* p. 232.

26. Eco, *Interpretation and Overinterpretation.*

27. Lorand, *Al Parshanut,* p. 243.

28. Schweickart, "Reading Ourselves," p. 42.

29. Scott, "Gender."

30. Ross, *Armon ha-Torah,* p. 419.

1. BACK TO THE BREAST

1. Foucault, *History of Sexuality,* pp. 140–141.

2. Bartky, "Foucault, Femininity"; Grosz, *Volatile Bodies;* Wolf, *Beauty Myth.*

3. Riley, *Am I That Name?,* p. 102.

4. For a discussion of the female breast in the spiritual world of the talmudic narrative, see Kosman, "Ha-Shad."

5. For a review of studies that emerged in the 1990s on the human body and Judaism, see Seidman, "Carnal Knowledge." For a more updated review and discussion, see Fonrobert, "On Carnal Israel."

6. See, e.g., Eilberg-Schwartz, *People of the Body.*

7. Literally, "a defect [both] for him and for her." The list of priestly defects in the Mishna and its halakhic and cultural significance is discussed by Rosen-Zvi in "Ha-Guf."

8. See, for example, "And Gehazi approached to thrust her away"—R. Jose b. Hanina said, "He pushed the glory of her beauty, her breasts," in Leviticus Rabba 24, 6, and also Palestinian Talmud Sanhedrin 10, 2 (29b).

9. See, for example, Ketubot 75a and elsewhere.

10. For an enlightening discussion on the subject of modesty from a gender perspective, see Hartman-Halbertal's article, "Kisui ve-Gilui," in which she argues, inter alia, in the wake of Foucault: "Such explicit and unceasing discussion of the obligation to cover the woman's body includes within itself a sort of feverish lack of modesty that may well be a symptom of the same problem that it is meant to address," p. 7.

11. Irigaray, *This Sex,* pp. 177–184.

12. See, for example, the discussion in Niddah 47a–48b.

13. Irigaray, *This Sex,* p. 28.

14. Bekhorot 7b.

15. See, for example, the story about Ula's mother in Bava Batra 9b, discussed by Kosman, "Ha-Shad," or the story of Miriam, daughter of Tanhum, in Lamentations Rabba, 1, or Hannah's reference to her breasts in Berakhot 31b, and elsewhere.

16. Sanhedrin 108b; Exodus Rabba 38, 4 and elsewhere.

17. Zakowitz, *Al Tefisat,* pp. 23, 78.

18. See Levinson, "Ha-Em ve-ha-Um." See also Levinson, *Ha-Sippur,* p. 65 (Genesis Rabba 53, 9 according to MS Vatican 30 and corrections in accordance with MS Vatican 60. The latter concludes with the words "the milk [meant] for Isaac").

19. On the poetics of the midrashic story, see Meir, *Ha-Sippur;* Levinson, *Ha-Sippur.*

20. See Levinson's comment on the hermeneutic circle created here: the story is created from the verses, while at the same time the story reinterprets the verses that nourished it. Levinson, *Ha-Sippur,* p. 68.

21. Bakhtin, *Rabelais,* pp. 238, 317.

22. Levinson emphasizes the nonnormative aspects of the story; see "Ha-Em ve-ha-Um," p. 474.

23. O'Brien, *Politics of Reproduction,* p. 8. My thanks to Rotem Wagner for this reference.

24. The Sages were certainly sensitive to the tension surrounding Abraham's fatherhood, as expressed also in other midrashim that describe Isaac's remarkable similarity to his father. For example, Bava Metzia 87b, Tanhuma Exodus 1, and elsewhere. Levinson, "Ha-Sippur ha-Mikra'i," p. 162, likewise maintains that the extensive tradition of the questioning of Isaac's paternity underlies this midrash.

25. My thanks to Noam Zion for this comment.

26. Levinson, "Ha-Sippur ha-Mikra'i," pp. 161–162.

27. Pardes, *Biography of Ancient Israel,* p. 34.

28. Freud, *General Introduction,* pp. 262–273.

29. On the female aspects of the Divine image, see Eilberg-Schwartz, *God's Phallus,* p. 115; Trible, *God and the Rhetoric,* p. 61.

30. Lorberbaum, "Al Da'atam."

31. Lorberbaum, *Tzelem Elo-him,* p. 400. See n. 40 and his reference to other studies on the inclusion of the female in the Divine image. Lorberbaum addresses the subject in a rather laconic way; his book lacks a satisfactory accounting of the androgynous or female elements of the image of God and the theological perceptions that may arise from this cultural depiction.

NOTES

32. Eliade, *Patterns in Comparative Religions,* pp. 239–264.

33. This does not mean to say that such appropriation is aimed exclusively at women; the fact is that God appropriates masculine human powers, such as seed, no less than He does the woman's breasts or womb.

34. A motif recalling the drawing of water from the rock in the wilderness; Num. 20:11.

35. This fascinating story is discussed by several scholars, including Frankel, *Darkei ha-Aggada,* pp. 303–308; Shinan, "Mi-derashat ha-Pasuk"; Levinson, *Ha-Sippur,* p. 299.

36. Pesahim 108b, and Rashi (ad loc.) links this teaching to our story.

37. Genesis Rabba 30, 8, Theodor-Albeck edition, p. 275.

38. Makhshirin 6, 7.

39. Concerning the possibility of a feminine identity for the Shekhina (Divine Presence), Urbach argues that rabbinic teachings concerning the Shekhina are completely devoid of any female element. This was an idea which, under Gnostic influences, came to occupy an important place in Kabbalah at a later time. The expression *Shekhina* (derived from the root *sh-kh-n,* meaning "to dwell") simply expresses God's closeness and immanence; Urbach, *Hazal,* p. 52. In contrast, Schäfer argues that the Shekhina is the female aspect of God; Schäfer, *Mirror,* pp. 86–91. The midrash under discussion, as shall be explained below, attributes a masculine gender to the Divine Presence.

40. Mekhilta de-Rabbi Shimon ben Yohai 15, 1.

41. The terms appear in I Sam. 15:3; "infant" (*olel*) appears to define a stage later than "suckling" (*yonek*).

42. Infants, by definition, lack perspective; they are too close.

43. Concerning this exegetical strategy see Frankel, *Darkei ha-Aggada,* p. 97.

44. Freud, *Moses and Monotheism,* pp. 179–180.

45. Palgi-Hacker, *Me-I-Mahut,* pp. 306–307.

46. Boyarin, *Carnal Israel,* p. 15.

47. See also the description of Gehazi's perverted behavior toward the Shunammite woman in the Palestinian Talmud, Sanhedrin 10, 2 (29b) and in Leviticus Rabba 24, 6.

48. Freud, *General Introduction;* see also Yalom, *History of the Breast,* p. 150.

49. Many attempts have been made to interpret the expression "knowledge of good and evil." For various proposals and a discussion of their stronger and weaker points, see, e.g., Callender, *Adam in Myth,* pp. 66–84; Barr, *Garden of Eden,* pp. 57–73. In Knohl's view (*Emunot ha-Mikra,* pp. 30–34), the term means "moral judgment and sexual awareness."

50. See this meaning for the expression also in Gen. 24:50; Gen. 31:24, 29.

51. Zakowitz, "Migvan De'ot."

52. An assumption whose validity is accepted to this day. Medical organiza-

tions around the world agree that an infant's nutrition at the earliest stages has a decisive influence on his physical, emotional, and intellectual development for the rest of his life.

53. The literary image of a child refusing to suckle from a foreign woman appears in Christian literature, too; see Baumgarten, *Imahot,* pp. 202–203.

54. Wickes, *History of Infant Feeding,* pp. 151–158; 416–422.

55. On the legal point contained in this story see Frankel, *Darkei ha-Aggada,* p. 495.

56. The author of the midrash is not troubled by the fact that the law was formulated in a later period, long after Moses's birth. This expresses the perception of halakhic laws as eternal and valid at all times.

57. On the main dimension of the distinction between ritual purity and impurity in religious life, see Douglas, *Purity and Danger;* Durkheim, *Elementary Forms,* p. 52.

58. Urbach addresses this sense of the concept in his book *Hazal,* p. 378, n. 23.

59. Kristeva and Moi, *Kristeva Reader,* pp. 74–88.

60. The motif of the "wonder child" who possesses wisdom and insight from infancy, is characteristic of stories of wonder heroes. It involves a skipping over infancy—in the sense of connection with the mother and the preverbal stage that is usually identified as preceding understanding. See, for example, the prophet Jeremiah at birth, in Pesikta Rabbati 26. A different sort of connection between the semiotic and the symbolic is expressed, for example, in the statement, "David was a psalmist even while still in the womb; he would suckle at his mother's bosom and gaze at her breasts, and utter song" (Berakhot 10a). The popular image of the "child wonder" finds expression in many stories, both in Jewish culture and outside of it; see, e.g., Horodotzky, "Yanuka"; Shahar, *Childhood in the Middle Ages;* Curtius, *European Literature,* pp. 98–101.

61. Rabbinic literature contains many references to Moses's stuttering. For example, the story of the test of the coals in Exodus Rabba 1:26, or the understanding of the expression "I am not a man of words" as a medical condition, in Deuteronomy Rabba 1, 1, etc.

62. The homology between ethnic identity and gender identity, familiar to us from other sources in rabbinic literature, aims to anchor fluid cultural meanings in categories that are supposedly fixed and constant. See the discussion of identical story lines based on this homology in Levinson's article, "Ha-Em ve-ha-Um," pp. 465–485.

63. Cixous and Clément, *Newly Born.*

64. On the feminine images of the Torah, see Kadari, "Tokho Ratzuf Ahava"; Green, "Bride, Spouse."

65. For more on this conflict, see Boyarin, *Carnal Israel,* pp. 134–166.

NOTES

66. The competition is religious in nature. See, for example, "'Why should you, my son, be ravished with a strange woman, and embrace the bosom of an alien?' (Prov. 5:20)—Better that you embrace the breasts of Torah, which bring you merit, than that you embrace the bosom of a foreign woman, who will lead you to sin," Midrash Proverbs 5.

67. Kadari, "Tokho Ratzuf Ahava," p. 401.

68. Kadari discusses the different interpretations offered in Song of Songs Rabba and their importance in the work's poetics; Kadari, "Li-Melekhet," pp. 169–203.

69. Pardes, *Ha-Beria*, pp. 108–109.

70. The juxtaposition of "synagogues and study halls" is very common in talmudic literature; see Erubin 21b; Pesahim 87a; Yoma 11b; Megilla 6a; Megilla 29a; Bava Batra 8a; Sifra Behukotai 2,6; Genesis Rabba 42,3; Genesis Rabba 63,6; Leviticus Rabba 11,7, and more.

71. On this homiletic genre, known as a *petirah,* see Raveh, *R. Peloni Patar.*

72. See Nidda 48b. A different and equally disturbing attempt to make the breasts subservient to the rules of a certain social and cultural order finds harsh expression in the attempt to synchronize the appearance of signs of puberty manifest in the woman's two sexual organs. See Nidda 48a.

73. Lorand, *Ha-Yofi,* pp. 257–268; 373–390.

74. An example of a comparative approach in the study of religions is to be found in the entry *twins* in the Hastings Encyclopedia of Religion and Ethics (see Hartland, "Twins").

75. See Rubak, "Be-Hayehem," p. 21.

76. Gross, *Berit ha-Lashon,* p. 13.

77. For feminist criticism of the identification of woman with nature, see Ortner, "Is Female to Male." For positive representations of this view, see Graves, *White Goddess,* and Patai, *Robert Graves and the Hebrew Myths,* pp. 70–75.

78. Stein, *Psychoanalytic Theories,* p. 84.

79. Ibid., p. 86.

80. Ibid., p. 98. The contrast between the good breast and the bad breast finds expression in certain psychological mechanisms known as "introjection" and "projection," where the infant's aim is to acquire and internalize the ideal object while distancing the bad object.

81. Pardes, *Biography of Ancient Israel,* p. 46.

82. Ibid.

83. The *gezera shava* (comparison) is based on the use of the identical word *kol* (all).

84. It should be noted, in the context of this discussion, that the poles of the Ark are themselves described in talmudic literature using the image of a woman's breasts. It is possible that this image is the background to the midrash here,

shaping the symbolic space within which it functions. See, for example, "R. Judah contrasted the following passages: 'And the ends of the staves were seen' (I Kings 8), but it is also written, 'But they could not be seen without' (Ibid.). How is that possible? They could be perceived, but not actually seen. Thus was it also taught: 'And the ends of the staves were seen'—one might propose that they did not protrude from their place; therefore Scripture [negates this and] says: 'And they drew out the staves' (Ibid.). One might propose that they tore the curtain and showed forth; Scripture [negates this and] says: 'They could not be seen without.' How then? They pressed forth and protruded against the curtain, appearing as the two breasts of a woman, as it is said: 'My beloved is unto me as a bag of myrrh that lies between my breasts [Song of Songs]'" (Yoma 54a).

85. In the midrash discussed previously, in which Moses refuses to suckle from the Egyptian women.

86. For example, in Deut. 32:18, 37; II Sam. 22:32, 47; Is. 26:4, and elsewhere. The literal meaning of the word is a great rock, precipice or fortress, and it is no surprise that this is one of the Names of God, who is a refuge and strong protector for His believers.

87. For interpretation of names in rabbinic literature see Heinemann, *Darkei ha-Aggada*, pp. 110–111; Harduf, *Yalkut ha-Shemot*; Harduf, *Milon u-Mafteah*.

88. Biale, *Eros ve-ha-Yehudim*, p. 40; see also Biale, "God with Breasts."

89. Albright, "Names Shaddai and Abraham."

90. See, for example, Gen. 28:3; Gen. 35:11.

91. Lutzky, "Shadday as a Goddess Epithet"; Biale, "God with Breasts"; Biale, *Eros ve-ha-Yehudim*, p. 40.

92. The idea of two mountains identified as the breasts of the earth, the ground, sits well with Canaanite mythology. This image may parallel Horeb and Sinai in the Bible. See Albright, "Names Shaddai and Abraham."

93. On these power struggles see Glander, *Ma'avakei ha-Koah*.

94. See chapter 7 for myths about the deep.

95. Irigaray, *This Sex*, pp. 106–118.

96. Carson, "Putting Her in Her Place," p. 153.

97. Rubin, *Reshit ha-Hayim*, p. 86.

98. Klein, *Love, Guilt*, pp. 306–307.

99. Urbach, *Hazal*, pp. 15–21.

2. DESIRE AND DOMINION

1. Yebamot 62b; Genesis Rabba 17, 2 and elsewhere.
2. Yebamot 63a.
3. Genesis Rabba 8, 9.
4. Millett, *Sexual Politics*, pp. 24–25.

NOTES

5. During my research on this subject I encountered the work of Esther Fisher, whose doctoral thesis also addresses feminine desire in rabbinic sources. The dialogue with her was most informative; see Fisher, "'Ve-el Ishekh."

6. Stern, "Captive Woman."

7. Wegner, *Chattel or Person?*

8. Ibid., and Boyarin, "Hirhurim al Betulot."

9. Rosen-Zvi, *Ha-Tekkes.*

10. For example, see Fonrobert, *Menstrual Purity,* who discusses the laws pertaining to a menstruating woman, and Rosen-Zvi, *Ha-Tekkes,* analyzing the ceremony prescribed for the *sotah* in the tannaic Mishna. Further areas of regulation of control, such as the separation between the sexes and the laws of covering the body, have also been addressed in research; see Rosen-Zvi, "Yetzer ha-Ra"; Satlow, "Jewish Constructions of Nakedness."

11. Rosen-Zvi, *Ha-Tekkes,* p. 31. For more on the curses of man and woman in the ancient literature, see Boyarin, *Carnal Israel,* p. 129; Baskin, *Midrashic Women,* pp. 73–79; Vogels, "Power Struggle," p. 197, and his numerous references ad loc., n. 1.

12. Zebahim 43b.

13. R. Isaac b. Abdimi introduces his teaching with the words, "Eve was cursed with ten curses," but goes on to enumerate only seven. The Gemara completes his list and provides a context that lies outside of our present discussion. For more on this matter in the Gemara, see Baskin, *Midrashic Women,* pp. 73–79. For a discussion about feminine desire in talmudic literature, which also mentions this Gemara, see Boyarin, "Rabbinic Resistance."

14. On the husband's absence in the context of fulfilling the wife's sexual desire, see Hanschke, "Ha-Yotze la-Derekh."

15. MacKinnon, "Desire and Power," p. 107.

16. Boyarin, *Carnal Israel,* p. 131, argues: "The 'curses' are women's state, not their estate. Not only is the curse not a justification for causing her to suffer, it is that very curse that creates the obligation for the husband to 'take care of her.' Once again it is clearly the case, however, that the gender relations are asymmetrical, that the position of women in sexuality is subordinate, and the position of men is dominant."

17. For the perception of feminine desire in other sources in rabbinic literature, see Hauptman, *Rereading the Rabbis.*

18. From this point onward the text reflects the version of only some of the manuscripts, as we shall see below.

19. See Kahana, "Shesh Moshzar," and Meir, "Gan be-Eden"; Meir, "Ma'aseh ha-Arikha"; Meir, "Retzifut ha-Arikha."

20. For the connection between the verse in Genesis and that in Songs, see

Trible, *God and the Rhetoric,* pp. 144–165. She views Songs in general, and this verse in particular, as an alternative (or perhaps "corrective") description of the relationship between man and woman in the Garden of Eden narrative, and proposes using chapters 2–3 of Genesis as the key to understanding Songs.

21. Song of Songs Rabba 7, 1.

22. For more on the contrast between masculine sexuality, based on oneness, and feminine sexuality based on multiplicity, see chapter 1.

23. One of the principal targets of feminist criticism is the religious tradition of monotheism, along with its gender distinction characterized by symbols and myths. For reference to contemporary research in this area, see Ross, *Armon ha-Torah,* p. 45, n. 31.

24. Pardes, *Ha-Beria,* p. 45.

25. As I learned from Fisher, "'Ve-el Ishekh.'"

26. Schremer interprets the strident rabbinic exhortations as to the great importance of marriage and the commandment to "be fruitful and multiply" as a polemic against tendencies to prefer a single existence, which the Sages view as dangerous. See Schremer, *Zakhar u-Nekeva,* p. 53. He refers mainly to men, but it is possible that the Sages also took a dim view of feminine celibacy.

27. Rosenthal, "Al Derekh Tippulam," p. 408.

28. Rich, "Compulsory Heterosexuality," p. 633.

29. The connection between violence and sexuality is a subject of ongoing discussion in gender studies; see MacKinnon, *Toward a Feminist Theory.* For a selected bibliography on the subject of rape within marriage, see Harmes, "Marital Rape."

30. For millstones as an allusion to women and the yoke of marriage, see Kiddushin 29b. For a lamp in the context of relations between the sexes, see Yalkut Shimoni, Proverbs 958; Leviticus Rabba 9, and elsewhere. See the comments of the redactor of Genesis Rabba concerning the identity of woman with millstones, ad loc.

31. This exegetical tradition would seem to be derived from several biblical verses (Job 31:9–10; Is. 47:2–3). See also Sanhedrin 32b and Palestinian Talmud Ketubot 25c; and Sotah 10a.

32. See, for example, Gittin 58a—"Two wicks in a single lamp"; Leviticus Rabba 9, 9—"She went home and found the lamp extinguished."

33. Brand, *Keli ha-Heres,* pp. 302, 311.

34. Ibid., p. 340, and see his references there to the pottery lamps in Pesahim 14b, Kelim 2, 8. He notes (p. 353) the possibility of a clay lamp being placed upon a golden candelabrum, but brings only our source in support. Elsewhere (p. 377) he talks about the similarity between the Greek terms for *husband* and *lamp.* Perhaps this similarity is what prompted the image in our midrash.

NOTES

35. Lubin, *Isha Koret Isha,* pp. 78–89.

36. The criterion of "multiple existence" defines a literary work as a popular work; Yassif, *Sippur ha-Am,* p. 5.

37. The editor of this manuscript claims that it "supersedes all other manuscripts in its accuracy," vol. III, p. 107.

38. On philological trends in the study of folklore, see Yassif, *Sippur ha-Am,* p. 564, n. 3.

39. MacKinnon, "Desire and Power."

40. Beauvoir, *Second Sex,* p. 9.

3. "THEY LET THE CHILDREN LIVE"

1. See, for example: Gen. 4:1; 4:17; 21:2; 30:17; 30:23; 38:3; I Sam. 2:21; Is. 8:3; Hos. 1:8, and elsewhere.

2. Rich, *Of Woman Born,* p. 184.

3. Mossman, *Politics and Narratives,* pp. 2–3.

4. O'Brien, *Politics of Reproduction.*

5. I learned much about the theoretization of childbirth from my friend Rotem Wagner, whose article on birth in Hebrew literature is in preparation.

6. Levinson, "Ha-Sippur," p. 297.

7. Pardes, *Biography of Ancient Israel.*

8. Exum, "'You Shall Let Every Daughter Live,'" pp. 63–82.

9. For a review of research on the redaction of aggadic midrashim, see Kadari, "Li-Melekhet," pp. 10–16.

10. An earlier text, paralleling this unit, is to be found in Sifri, Beha'alotekha 78, Horowitz edition, p. 74.

11. An earlier parallel text of this midrash is to be found in Mekhilta de-Rabbi Yishmael, 6, 2, Epstein-Melamed edition, Jerusalem, 5715, p. 6. Another parallel is the beraita in the Babylonian Talmud, Sotah 12a. For a discussion of the parallels and the Second Temple–period legends on this subject, see Blidstein, "Midrashei Amram."

12. On the sisterhood of women as a political force, see hooks, "Sisterhood."

13. The connection between the Hebrew midwives and Shifra and Pu'a is given expression in the realm of the plastic arts in the frescoes of the Dura-Europos synagogue, where the two pairs look very similar. See Weitzmann and Kessler, *Frescoes,* p. 27.

14. Zakowitz, *Tzevat bi-Tzevat,* p. 198.

15. See Exodus Rabba, Shinan, p. 56, n. 18, and his reference there to Heinemann, *Darkei ha-Aggada.*

16. On the profession of midwifery in the Bible, see Philip, "Mi-Ledah."

17. The expression *hofi'ah panim* occurs only in relation to Pu'a. Another

expression with similar meaning is *he'iz panim*—see Berakhot 62b. For a discussion of the character of Miriam in the midrash, see Steinmetz, "A Portrait of Miriam."

18. The identification of the background of a hero or leader with a family of high social status is found in many classical works. For example, Sargon was the son of a woman of the highest nobility. Paris is the son of Priam, king of Troy, and Hecuba; Perseus is the son of Zeus and Danaë, daughter of Acrisius, king of Argon. In Hindu mythology Karna is the son of the princess Kunti and the deity Surya. See: Rank, "Myth of the Birth," pp. 13–48.

19. See Blidstein, "Midrashei Amram," p. 9, and especially the possibility of interpreting this legend as an expression of rabbinic anti-asceticism, opposing the ethos of halting reproduction in view of the harsh political situation in which the nation found itself.

20. Thematically, this relates to the exegetical teachings surrounding Miriam's chiding of her brother, Moses, concerning his abstinence from marital relations with his wife, Zippora. See Sifri, Beha'alotekha 99.

21. Levinson, "Ha-Sippur ha-Mikra'i," p. 305, addresses the parallel narrative in the Babylonian Talmud, and his view is echoed extensively in the teachings from Exodus Rabba to be discussed below.

22. Gilligan, *In a Different Voice,* chapters 2–3.

23. The text has been completed here on the basis of MS 4.

24. See Exodus Rabba Shinan, ad loc.

25. Based on the narrative in Gen. 18:1–14. Shinan, ad loc, provides references to other rabbinic discussions on this theme.

26. Lubin, *Isha Koret Isha,* p. 216.

27. Ibid., pp. 219, 223.

28. He was the first to present it as a fundamental developmental experience in one of his important works; see Freud, *Interpretation of Dreams.*

29. Elitzur, *Lifnai ve-Lifnim,* pp. 173–211, and references there.

30. Ruddick, *Maternal Thinking,* takes an essentialist view of motherhood and femininity.

31. For a perspective on and criticism of Ruddick's thought in the context of feminist theories of motherhood, see Brunner, "Kolah shel Imma," p. 13. For a more comprehensive discussion of her thought, see Bailey, "Mothering, Diversity."

32. As described, for example, by Rich, *Of Woman Born.*

33. The nation is a political entity imagined as a community. See Anderson, *Imagined Communities.*

34. Tzamir, "Lilit, Hava," p. 138.

35. Jay, *Throughout Your Generations.*

36. Ibid. p. 147.

NOTES

37. Ibid., p. 149. See also her interpretation of the Binding of Isaac in this context, as a rebirth at the hand of the father who is guided by God, with no feminine input or assistance; ibid., p. 102.

4. JUDITH, WIFE OF R. HIYYA

1. Ilan, *Jewish Women*, pp. 32–36; Veller, *Nashim be-Hevra*, pp. 113–114.
2. Pardes, *Ha-Beriah*, p. 16.
3. For a detailed description of the descriptive poetics of the genre, see Raveh, *Me'at mi-Harbeh*.
4. Text of MS Munich 141.
5. On the centrality of dialogics as a literary strategy in legends of the Sages, see Raveh, *Me'at mi-Harbeh*, pp. 57–77.
6. This choice is a departure from the more prevalent tendency in talmudic narratives to refer to a woman simply as "the wife of so-and-so."
7. As discussed in chapter 3.
8. An example of this motif is to be found in the biblical story of Tamar (Gen. 38), in which the weak woman manages to deceive the man and become impregnated with his seed by means of her disguise. It must be emphasized that Judith's story inverts the purpose for which the feminine disguise is intended by Tamar: there the purpose was to achieve a pregnancy; here it is to prevent a pregnancy. On this motif and its appearances in aggadah literature, see Shinan, "Isha, Masekha."
9. There are different theories as to the origin of the term *drag*. One view traces it to the Shakespearean period, in which it was used as a description of men wearing women's clothing onstage. Originally a mnemonic for the expression *Dressed As a Girl*, in time the term was extended to include both sexes. Other sources date the term *drag* to the 1870s. There are other possible explanations as well: the Yiddish term *trogn*, "to wear"; or even "dragging" skirts on the floor. Eliade, *Patterns in Comparative Religion* (p. 424) notes the ceremonies of "exchanging clothing" in India, Persia, and other parts of Asia as a softer version of the mythos of human androgyny.
10. Butler, *Gender Trouble*.
11. Butler, "Imitation and Gender Insubordination," p. 318. In her article "Critically Queer" she argues, based on Michel Foucault's concept of "power," that the categories of "male" and "female" are socially generated, and that one of the ways of changing the existing situation is gender parody, in the style of drag performances, in which men masquerade as women, thereby illustrating how gender roles are simply social conventions. These parodies subvert the power of the gender conventions and present them as arbitrary, thereby introducing the possibility of changing them.

12. The story illustrates the "gaps" or "loopholes" in the halakhic system, which women can exploit in the pursuit of a subversive interpretation of the law that suits them. Unquestionably, in order to approach this role, a woman must know the law, along with its loopholes and the creative possibilities for its interpretation.

13. Apparently the same contraceptive potion referred to elsewhere as the "cup of sterility"—see Tosefta Yebamot 8b; Shabbat 109b.

14. Sometimes this potion was used to cure other illnesses, such as jaundice and gonorrhea, although it did indirectly cause sterility—see Mishna Shabbat 14:3. According to the Sages, the potion was known and commonly used in the earliest period of human history: Lamech gave it to Zilla to drink so that he could have intercourse with her and she would not become pregnant; a similar account concerns the generation of the Flood. See Genesis Rabba 23:3.

15. The use of the word *keres* (literally, "belly") is quite common in the context of fertility; see Mekhilta de-Rashbi 14, 13; Mekhilta de-Rabbi Isaac Bo; Massekhta de-Pis'ha 12; Berakhot 63b; Sotah 31a, and elsewhere.

16. Gilligan, *In a Different Voice,* chapter 5.

17. The Gemara then goes on to record instances in which it was specifically the woman who demanded children, and the husband who was unable to provide them.

18. Mishna Yebamot 6, 6; Tosefta Yebamot 8, 3. The ruling in halakha is that one fulfills the obligation with a son and a daughter. See Maimonides, Laws of Intimate Relations, 15, 4.

19. The plain meaning of the text here implies a blessing rather than a commandment; see Schremer, *Zakhar u-Nekeva,* p. 51.

20. On the image of God and childbearing, see Lorberbaum, *Tzelem Elohim,* pp. 386–397.

21. This is one of the most astounding examples of an interpretation that excludes women in the realm of halakha. The general consensus among halakhic decisors over the generations has been that the commandment, "Be fruitful and multiply" does not obligate women. See Maimonides, Laws of Intimacy 15, 2 and 10. For further discussion see Leibowitz, "Peri u-Revi."

22. Fisher, *Petor Nashim.*

23. This represents the approach of, for example, R. Meir Simha of Dvinsk; see Simha, Meshekh 58 9, 7.

24. In this context it is important to note that the rabbinic tradition of the Land of Israel supports the opinion of R. Yohanan b. Baroka; see Palestinian Talmud Yebamot 6, 6 and Genesis Rabba 8, 12.

25. The phenomenon of seemingly unrelated teachings inserted at a certain point in the text, because they are attributed to the same Sage who has just been quoted, is quite common in talmudic literature, but I wish to argue that

NOTES

beyond this technical matter, in our instance there is also a more fundamental connection between the elements comprising the discussion. Wermut, "Ha-im Hala," too, argues that citing three teachings by the same Sage may anticipate elements that appear later on in the talmudic discussion.

26. Aside from the instance of Abraham and Sarah, see the matter of the *sotah* in Sifri Numbers 42, and Numbers Rabba 11, 7 concerning Manoah and his wife. In a different gender context, see the well-known debate concerning the praise for a "beautiful and personable bride" in Ketubot 11a.

27. Fisher, *Petor Nashim*, p. 209.

28. See on this matter Ross, *Armon ha-Torah*, p. 406.

29. Boyarin, *Carnal Israel*, p. 15

30. Goshen-Gottstein, *Sinner and the Amnesiac*, pp. 8, 14; see his general reservation concerning the classical concept of biography in the context of rabbinic literature: ibid., pp. 10–11. On the perception of biography in the ancient world, see also Rubenstein, *Talmudic Stories*, p. 6.

31. Even, *Milon Munahei*, p. 27, defines a "biographical narrative" as a work that is usually of considerable scope. Rubenstein, *Talmudic Stories*, pp. 5–8, presents the biographical model as an important tool for reading legends of the Sages, and notes that the difference between biographies in the ancient world and the legends of the Sages is that the former are longer.

32. Meir, "Ha-Demuyot," p. 375. Yassif, *Sippur ha-Am*, pp. 122–137, examines Hebrew folktales and categorizes a large portion of what we refer to here as "legends of the Sages" as "biographical tales."

33. Tomashevsky, "*Thematics*."

5. THE VOICE OF DOUBT

1. Gafni, *Safek*, p. 27.

2. My thanks to Dr. Ronit Shoshani, whose comments contributed greatly to the discussion here.

3. There is no clear consensus as to what the *ilusis* (or *ilsis*) of Tiberias was. From the sources, we deduce that it was an open area within the boundaries of Tiberias where Torah study and prayer activities were conducted. For discussion and review of the research, see Eliav, *Atarim*, pp. 11–15.

4. In accordance with the Vilna edition. The M. B. Lerner edition of Ruth Rabba (Jerusalem 5731, 88–92) has some slight variations, but they do not impact on the subject of our discussion.

5. The citation in the name of Resh Lakish is problematic from a chronological point of view because he lived after the generation of R. Judah. Lerner, in his critical edition, posits that this is a later addition. In the later parallel to this text, in Exodus Rabba 52, 3, the woman's statement expresses her own view.

6. Gilligan, *In a Different Voice,* p. xvi.

7. To my mind her ironic tone is highlighted in the version found in MS Oxford: "She said to him: My teacher, Rabbi, our holy Rabbi, R. Judah the Prince, the five titles by which you are known:..."

8. Buber edition, Pekudei 7 66b.

9. Found in Ta'anit 25a, as discussed, inter alia, by Frankel, *Darkei ha-Aggada,* pp. 278–280; and Kosman, *Massekhet Nashim,* pp. 24–26.

10. The later parallels in Tanhuma and in Exodus Rabba 52, 3 are in fact paraphrases that soften the biting criticism of R. Judah; see ad loc. A similar phenomenon of weakening the critical dimension of the story in later versions is noted by Shinan, "Ma'aseh be-Etrogim."

11. Concerning R. Judah's wealth, see Meir, *Rabbi Yehuda,* pp. 243–247.

12. R. Judah's lack of social awareness is also attested to by the story in Bava Batra 8a. It should also be noted that the legends of the Sages do not spare criticism of wealthy Sages who are oblivious to the situation of the common people. See, for example, R. Joshua's words to Rabban Gamliel in Berakhot 28a: "Woe to the generation that has you as its leader, for you are unaware of the suffering of the scholars, how they support themselves, and what they live on."

13. I understand the expression *kasheh* (literally, "difficult") as having the same meaning as in "... as difficult [that is, "as great," or "as impressive"] as the parting of the Reed Sea" (Genesis Rabba 61, 3–4); see also Shinan, "Kasheh ke-Keri'at," pp. 23–37.

14. Incidentally, it is not only R. Simeon, R. Judah, and God Himself who are deaf to this criticism regarding the absence of social justice and solidarity. Ofra Meir, a contemporary scholar who discusses this story as part of her research on R. Judah, is likewise oblivious to the disturbing voice of the anonymous woman who is the heroine of our story. See Meir, *Rabbi Yehuda,* pp. 152–153.

15. Freud, *The Uncanny.*

16. On the view of the *Uncanny* in the gender context, see Benyamini, "The Manhood Anxiety"; and in the literary gender context, see Pellman, "Ha-Min shel ha-Keria."

17. Lubin, *Isha Koret Isah,* p. 74 onwards.

6. OPEN TO CONQUEST

1. Feig-Vishnia, "Benot Afrodita," pp. 6–9.
2. Lionstam, "Zenut u-Zenunim."
3. Yebamot 61b.
4. Ilan, *Jewish Women,* pp. 115–214.
5. Bar Ilan, *Some Jewish Women,* pp. 134–160.

NOTES

6. Feig-Vishnia, "Benot Afrodita," p. 6.

7. Shalev, "Al Shivyon," pp. 893–897.

8. For a discussion of the biblical narrative, see Ashman, *Toldot Hava,* pp. 109–116, and references there.

9. Kosman, "Ha-Isha she-Hafkha," p. 91.

10. Maloul, "Gisha Holistit-Inegrativit," pp. 150–151.

11. See Ashman, *Toldot Hava,* p. 112.

12. Zakowitz, "Humor and Theology"; see also Sherwood, "A Leader's Misleading," who adopts his line of interpretation.

13. Newman, "Rahab and the Conquest."

14. Gilbert and Gubar, *Madwoman in the Attic.*

15. In the Middle Ages, too, prostitutes were to be found in such liminal areas; see Shahar, *The Fourth Estate,* p. 87.

16. For a discussion of the implementation of the *gezerah shavah* in aggadah, see Frankel, *Darkei ha-Aggada,* p. 179.

17. Ashman, *Toldot Hava,* p. 113.

18. Levinson, "Ha-Em ve-ha-Um," pp. 465–466.

19. Proselytism as a phenomenon began in the second century CE, according to S. Cohen, *Beginnings of Jewishness,* pp. 135–139.

20. S. Cohen, "Crossing the Boundary," p. 15.

21. My thanks to Valeria Seigalshifer for the introductions to feminist theory at the Seder Nashim beit midrash, which helped me understand the importance of these distinctions.

22. Beauvoir, *Second Sex,* p. 612.

23. In this regard it is interesting to note the kabbalistic teaching of the school of Rabbi Isaac Luria, that Rahab was later reincarnated as a man; see Kosman, "Ha-Isha she-Hafkha," p. 102.

24. Concerning the place of this aspect within the phenomenon of proselytism during the mishnaic and talmudic periods, see S. Cohen, *Beginnings of Jewishness,* pp. 142–146.

25. Ashman, *Toldot Hava,* p. 116.

26. Hirschman, *Torah le-Khol* (p. 75), illuminates this teaching as part of his explanation of R. Eliezer's approach, which has all the nations and peoples of the world invited to join the children of Israel, except for Amalek.

27. As Boyarin, "Hirhurim al Betulot" (p. 12, n. 13) notes, harlotry is employed as a sustained metaphor in discussing the world of heresy and idolatry.

28. Foucault, "Of Other Spaces", talks about the sphere of prostitution as an example of a special type of "heterotopia." Heterotopias are "something like counter-sites, a kind of effectively enacted utopia in which the real sites, all the other real sites that can be found within the culture, are simultaneously represented, contested, and inverted . . . Either their role is to create a space of illu-

sion that exposes every real space, all the sites inside of which human life is partitioned, as still more illusory (perhaps that is the role that was played by those famous brothels of which we are now deprived). Or else, on the contrary, their role is to create a space that is other, another real space, as perfect, as meticulous, as well arranged as ours is messy, ill constructed, and jumbled." For illumination of the subject of prostitution in rabbinic literature in the heterotopic context, see Balberg, "Bein Heterotopia." Elsewhere in rabbinic literature, prostitution is the epitome of heterotopia, serving as a metaphor for all that is non-Jewish and threatening to the Jewish community. Mention must be made here of Laurie Davis's apt description of the Sages as viewing themselves as "virgins in a brothel"; quoted by Boyarin, "Hirhurim al Betulot," p. 12, and see n. 13 ad loc.

29. Butler, *Gender Trouble*.

30. The Mishna, in Shabbat 2, 6, enumerates these three commandments as incumbent upon women. On observance of the commandments as one of the central aspects of conversion, see S. Cohen, *Beginnings of Jewishness*, pp. 149–150.

31. See, for example, Sifri Num. 115.

32. Josh. 6:25; 8:26; Deut. 7:1–6; 20:10–18.

33. Ex. 12:22

34. Ashman, *Toldot Hava*, p. 116.

35. For a discussion of marriage as a way of integrating into the community within the framework of conversion, see S. Cohen, *Beginnings of Jewishness*, pp. 155–156.

36. Matthew 1:5.

37. Pardes, *Biography of Ancient Israel*, pp. 115–116.

38. A harlot from the city of Uruk is dispatched to the forest to turn the wild Enkidu into a civilized man. See Shifra and Klein, *Ba-Yamim*, pp. 198–200.

39. Levinson, "Ha-Em ve-ha-Um," pp. 466–467, and see his reference to other studies in this area, n. 9, ad loc.

40. Different scholars have sought to differentiate between different types of characters on the basis of their nature, their stature in the story, or their role. E. M. Forster proposes drawing a distinction between flat characters and round ones. "Flat" characters possess few traits and by the end of the work still represent nothing beyond what we know about them when they first appeared. "Round" characters gradually develop, and from time to time they reveal some new aspect of themselves. Other scholars present the distinction as a contrast between a "complex" character and a "simple" one, or between "static" and "developing" characters. Even, *Milon Munahei*, pp. 51–52.

7. THE MYTH IN THE ATTIC

1. Segal, *Theorizing about Myth*.
2. Brevard, *Myth and Reality*, p. 74.
3. See Urbach, *Hazal*, pp. 203–204; Scholem, *On the Kabbalah*, p. 87. These two positions gave rise to a polemic between Liebes and Shalom Rosenberg. See Rosenberg, "Mitos ha-Mitosim," and Liebes, "Mitos ve-Ortodoksia."
4. Scholem, *On the Kabbalah*, p. 88.
5. Greenwald, "Nokhehuto," p. 14.
6. Stein, *Mimra, Magia, Mitos*, p. 269.
7. See, for example, Boyarin, *Intertextuality*, pp. 93–104; Goshen-Gottstein, "Mitos Ma'aseh," p. 60; and further references in Stein, *Mimra, Magia, Mitos*, p. 271, n. 28.
8. See Liebes's strident words in this regard: Liebes, "*De Natura Dei*," as well as Lorberbaum, *Tzelem Elo-him*, pp. 78–82.
9. Pardes, *Ha-Beria*, p. 76
10. I adopt here Bronislaw Malinowski's view of the function of myth; see Segal, *Theorizing about Myth*, p. 44.
11. For a discussion of this teaching, see Goshen-Gottstein, "Mitos Ma'aseh," p. 61.
12. Eliade, *Patterns in Comparative Religion*, p. 188.
13. See Glander, *Mavo la-Mikra*, pp. 82–83. For a summary and references to studies, see recently also Routledge, "Did God Create Chaos?," p. 70.
14. Shifra and Klein, *Ba-Yamim*, p. 9.
15. *Enǔma Eliš*.
16. Renan, *Elot ve-Gibborim*, p. 113.
17. Gunkel, *Genesis*, p. 105. Tsumura disagreed with Gunkel in this regard; see Tsumura, *Creation and Destruction;* Heidel, *The Babylonian Genesis*, pp. 82–140.
18. Fenton, *Gishot Shonot*.
19. Patai, *Ha-Mayim*, p. 150.
20. Ortner, "Is Female to Male," p. 72. For positive representations of this view see Graves, *White Goddess,* and Patai, *Robert Graves and the Hebrew Myths*.
21. See the editorial comment, ibid. p. 123, concerning the presence of this teaching already in the *Sefer Hinukh*.
22. In this regard see also, "From when do we recite the blessing over rain? From the time when the bridegroom goes out to meet the bride," Berakhot 59b and Ta'anit 6b.
23. The same idea finds expression in the molding of the character of Rahab, the harlot, as discussed in chapter 6.
24. And adopted as the epigram to Beauvoir's book, *The Second Sex*.
25. Irigaray, *This Sex,* pp. 106–118. The gender context in which Irigaray

views solidity and fluidity may provide a response to Goshen-Gottstein's questioning ("Mitos Ma'aseh," p. 67) of the contrast between water and stone in these sources, seemingly less self-evident than the other possibility that he raises: the contrast between water and fire.

26. Theodor-Albeck explains—"'Of the same sort'—in other words, of the same type. Sheol is darkness, and the deep covering over it is darkness, and the wicked within it are darkness."

27. See also the editorial note concerning the corruption of the order of the units in this midrash.

28. For a discussion of this *petihta,* see Frankel, *Midrash ve-Aggada,* pp. 206–216, and his references to additional research.

29. Beauvoir, *Second Sex,* vol. 1, p. 166

30. Yalkut Shimoni, Prov. 948.

31. Human sacrifice is forbidden in several places in the Pentateuch: Deut. 12; 31; 18:10; Lev. 18:21; 20:2–5; see also the law of redemption of the firstborn in Ex. 34:9–20 and 13:11–15. It is decried in the Book of Psalms, too: "They sacrificed their sons and daughters to idols, and shed innocent blood—the blood of their sons and of their daughters, whom they sacrificed to the idols of Canaan, and the land was polluted with blood" (Ps. 106:37–38). In biblical historiography, Ahaz and Menashe, kings of Judah, are accused of having passed their children through fire in the manner of the abominations of the nations (II Kings 16:3; 21:6; II Chron. 33:6), while concerning Josiah we are told that "he defiled the Tophet, which is in the valley of Ben-Hinnom, so that no man might cause his son or his daughter to pass through the fire for Molekh" (II Kings 23:10). Child sacrifice is denounced by Isaiah: ". . . slaying the children in the valleys under the clefts of the rocks" (Is. 57:5), and Ezekiel defines such an act as an abomination and a profanation of the Temple (Ez. 16:20–21; 23:37, 39). These repeated protests indicate that this was, in fact, a prevalent form of worship, and they testify to ongoing, outspoken attempts to uproot it; see Amit, *Galui ve-Nistar,* p. 80. Of course, the issue of child sacrifice is central to the story of the Binding of Isaac, whose message is ultimately an indirect rejection of this practice.

32. I employ the term *gezera shava* here in accordance with its definition in the Talmudic Encyclopedia: "The deduction of a law in one area from a different area on the basis of similar words mentioned in the Torah in both places." Rosen-Zvi addresses this teaching in *Ha-Tekkes,* p. 146, and refers (n. 52) to additional examples of the highlighting of appropriate retribution through symmetrical linguistic molding.

33. Philip, "Mi-Leda u-mi-Beten," p. 67.

34. Rosen-Zvi, *Ha-Tekkes,* p. 148. He describes the principle of "measure for measure" as an exegetical convention applied in tannaic literature only to historical narratives.

NOTES

35. For other rabbinic teachings concerning the midwives and the attitude they express toward the gender issue, see chapter 3.

36. Pardes, *Biography of Ancient Israel,* p. 31.

37. Mekhilta de-R. Shimon bar Yohai 15, 5.

38. Eliade, *Myth of the Eternal Return.*

39. Pedaya, "Temurot be-Kodesh," p. 55.

40. Halbertal and Naeh, "Ma'ayanei ha-Yeshu'a" (p. 184), review these traditions.

41. See Rashi's commentary on Song of Songs 7:2.

42. See Song of Songs Rabba, 1:6; ibid. 8:12, and elsewhere.

43. For a review of midrashic traditions concerning the foundation stone, see Noy, "Even ha-Shetiya."

44. See Halbertal and Naeh, "Ma'ayanei ha-Yeshu'a" (p. 184), and their references to research on the perception of the Temple in Jerusalem as the center of the world, n. 29.

45. In his commentary, Rashi has trouble with the apparent contradiction between the traditions that speak of the shafts as existing from the time of the Creation, and the fact that this source suggests that it is David himself who digs them. Rashi seeks to resolve this problem by suggesting that "perhaps they filled with earth, or stones, such that they had to be dug out again." Pedaya, "Temurot be-Kodesh" (p. 77), maintains that the digging of the shafts refers to the excavation of the tunnels and the structure of underground channels beneath the Temple that supplied its water.

46. Suffocation is one of the four forms of death, which, according to biblical law and halakha, may be meted out as a death penalty by the High Court.

47. In the eyes of the Sages, Ahitophel is the prototype of a wise man of flawed character. He is presented as a negative figure, a companion of Doeg the Edomite. Thus, for example, a midrash aggada in Genesis Rabba 32:7 teaches: "Doeg and Ahitophel would speak lies"; and in the Jerusalem Talmud, Peah, chapter 1, 16a we find: "Doeg and Ahitophel spoke slander." On the one occasion when Ahitofel's good advice is rejected, he understands that Absalom's rebellion against David has failed; he returns home and strangles himself (II Sam. 17:23).

48. "Peace between husband and wife" may be a code loaded with meaning in the case of the relationship between David and Ahitophel. Bathsheba, wife of Uriya the Hittite, was the daughter of Eliam (II Sam. 11:3). Yavin suggests that the man in question is Eliam son of Ahitophel—such that Bathsheba was Ahitophel's granddaughter; Yavin, "Reshito shel Beit David."

49. See, for example, the philological, historical orientation of the exegesis of Heinemann, "David ha-Melekh," contrasting with the psychoanalytic exegesis of Ruah-Midbar, "Aggadat David."

50. See Gurevich's fascinating discussion of the characteristics of boundaries: Gurevich, *Al ha-Makom,* pp. 184–185.

51. Ibid.

52. Ibid., p. 192.

53. Storr, *Jung,* p. 44.

54. For more on Ezekiel's vision, Zachariah's prophecy, and the Sages' view of the connection between the deep and the Temple, see Halbertal and Naeh, "Ma'ayanei ha-Yeshu'a," pp. 182–183.

55. Pedaya, "Temurot be-Kodesh," p. 89.

8. THE CREATION OF WOMAN

1. On the Sages' attitude toward non-Jews, see Lieberman, *Yevanit ve-Yevanut,* pp. 52–68. Herr, "Historical Significance," takes a historical view of these dialogues and others between Jewish Sages and non-Jews. For references to additional studies, see Y. Cohen, *Ha-Yahas le-Nokhri,* p. 16, nn. 13–21.

2. This is one of sixteen stories, appearing in different midrashic sources, which present an encounter between R. Jose and the Roman noblewoman.

3. A recent important work by Deutsch (*Ha-Matrona*) traces the various appearances of this character in the different midrashic collections and over the different periods of rabbinic literature and offers an up-to-date review of the relevant historical and literary research. Deutsch's discussion does not give full attention to the gender aspects of the encounters.

4. The prevalent view in the research is that the *matronot* were not Jewish. An exception is Ilan (and some other scholars, such as Raviv, "Sippur ha-Dialog," and Labendz, *Socratic Torah,* who follow her view) that the *matrona* who speaks with R. Jose is Jewish.

5. Herr, "Historical Significance," attempts to explain the significance of the dialogues between Jews and non-Jews, arguing that they reflect a conflict between the Jewish worldview of the tannaic Sages and the gnostic—or, sometimes, Christian—view of their interlocutors. Artman, *Dialog,* treats this story from a "Bakhtinian" perspective, and her insights have influenced my understanding of it.

6. A view that finds expression, for example, in the Mishna, Kiddushin 1:1: "A woman is betrothed (literally, 'acquired') in three ways..." It should be noted, however, that throughout the rest of this tractate, *betrothal* is not *acquisition:* the transaction is not carried out between the groom and the woman's father, but rather between the groom and the bride herself, and it is not valid if she is not agreeable to it.

7. Rosh Ha-Shana 11a; Ta'anit 8b; Sanhedrin 91b, and elsewhere.

8. The molding of feminine secondariness is not unique to this source. Gil-

NOTES

bert and Gobar, *Madwoman in the Attic,* offer a feminist accounting of it, as does Abarbanel, *Hava ve-Lilit.*

9. See also Boyarin, *Socrates and the Fat Rabbis,* pp. 205–206.

10. The mention of mucus and blood in the context of birth is also to be found in Pesikta de-Rav Kahana 9:10: "Even though a newborn emerges from his mother's womb soiled and dirty, full of mucus and blood, everyone embraces him and kisses him—especially if it is a male."

11. Another context in which we find concern over possible aversion toward the woman as a result of exposure to mucus and blood is that of menstruation; see Ketubot 65b: "The worn-out clothes may be given to a woman—for what would she want them? Rehaba said: For her to use during her days of menstruation, so that she does not become loathsome to her husband."

12. *Bihsha* in Aramaic—translated by Melamed, *Milon Arami-Ivri,* as a "cooking ladle." Sokoloff, *Dictionary of Jewish Babylonian Aramaic,* translates it as: "She placed it in her armpit." If we accept this latter translation, it seems that the Emperor's daughter, by touching the chunk of meat to her body, offers a powerful demonstration of the "meaty" appearance of the side taken from Adam prior to the woman being created from it. Despite the attraction of this proposal, it seems to me a less likely translation.

13. Concerning the possibility that she is the daughter of Rabban Gamliel, see the important comment by Hirshman, *Torah le-Khol,* p. 159, regarding the fact that in tannaic literature, dialogue with a non-Jew is generally undertaken by the House of the President of the Sanhedrin. See also his attention to another dialogue involving R. Jose that he regards as unusual.

14. Deutsch, *Ha-Matrona,* p. 159.

15. "Whatever a man wishes to do with his wife, he may do; this may be compared to meat that comes from the slaughter-house: he may eat it salted, roasted, cooked, or seethed, as he wishes." (Nedarim 20b). For further discussion of this point see Satlow, *Tasting the Dish* and Boyarin, *Carnal Israel.*

16. He maintains that the spiritual survival of the Sages is presented as employing tactics and schemes usually associated with women; see Boyarin, "Masada or Yavneh?," pp. 306–309. Concerning the development of this view in the modern age, see Boyarin, "Neshef ha-Masekhot," and Boyarin, *Unheroic Conduct,* pp. 123–144.

BIBLIOGRAPHY

MIDRASHIC SOURCES

Genesis Rabba

Theodor, J., and C. Albeck. 5756. *Midrash Bereishit Rabba: al-pi Ketav-Yad be-British Museum im Shinuyei Nus'haot mi-Shemonah Kitvei Yad Aherim u-mi-Defusim Rishonim u-Perush Minhat Yehuda,* vols. 1–3. Jerusalem: Shalem.

Leviticus Rabba

Margaliot, M. 5753. *Midrash Vayikra Rabba: Yotze le-Or al-pi Kitvei Yad u-Seridei ha-Geniza, im Hilufei Nus'haot, He'arot u-Biurim,* vols. 1–5. New York and Jerusalem: Jewish Theological Seminary.

Ruth Rabba

Lerner, M. B. 5731. "Midrash Rut Rabba." PhD dissertation, Hebrew University of Jerusalem (unpublished).

Mekhilta de-Rabbi Ishmael

Epstein, N., and E. Z. Melamed. 5715. *Mekhilta de-Rabbi Shim'on ben Yohai: al-pi Kitvei Yad min ha-Geniza u-mi-Midrash ha-Gadol im Mavo, Hilufei Girsaot ve-Hearot.* Jerusalem: Mekizei Nirdamim.

Tanhuma

Buber, S. 5724. *Midrash Tanhuma: Ha-Kadum ve-ha-Yashan al Hamisha Humshei Torah, Hearot ve-Tikkunim u-Mareh Mekomot.* Jerusalem: Orzal.

ACADEMIC SOURCES

Abarbanel, Nitza. 5754. *Hava ve-Lilit.* Ramat Gan: Bar-Ilan University.
Adler, Rachel, 2008. *Feminism Yehudi.* Tel Aviv: Yedioth Aharonoth.
Albright, William Foxwell. 1935. "The Names Shaddai and Abraham." *Journal of Biblical Literature* 54: 173–204.
Alexander, Elizabeth Shanks. 2000. "The Impact of Feminism on Rabbinic Studies." In Jonathan Frankel, ed., *Jews and Gender: The Challenge to Hierarchy.* New York: Oxford University Press, pp. 101–118.
Amit, Yaira. 2003. *Galui ve-Nistar ba-Mikra: Pulmusim Geluyim, Akifim u-ve-Ikar Semuyim.* Tel Aviv: Miskal.

BIBLIOGRAPHY

Anderson, Benedict. 1991. *Imagined Communities: Reflections on the Origin and Spread of Nationalism*, rev. and extended ed. London: Verso.

Artman, Tali. 2002. *Dialog, Mitos ve-Yitzug Demui Historia: Keria be-Shiv'a Mifgashim Bein Matrona le-R. Yossi be-Bereishit Rabba*. MA research paper, Hebrew University, Jerusalem.

Ashman, Ahuva. 2008. *Toldot Hava: Banot, Imahot ve-Nashim Nokhriot ba-Mikra*. Tel Aviv: Yediot Sefarim.

Bailey, Alison. 1994. "Mothering, Diversity and Peace Politics: A Critical Analysis of Sara Ruddick's Maternal Thinking: Toward a Politics of Peace." *Hypatia* 9 (2): 188–198.

Bakhtin, Mikhail Mikhailovich. 1968. *Rabelais and His World*. Translated by Helene Iswolsky. Cambridge, Mass: MIT Press.

Balberg, Mira. 5768. "Bein Heterotopia le-Utopia: Keria bi-Shenei Sippurei Masa' el Zonot u-ve-Hazara." *Mehkarei Yerushalayim be-Sifrut* 22: 191–213.

Bar Illan, Meir. 1998. *Some Jewish Women in Antiquity*. Atlanta: Scholars Press.

Barr, James. 1992. *The Garden of Eden and the Hope of Immortality*. London: SCM Press.

Bartky, Sandra. 1998. "Foucault, Femininity, and the Modernization of the Patriarchal Power." In Rose Weitz, ed., *The Politics of Women's Bodies: Sexuality, Appearance and Behavior*. New York: Oxford University Press, pp. 61–86.

Baskin, Judith Reesa. 2002. *Midrashic Women: Formation of the Feminine in Rabbinic Literature*. Waltham, Mass.: Brandeis University Press.

Baumgarten, Elisheva. 2005. *Imahot ve-Yeladim: Haye Mishpaha be-Ashkenaz bi-Yemei ha-Benayim*. Jerusalem: Shazar Center for Jewish History.

Beauvoir, Simone de. 2011. *The Second Sex*. Vintage Books edition. New York: Random House

Ben Amos, Dan. 1975. "Kategoriot Analitiyot ve-Zhanerim Etniyim." *Ha-Sifrut* 20: 136–149.

Ben Yehuda, Eliezer. 1948–1959. *Milon ha-Lashon ha-Ivrit ha-Yeshana ve-ha-Hadasha*. Jerusalem: Ben Yehuda.

Benyamini, Itzhak. 2013. "The Manhood Anxiety: On the Male Fear of Female Domesticality in Sigmund Freud's 'The Uncanny.'" *History and Theory, Bezalel*, issue no. 27—The Uncanny.

Biale, David. 1982. "The God with Breasts: El Shaddai in the Bible." *History of Religion* 21 (3): 240–256.

———. 1994. *Eros ve-ha-Yehudim*. Tel Aviv: Am Oved.

Bialik, Haim Nahman. "Halachah and Aggadah." *Revealment and Concealment: Five Essays*. Jerusalem: Ibis Editions, 2000, pp. 45–87.

Blidstein, Yaakov. 5764. "Midrashei Amram u-Miriam." In Zeev Gries, Haim Kreisel, and Boaz Huss, eds., *Shefa Tal: Iyyunim be-Mahshevet Yisrael u-ve-*

Tarbut Yehudit, Mugashim le-Bracha Sack. Beer Sheba: Ben Gurion University Press, pp. 1–12.

Boyarin, Daniel, 1990. *Intertextuality and the Reading of Midrash.* Bloomington: Indiana University Press.

———. 1995. *Carnal Israel: Reading Sex in Talmudic Culture.* Berkeley: University of California Press.

———. 1996. "Rabbinic Resistance to Male Domination: A Case Study in Talmudic Cultural Poetics." In Steven Keapnes, ed., *Interpreting Judaism in a Postmodern Age.* New York: New York University Press, pp. 126–135.

———. 1997. "Masada or Yavneh? Gender and the Arts of Jewish Resistance." In Jonathan Boyarin and Daniel Boyarin, eds., *Jews and Other Differences.* Minneapolis: University of Minnesota Press, pp. 306–329.

———. 1997. "Ta'alulanim, Mikdeshei ha-Shem u-Paisanim—'Tasritim Nistarim' u-Meyumanuyot ha-Hitnagdut shel ha-Pezura." *Teoria u-Bikkoret* 10: 145–162.

———. 1997. "Neshef ha-Masekhot ha-Koloniali: Tzionut, Migdar, Hikui." *Teoria u-Bikkoret* 11:123–144.

———. 1997. *Unheroic Conduct: The Rise of Heterosexuality and the Invention of the Jewish Man.* Berkeley: University of California Press.

———. 5759. "Hirhurim al Betulot u-Migdar—Bein Hazal le-Avot ha-Kenesiya." *Historia* 3: 5–31.

———. 2009. *Socrates and the Fat Rabbis.* Chicago: University of Chicago Press.

Brand, Yehoshua. 5713. *Keli ha-Heres be-Sifrut ha-Talmud.* Jerusalem: Mossad ha-Rav Kook.

Brenner, Athalya. 1997. *The Intercourse of Knowledge: On Gendering Desire and 'Sexuality' in the Hebrew Bible.* Leiden: Brill.

Brevard, Childs. 1962. *Myth and Reality in the Old Testament.* London: Studies in Biblical Theology.

Brunner, Jose. 1993. "Kolah shel Imma, O: Dialektikot shel Toda'a Atzmit." *Zemanim* 46 (Winter): 4–17.

Butler, Judith. 1990. *Gender Trouble: Feminism and the Subversion of Identity.* New York: Routledge.

———. 1993. *Bodies That Matter: On the Discursive Limits of "Sex."* New York: Routledge.

———. 1993. "Imitation and Gender Insubordination." In H. Abelove, M. A. Barale, and D. M. Halperin, eds., *The Lesbian and Gay Studies Reader.* New York: Routledge.

———. 1999. "Critically Queer." In J. Wolfreys, ed., *Literary Theories: A Reader and Guide.* New York: New York University Press.

Callender, Dexter Eugene. 2000. *Adam in Myth and History: Ancient Israelite Perspectives on the Primal Human.* Winona Lake, Ind: Eisenbrauns.

BIBLIOGRAPHY

Carson, Anne. 1990. "Putting Her in Her Place: Woman, Dirt and Desire." In David M. Halperin, ed., *Before Sexuality: The Construction of Erotic Experience in the Ancient Greek World*. Princeton, N.J.: Princeton University Press.

Cixous, Hélène, and Catherine Clément. 1986. *The Newly Born Woman*. Minneapolis: University of Minnesota Press.

Cohen, Aryeh. 1998. *Rereading Talmud: Gender, Law, and the Poetics of Sugyot*. Atlanta: Scholars Press.

Cohen, Shaye J. D. 1989. "Crossing the Boundary and Becoming a Jew." *Harvard Theological Review* 82 (1): 13–33.

———. 1999. *The Beginnings of Jewishness: Boundaries, Varieties, Uncertainties*. Berkeley: University of California Press.

Cohen, Yehezkel. 1975. *Ha-Yahas le-Nokhri ba-Halakha u-ve-Metziut bi-Tekufat ha-Tannaim*. PhD dissertation, Hebrew University, Jerusalem.

Curtius, Enrst Robert. 1935. *European Literature and Latin Middle Ages*. Translated by Willard R. Trask. Princeton, N.J.: Princeton University Press.

Deutsch, Hayuta. 5771. *Ha-Matrona Rabbat ha-Panim: Degamim Kevu'im u-Mishtanim shel Mifgashim bein Hakhamim ve-Nashim Nokhriot be-Midrashim u-ve-Talmudim*. PhD dissertation, Bar-Ilan University, Ramat Gan.

Douglas, Mary. 2002. *Purity and Danger*. New York: Routledge Classics.

Durkheim, Emile. 1965. *The Elementary Forms of Religious Life*. New York: Free Press.

Eco, Umberto. 1992. *Interpretation and Overinterpretation*. Cambridge, UK: Cambridge University Press.

Eilberg-Schwartz, Howard, ed. 1992. *People of the Body: Jews and Judaism from an Embodied Perspective*. Albany: State University of New York Press.

———. 1992. "The Problem of the Body for the People of the Book." In Howard Eilberg-Schwartz, ed., *People of the Body: Jews and Judaism from an Embodied Perspective*. Albany: State University of New York Press, pp. 17–46.

———. 1994. *God's Phallus and Other Problems for Men and Monotheism*. Boston: Beacon Press.

Eliade, Mircea. 1958. *Patterns in Comparative Religions*. Translated by Rosemary Sheed. Lincoln: University of Nebraska Press, 1996.

———. 1971. *The Myth of the Eternal Return: Cosmos and History*. Princeton, N.J.: Princeton University Press.

Eliav, Yaron Z. 1995. *Atarim, Mosdot ve-Haye Yom-Yom bi-Teveria bi-Tekufat ha-Talmud*. Tiberias: Ha-Merkaz le-Heker Teveria and Bar-Ilan University, Department of Jewish History

Elitzur, Avshalom K. 1987. *Lifnai ve-Lifnim: Iyyunim Psychoanalitiim be-Mikra u-va-Yahadut*. Tel Aviv: Yarum.

Enûma Eliš: The Seven Tablets of Creation, translated by Leonard William King.

London, 1902. http://theknowledgeden.com/wp-content/uploads/2011/11/Seven-Tablets-of-Creation-the.-Leonard-King-1902.pdf.

Even,Yosef. 5738. *Milon Munahei ha-Sipporet*. Jerusalem: Akademon.

Exum, Cheryl J. 1983."'You Shall Let Every Daughter Live': A Study of Exodus 1:8–2:10." *Semeia* 28: 63–82.

Feig-Vishnia, Rachel. 2005. "Benot Afrodita—Zenut ve-Zonot ba-Olam ha-Atik." *Zemanim* 90: 6–9.

Fenton, Terry. 1978. "Gishot Shonot shel Sofrei ha-Mikra le-Mitos ha-Teomakhia." *Mehkarim ba-Mikra u-va-Mizrah ha-Kadmon*: 337–381.

Fisher, Esther. 2005. "Petor Nashim mi-Mitzvat 'Peru u-Revu.'" *Lihyot Isha Yehudiya* 3: 199–212.

———. Forthcoming. "'Ve-el Ishekh Teshukatekh ve-Hu Yimshol Bakh'—Havnayot shel ha-Teshuka ha-Minit shel Nashim be-Sifrut Hazal u-Mashma'uyoteihen ha-Migdariot." MA dissertation.

Fonrobert, Charlotte E. 2000. *Menstrual Purity: Rabbinic and Christian Reconstruction of Biblical Gender*. Stanford, Calif.: Stanford University Press.

———. 2005. "On Carnal Israel and the Consequences: Talmduic Studies Since Foucault," *Jewish Quarterly Review* 95: 462–469.

Foucault, Michel. 1980. *The History of Sexuality*, vol. 1: An Introduction. Trans: Robert Hurley. Vintage Books edition, New York: Random House.

———. 1984. "Of Other Spaces: Utopias and Heterotopias." Translated by Jay Miskowiec. *Architecture/Mouvement/Continuité* 5: 46–49. http://web.mit.edu/allanmc/www/foucault1.pdf

Frankel,Yona. 5757. *Midrash ve-Aggada*. Tel Aviv: Open University.

———. 1991. *Darkei ha-Aggada ve-ha-Midrash*. Givatayim, Israel:Yad le-Talmud.

Freud, Sigmund. 1899. *The Interpretation of Dreams*. Translated by Joyce Crick, with an introduction and notes by Ritchie Robertson. Oxford, UK: Oxford University Press; reprint ed. 1999.

———. 1919. *The Uncanny*. Translated David Mclintock with an introduction by Hugh Haughton. London: Penguin; reprint ed. 2003.

———. 1920. *A General Introduction to Psychoanalysis*. Translated by G. Stanley Hall. (Project Gutenberg EBook #38219; reprint ed. 2011.)

———. 1937. *Moses and Monotheism*. Translated by Katherine Jones. New York: Alfred A. Knopf.

Gadamer, Hans-Georg. 1975. *Truth and Method*. New York: Seabury.

Gafni, Mordechai. 2001. *Safek: Hashavat I-ha-Vadaut ke-Erekh Ruhani*. Ben Shemen, Israel: Modan.

Gilbert, Sandra, and Susan M. Gubar. 1979. *The Madwoman in the Attic: The Woman Writer and the Nineteenth-Century Literary Imagination*. New Haven, Conn.:Yale University Press.

Gilbert, Susan M. 1985. "What Do Feminist Critics Want?" In Elaine Showalter, ed., *New Feminist Criticism: Essays on Women, Literature, and Theory.* New York: Pantheon, pp. 29–45.

Gilligan, Carol. 1993. *In a Different Voice: Psychological Theory and Women's Development.* Cambridge, Mass.: Harvard University Press.

Glander, Shamai. 1990. *Mavo la-Mikra*, vol 1. Tel Aviv: Open University.

———. 5765. "Ma'avakei ha-Koah be-Mitosim ha-Mesopotamiyim ve-ha-Kena'aniyim u-ve-Tiurei ha-Beria ha-Mikriyim." In Uzi Shavit, et al., eds., *Ha-Yashan Yit'hadesh ve-ha-Hadash Yitkadesh: Al Zehut, Tarbut ve-Yahadut, Asufa le-Zikhro shel Meir Ayali.* Tel Aviv: Ha-Kibbutz ha-Meuhad, pp. 46–59.

Goshen-Gottstein, Alon. 1996. "Mitos Ma'aseh Bereishit be-Sifrut ha-Amorait." *Eshel Beer Sheva* 4:58–77.

———. 2000. *The Sinner and the Amnesiac: The Rabbinic Invention of Elisha Ben Abuya and Elazar Ben Arach.* Stanford, Calif.: Stanford University Press.

Graves, Robert. 1948. *The White Goddess: A Historical Grammar of Poetic Myth.* London: Faber & Faber.

Green, Arthur. 1995. "Bride, Spouse, Daughter: Images of the Feminine in Classical Jewish Sources." In Susannah Heschel, ed., *On Being a Jewish Feminist.* New York: Schocken, pp. 248–260.

Greenwald, Itamar. 5756. "Nokhehuto ha-Bilti Nimna'at shel ha-Mitos—Masat Petiha." *Eshel Be'er Sheva* 4:1–14.

Gross, Benjamin. 2007. *Berit ha-Lashon: Ha-Dibbur be-Mahshevet Yisrael.* Jerusalem: Reuven MA.

Grosz, Elizabeth. 1994. *Volatile Bodies: Toward a Corporeal Feminism.* Bloomington: Indiana University Press.

Gunkel, Hermann. 1901. *The Legends of Genesis.* Translated by William Herbert Carruth. Chicago: The Open Court Publishing Co.

———. 1910. *Genesis.* Translated by Mark E. Biddle. Macon, GA: Mercer University Press; reprint ed. 1997.

Gurevich, Zali. 2007. *Al ha-Makom.* Tel Aviv: Am Oved.

Halbertal, Moshe. 5757. *Mahapekhot Parshaniyot be-Hithavutan: Arakhim ke-Shikulim Parshaniyim be-Midrashei Halakha.* Jerusalem: Magnes.

Halbertal, Moshe, and Shelomo Naeh. 5767. "Ma'ayanei ha-Yeshu'a: Setira Parshanit u-Teshuvat ha-Minim." In Yehoshua Levinson, ed., *Higayon le-Yona.* Jerusalem: Magnes, pp. 179–197.

Hanschke, David. 5764. "Ha-Yotze la-Derekh: Al Du-Mashma'ut ve-al Totzeoteiha." *Leshonenu* 66 (1–2): 87–102.

Harduf, David M. 5724. *Yalkut ha-Shemot ha-Peratiyim she-be-Tanakh u-Midrasheihem.* Tel Aviv: Yizreel.

———. 1960. *Milon u-Mafteah le-Midrashei ha-Shemot ha-Tanakhiyim ba-Aggada.* Tel Aviv: Yizreel.

Harmes, Roberta. 1999. "Marital Rape: A Selected Bibliography." *Violence Against Women* 5: 1082–1083.

Hartland, Sidney E. 1921. "Twins." In James Hastings, ed., *Encyclopedia of Religion and Ethics*, vol. 12. New York: Edinburg, pp. 491–500.

Hartman-Halbertal, Tova. 5764. "Kisui ve-Gilui be-Isha: Al ha-Tzorekh be-Gidrei Tzeni'ut Aherim, ha-Yotzrim Yehasim Nekhonim Yoter Bein Gevarim ve-Nashim." *De'ot* 17: 6–11.

Hauptman, Judith, 1998. *Rereading the Rabbis: A Woman's Voice*. Boulder, Colo.: Westview Press.

Heidel, Alexander. 1951. *The Babylonian Genesis*. Chicago: University of Chicago Press.

Heinemann, Yosef. 5714. *Darkei ha-Aggada*. Jerusalem: Magnes.

———. 5733. "David ha-Melekh ve-Hitpartzut Mei ha-Tehom." In Ezra Fleischer, ed., *Mehkerei Sifrut, Mugashim le-Shimon Halkin*. Jerusalem: Magnes, pp. 23–34.

Herr, Moshe David. 1971. "The Historical Significance of the Dialogues between Sages and Roman Dignitaries." *Scripta Hierosolymitana* 22: 123–150.

Hirshman, Menachem. 1999. *Torah le-Khol Baei Olam: Zerem Universali be-Sifrut ha-Tannaim ve-Yahaso le-Hokhmat ha-Amim*. Tel Aviv: Ha-Kibbutz ha-Meuhad.

hooks, bell. 1986. "Sisterhood: Political Solidarity Among Women." *Feminist Review* 23: 125–138.

Horodotzky, Shemuel Abba. 5689. "Yanuka." *Moznayim* 10: 7–9; 12: 8–10.

Ilan, Tal. 1995. *Jewish Women in Greco-Roman Palestine: An Inquiry into Image and Status*. Translated by Jonathan Price. Tübingen, Germany: J.C.B. Mohr.

———. 2001. "Sifrut Hazal ve-Limmudei Nashim." In Rina Levin Melamed, ed., *Harimi Be-Koah Kolekh: Al Kolot Nashiim u-Parshanut Feministit be-Limmudei ha-Yahadut*. Tel Aviv: Miskal, pp. 48–50.

Irigaray, Luce. 1985. *This Sex Which Is Not One*. Ithaca, N.Y.: Cornell University Press.

Jay, Nancy. 1992. *Throughout Your Generations Forever: Sacrifice, Religion, and Paternity*. Chicago: University of Chicago Press.

Kadari, Tamar. 5764. "Li-Melekhet ha-Arikha be-Midrash Shir ha-Shirim Rabba." PhD dissertation, Hebrew University, Jerusalem.

Kadari, Tamar. 5762. "Tokho Ratzuf Ahava: Al ha-Torah ke-Ra'aya bi-Derashot Tannaim le-Shir ha-Shirim." *Tarbitz* 71 (3–4): 391–404.

Kahana, Menahem. 5767. "Shesh Moshzar: Le-Siddurah shel Parshat 'Bereishit bara' be-Midrash Bereishit Rabba." In Yehoshua Levinson, ed., *Higayon le-Yona: Hebetim Hadashim be-Hekker Sifrut ha-Midrash, ha-Aggada ve-ha-Piyyut*. Jerusalem: Magnes, pp. 347–376.

Klein, Melanie. 1975. *Love, Guilt and Reparation and Other Works 1921–1925*. New York: Free Press, Simon & Schuster.

Knohl, Yisrael. 5767. *Emunot ha-Mikra: Gevulot ha-Mahapekha ha-Mikrait*. Jerusalem: Magnes.

Konstan, David. 1994. *Sexual Symmetry: Love in the Ancient Novel and Related Genres*. Princeton, N.J.: Princeton University Press.

Kosman, Admiel. 1999. "Ha-Isha she-Hafkha le-Gever: Demutah shel Rahav ba-Midrash." In Maya Leibowitz, et al., eds., *Barukh she-Asani Isha? Ha-Isha be-Yahadut me-ha-Tanakh ve-Ad Yamenu*. Tel Aviv: Miskal, pp. 91–102.

Kosman, Admiel. 2005. *Massekhet Nashim, Hokhma, Ahava, Neemanut, Teshuka, Yofi, Min, Kedusha: Keria be-Sippurim Talmudiyim ve-Rabaniyim ve-Shenei Midrashei Shir*. Tel Aviv: Alma and Am Oved.

———. 5768. "Ha-Shad ha-Nashi ve-ha-Peh ha-Niftah bi-Tefilla." In Admiel Kosman, ed., *Nashiut be-Olamo ha-Ruhani shel ha-Sippur ha-Talmudi*. Tel Aviv: Ha-Kibbutz ha-Meuhad, pp. 154–176.

Kristeva, Julia, and Toril Moi, eds. 1986. *The Kristeva Reader*. New York: Columbia University Press.

Labendz, Jenny R. 2010. "Socratic Torah: Non-Jews in Intellectual Culture." Submitted in partial fulfillment of PhD requirements in Talmud and Rabbinics, Graduate School of the Jewish Theological Seminary, New York.

Lauretis, Teresa de. 1987. *Technologies of Gender: Essays on Theory, Film, and Fiction*. Indiana University Press.

Leibowitz, Maya. 1999. "Peri u-Revi u-Mil'i et ha-Aretz: Mi Metzuveh be-Mitzvat Peru u-Revu?" In David Yoel Ariel, et al., eds., *Barukh she-Asani Isha? Ha-Isha be-Yahadut me-ha-Tanakh ve-Ad Yamenu*. Tel Aviv: Miskal, pp. 129–137.

Leibowitz, Yeshayahu. *Emuna, Historia ve-Arakhim*. Jerusalem: Akademon.

Leonstam, Shmuel E. 1954. "Zenut u-Zenunim." *Encyclopedia Mikrait*, vol. 2. Jerusalem: Bialik Institute, pp. 935–938. Levinson, Yehoshua. 1994. "Ha-Sippur ha-Mikra'i be-Itzuvo ha-Midrashi-Aggadi." PhD dissertation, Hebrew University, Jerusalem.

———. 2004. "Ha-Em ve-ha-Um: Zehuyot Sifrutiyot bi-Metziut Mishtaneh." In Yisrael Levin, ed., *Retzef u-Temura: Yehudim ve-Yahadut be-Eretz Yisrael ha-Bizantit-Notzrit*. Jerusalem: Dinur Center for Research in Jewish History, pp. 465–485.

———. 2005. *Ha-Sippur she-Lo Suppar*. Jerusalem: Magnes

Lieberman, Shaul. 5723. *Yevanit ve-Yevanut be-Eretz Yisrael*. Jerusalem: Bialik Institute.

Liebes, Yehuda. 1994. "De Natura Dei—Al ha-Mitos ha-Yehuda ve-Gilgulo." *Mishvaot*: 243–297.

———. 5758. "Mitos ve-Ortodoksia: Teshuva le-Shalom Rosenberg." *Mada'ei ha-Yahadut* 38: 181–186.
Lorand, Ruth. 5767. *Ha-Yofi be-Re'i ha-Filosofia*. Haifa: Haifa University Press.
———. 2010. *Al Parshanut ve-Havana*. Tel Aviv: Tel Aviv University Press.
Lorberbaum, Yair. 2000. "Al Da'atam shel ha-Hakhamim z"l Lo Alta ha-Hagshama Meolam (Moreh Nevukhim 1, 46): Antropomorfiyut be-Sifrut Hazal—Sekirat Mehkar Bikortit." *Mada'ei ha-Yahadut* 40: 3–54.
———. 2004. *Tzelem Elo-him*. Jerusalem and Tel Aviv: Schocken.
Lubin, Orly. 1993. "Isha Koret Isha." *Teoriya u-Bikkoret* 3: 65–78.
———. 2003. *Isha Koret Isha*. Haifa: University of Haifa Press.
Lutzky, Harriet. 1998. "Shadday as a Goddess Epithet." *Vetus Testamentum* 48: 15–36.
MacKinnon, Catharine. 1988. "Desire and Power: A Feminist Perspective." In Cary Nelson and Lawrence Grossberg, eds., *Marxism and the Interpretation of Culture*. Urbana: University of Illinois Press, 105–121.
———. 1989. *Toward a Feminist Theory of the State*. Cambridge, Mass.: Harvard University Press.
Maloul, Moshe. 2004. "Gisha Holistit-Integrativit be-Heker ha-Tarbut ha-Mikrait: Le-Hadgama—Motiv ha-Riggul ve-Kibbush Teritoria ba-Mikra." *Shenaton le-Heker ha-Mikra ve-ha-Mizrah ha-Kadum* 14: 141–157.
Meir, Ofra, 5737. "Ha-Demuyot ha-Po'alot be-Sippurei ha-Talmud ve-ha-Midrash (al pi midgam)." PhD dissertation, Hebrew University, Jerusalem.
———. 1987. *Ha-Sippur ha-Darshani be-Bereishit Rabba*. Tel Aviv: Ha-Kibbutz ha-Meuhad.
———. 5749. "Gan be-Eden: Hearot le-Ofen ha-Arikha shel Bereishit Rabba." *Dapim le-Mekhkar be-Sifrut* 5–6: 309–330.
———. 5750. "Retzifut ha-Arikha ke-Itzuv Hashkafat Olam." In Menachem Hirshman, ed., *Mahshevet Hazal: Divrei ha-Kenes ha-Rishon*. Jerusalem: Magnes, pp. 85–100.
———. 5756. "Ma'aseh ha-Arikha be-Bereishit Rabba, u-ve Vayikra Rabba." *Te'uda* 11: 61–90.
———. 1999. *Rabbi Yehuda ha-Nasi: Diukano shel Manhig be-Masorot Eretz Yisrael u-Bavel*. Tel Aviv: Ha-Kibbutz ha-Meuhad.
Melamed, Ezra Z. 5752. *Milon Arami-Ivri le-Talmud Bavli*. Jerusalem: Samuel and Odette Levy Institute.
Millett, Kate. 2000. *Sexual Politics*. Champaign: University of Illinois Press.
Moi, Toril. 2002. *Sexual/Textual Politics: Feminist Literary Theory*. New York: Routledge.
Morrison, Toni. 1993. *Playing in the Dark*. Vintage.
Mossman, Carol A. 1993. *Politics and Narratives of Birth: Gynocolonization from Rousseau to Zola*. Cambridge, UK: Cambridge University Press.

BIBLIOGRAPHY

Newman, Murray L. 1985. "Rahab and the Conquest." In James T. Butler, et al., eds., *Understanding the Word: Essays in Honor of Bernhard W. Anderson.* Sheffield, UK: JSOT Press, pp. 167–181.

Noy, Dov. 5728. "Even ha-Shetiya ve-Reshit ha-Beria." In Gedalia Alkoshi, et al., eds., *Ve-li-Yerushalayim: Divrei Sifrut ve-Hagut Likhvod Yerushayalim ha-Meshuhreret.* Jerusalem: Agudat ha-Sofrim ha-Ivrim bi-Medinat Yisrael, pp. 360–394.

O'Brien, Mary. 1981. *The Politics of Reproduction.* London: Routledge and Kegan Paul.

Ortner, Sherry. 1972. "Is Female to Male as Nature is to Culture?" In M. Z. Rosaldo and L. Lamphere, eds., *Woman, Culture & Society.* Stanford, Calif.: Stanford University Press, pp. 67–87.

Palgi-Hacker, Anat. 2005. *Me-I-Mahut le-Imahut.* Tel Aviv: Am Oved.

Pardes, Ilana. 1996. *Ha-Beria al-pi Hava.* Tel Aviv: Ha-Kibbutz ha-Meuhad.

———. 2002. *The Biography of Ancient Israel.* Berkeley: University of California Press.

Patai, Raphael. 1992. *Robert Graves and the Hebrew Myths.* Detroit: Wayne State University Press.

———. 5696. *Ha-Mayim: Mehkar li-Yedi'at ha-Aretz u-le-Folklor Eretzyisraeli bi-Tekufot ha-Mikra ve-ha-Mishna.* Tel Aviv: Dvir.

Pedaya, Haviva. 1997. "Temuorot be-Kodesh ha-Kodashim: Min ha-Shulayim la-Merkaz." *Mada'ei ha-Yahadut* 37: 53–110.

Pellman, Shoshana. 1993. "Ha-Min shel ha-Keria—Hevdel ha-Minim ve-Hokhmat ha-Sifrut." *Zemanim* 46–47: 107–119.

Peskowitz, Miriam Beth. 1997. *Spinning Fantasies: Rabbis, Gender, and History.* Berkeley: University of California Press.

Philip, Tarja S. 5768. "Mi-Leda u-mi-Beten u-mi-Herayon (Hosea 9:11): Meyaldot ba-Olam ha-Mikra." *Shenaton le-Heker ha-Mikra ve-ha-Mizrah ha-Kadum* 18: 59–78.

Rank, Otto. 1990. "The Myth of the Birth of the Hero." In Robert A. Segal, ed., *Quest of the Hero.* Princeton, N.J.: Princeton University Press, pp. 3–86.

Raveh, Inbar. 1996. "R. Peloni Patar Keriya be . . . : Ha-Petira be-Midrashei ha-Aggadah ha-Eretz-Yisraelit." MA dissertation, Department of Hebrew Literature, Hebrew University, Jerusalem.

———. 2008. *Me'at mi-Harbeh.* Tel Aviv: Ben Gurion University and Dvir.

Raviv, Rivka. 5768. "Sippur ha-Dialog Bein R. Yossi ben Halafta la-Matrona—Ben Bereishit Rabba, le-Vayikra Rabba." *Sidra* 23: 121–132.

Renan, Yael. 2001. *Elot ve-Gibborim: Mitosim al Gevulot ha-Koah.* Tel Aviv: Am Oved.

Rich, Adrienne. 1976. *Of Woman Born: Motherhood as Experience and Institution.* New York: W.W. Norton.

———. 1980. "Compulsory Heterosexuality and Lesbian Existence." *Signs* 5, no. 4 (Summer): 631–660.
Riley, Denise. 1988. *"Am I That Name?" Feminism and the Category of "Women" in History.* Minneapolis: University of Minnesota Press.
Rosenberg, Shalom. 5758. "Mitos ha-Mitosim." *Mada'ei ha-Yahadut* 38: 145–179.
Rosenthal, David. 1983. *"Al Derekh Tippulam shel Hazal be-Hilufei Nussah ba-Mikra."* In Yair Zakowitz and Alexander Rofe, eds., *Sefer Yitzhak Aryeh Zeligman,* vol. 2. Jerusalem: A. Rubinstein, pp. 395–417.
Rosen-Zvi, Ishay. 5766. "Ha-Guf ve-ha-Mikdash: Rshimat Mumei ha-Kohanim ba-Mishna u-Mekomo shel ha-Mikdash be-Beit ha-Mikrash ha-Tannai." *Mada'ei ha-Yahadut* 43: 49–87.
———. 5768. *Ha-Tekkes she-Lo Haya: Mikdash, Midrash u-Migdar be-Massekhet Sotah.* Jerusalem: Magnes.
———. 1999. "Yetzer ha-Ra, Miniut, ve-Issurei Yihud: Perek be-Antropologia Talmudit." *Teoria u-Bikkoret* 14: 55–84.
———. 2005. "Misogyny and its Discontents." *Prooftexts* 25 (1–2): 217–227.
Ross, Tamar. 2007. *Armon ha-Torah mi-Ma'al Lah: Ortodoksia u-Feminism.* Tel Aviv: Am Oved.
Routledge, Robin L. 2010. "Did God Create Chaos?: Unresolved Tension in Genesis 1:1–2." *Tyndale Bulletin* 61 (1): 69–88.
Ruah-Midbar, Marianna. 2001. "Aggadat David ve-ha-Tehom." *Nefesh* 7:11–18.
Rubenstein, Jeffrey L. 1999. *Talmudic Stories: Narrative Art, Composition, and Culture.* Baltimore: Johns Hopkins University Press.
Rubak, Sharon. 5763. "Be-Hayeihem u-ve-Motam Lo Nifradu—Ra'ayon ha-Teomut be-Notzrut ha-Ma'aravit." PhD dissertation, Hebrew University, Jerusalem.
Rubin, Nissan. 1995. *Reshit ha-Hayim: Tiksei Leida, Mila u-Pidyon ha-Ben bi-Mekorot Hazal.* Tel Aviv: Ha-Kibbutz ha-Meuhad.
Ruddick, Sara. 1989. *Maternal Thinking: Towards a Politics of Peace.* Boston: Beacon Press.
Satlow, Michael L. 1995. *Tasting the Dish: Rabbinic Rhetoric of Sexuality.* Atlanta: Scholars Press.
———. 1997. "Jewish Constructions of Nakedness in Late Antiquity." *Journal of Biblical Literature* 116: 429–454.
Schäfer, Peter. 2002. *Mirror of His Beauty: Feminine Images of God from the Bible to the Early Kabbala.* Princeton, N.J.: Princeton University Press.
Scholem, Gershom. 1996. *On the Kabbala and its Symbolism.* New York: Schocken.
Schremer, Adi. 5764. *Zakhar u-Nekeva Beraam: Ha-Nissuim be-Shalhei Yemei ha-Bayit ha-Sheni u-bi-Tekufat ha-Mishna ve-ha-Talmud.* Jerusalem: Shazar Center for Jewish History.
Schweickart, Patrocinio P. 1986. "Reading Ourselves: Towards a Feminist The-

ory of Reading." In Elizabeth A. Flynn and Patrocinio P. Schweickart, eds., *Gender and Reading: Essays on Readers, Texts, and Contexts.* Baltimore: Johns Hopkins University Press, pp. 31–62.

Scott, Joan. 1986. "Gender: A Useful Category of Historical Analysis." *The American Historical Review* 91, no. 5 (December): 1053–1075.

Segal, Robert A. 2007. *Theorizing about Myth.* Amherst: University of Massachusetts Press.

Seidman, Naomi. 1994. "Carnal Knowledge: Sex and the Body in Jeiwsh Studies." *Jewish Social Studies* 1.1: 41–115.

Shahar, Shulamith. 1990. *Childhood in the Middle Ages.* New York: Routledge.

———. 2003. *The Fourth Estate.* New York: Routledge.

Shalev, Carmel. 1995. "Al Shivyon, Shonut ve-Haflayat Min." In Barak Aharon, et al., eds., *Sefer Landau,* vol. 2. Tel Aviv: Borsi, pp. 893–930.

Sherwood, Aaron. 2006. "A Leader's Misleading and a Prostitute's Profession: A Re-examination of Joshua 2." *Journal for the Study of the Old Testament* 31 (1): 43–61.

Shifra, S., and Jacob Klein. 5756. *Ba-Yamim ha-Rehokim ha-Hem: Antologia me-Shirat ha-Mizrah ha-Kadum.* Tel Aviv: Am Oved.

Shinan, Avigdor, 5744. "*Mi-Derashat ha-Pasuk el ha-Aggada ha-Hofshit: Perek be-Toldot ha-Sippur ha-Mikrai ha-Murhav.*" *Mehkarei Yerushalayim be-Sifrut Ivrit* 5: 203–220.

———. 5752. "'Ma'aseh be-Etrogim': Sippur min ha-Midrash (Vayikra Rabba, 37:2) u-mi-Ketzat Gilgulav." *Mehkarei Yerushalayim be-Folklor Yehudi* 13–14: 61–79.

———. 5756. "Isha, Masekha ve-Tahposet be-Sifrut ha-Aggada shel Hazal." *Migvan De'ot ve-Hashkafot be-Tarbut Yisrael* 6: 29–52.

———. 5757. "Kasheh ke-Keri'at Yam Suf: O—Ma le-Mosad ha-Nissuin ve-li-Keri'at Yam Suf?" In Yair Zakowitz and Avigdor Shinan, eds., *Keri'at Yam Suf.* Jerusalem: Beit ha-Nassi, pp. 23–37.

Showalter, Elaine E., ed. 1985. *New Feminist Criticism: Essays on Women, Literature, and Theory.* 8th edition. New York: Pantheon.

Simha, R. Meir, of Dvinsk. 5754–5760. *Meshekh Hokhma.* Bnei Brak: Beit Talmud Gavoha Siah Yitzhak.

Sokoloff, Michael. 2002. *A Dictionary of Jewish Babylonian Aramaic of the Talmudic and Geonic Periods.* Ramat-Gan: Bar-Ilan University Press.

Stein, Dina. 2004. *Mimra, Magia, Mitos: Pirkei de-Rabbi Eliezer le-Or Mehkar ha-Sifrut ha-Amamit.* Jerusalem: Magnes.

Stein, Ruth. 1991. *Psychoanalytic Theories of Affect.* Westport, CT: Praeger.

Steinmetz, Devora. 1988. "A Portrait of Miriam in Rabbinic Midrash." *Prooftexts* 8: 35–65.

Stern, David. 1998. "The Captive Woman: Hellenization, Greco-Roman Erotic Narrative and Rabbinic Literature." *Poetics Today* 19: 91–127.
Storr, Anthony. 1991. *Jung*. New York: Routledge.
Tomashevsky, Boris. 1965. *"Thematics" in Russian Formalist Criticism: Four Essays*. Translated by Lee T. Lemon and Marion J. Reis. Lincoln: University of Nebraska Press.
Trible, Phyllis. 1992. *God and the Rhetoric of Sexuality*. London: SCM Press.
Tsumura, David Toshio. 2005. *Creation and Destruction: A Reappraisal of the Chaoskampf wTheory in the Old Testament*. Winona Lake, Ind.: Eisenbrauns.
Tzamir, Hamutal. 2009. "Lilit, Hava ve-ha-Gever ha-Mit'apek: ha-kalkala la-Libidinalit shel Bialik u-vnei doro." *Mehkerei Yerushalayim be-Sifrut Ivrit* 23: 133–182.
Urbach, Ephraim E. 5746. *Hazal, Pirkei Emunot*. Jerusalem: Magnes.
Veller, Shulamit. 2000. *Nashim be-Hevra ha-Yehudit: Bi-Tekufat ha-Mishna ve-ha-Talmud*. Tel Aviv: Ha-Kibbutz ha-Meuhad.
Vogels, Walter. 1996. "The Power Struggle between Man and Woman (Gen. 3: 16b)." *Biblica* 77 (2): 197–209.
Wegner, Judith Romney. 1988. *Chattel or Person? The Status of Women in the Mishna*. New York: Oxford University Press.
Wermut, Tikva. 5761. "Ha-im Hala Mitzvat Periya u-Reviya al Nashim—Yevamot 65b–66a," *Dibbur ha-Mat'hil* 1:47–52.
Weitzmann, Kurt, and Herbert L. Kessler. 1990. *The Frescoes of the Dura Synagogue and Christian Art*. Washington, D.C.: Dumbarton Oaks Research Library and Collection.
Wickes, Ian G. 1953. "A History of Infant Feeding. Part I. Primitive Peoples: Ancient Works: Renaissance Writers." *Arch Dis Child* 28:151–158.
Winkler, John J. 1990. *The Constraints of Desire: The Anthropology of Sex and Gender in Ancient Greece*. New York: Routledge.
Wolf, Naomi. 2002. *The Beauty Myth*. New York: Harper Perennial.
Woolf, Virginia. 1929. *A Room of One's Own*. London: Hogarth Press.
Yalom, Marilyn. 1999. *A History of the Breast*, 2nd ed. London: Rivers Oram Press.
Yassif, Eli. 1994. *Sippur ha-Am ha-Ivri: Toldotav, Sugav u-Mashma'uto*. Jerusalem: Bialik Institute.
Yavin, Shemuel. 5735. "Reshito shel Beit David." In *Ha-Melukha ha-Yisraelit be-Reshitah*. Jerusalem: Shazar Center for Jewish History, pp. 60–90.
Zakowitz, Yair. 1987. *Al Tefisat ha-Nes ba-Mikra*. Tel Aviv: Ministry of Defense.
———. 1990. "Humor and Theology or the Successful Failure of Israelite Intelligence: A Literary-Folkloric Approach to Joshua 2." *Text and Tradition*: 75–98.

BIBLIOGRAPHY

———. 5757. "Migvan De'ot ve-Hashkafot al ha-Gevul be-Sifriyot Tarbutenu." In *Migvan De'ot ve-Hashkafot be-Tarbut Yisrael,* Book 7. Jerusalem: Ministry of Education, Culture and Sport.

———. 2009. *Tzevat bi-Tzevat Asuya.* Tel Aviv: Am Oved.

Zohar, Noam, 5767. *Be-Sod ha-Yetzira shel Sifrut Hazal: Ha-Arikha ke-Mafteah le-Mashma'ut.* Jerusalem: Magnes.

Zunz, Yom-Tov L. 1832. *Die Gottesdienstlichen Vortrage der Juden (The Sermons of the Jews in their Historic Evolution).* Berlin: A. Asher.

BIBLICAL SOURCES

Pentateuch

Genesis
- 1:1   133
- 1:2   119
- 1:7   122
- 1:28   76, 82, 84
- 2:9   18
- 2:21   166
- 2:21–23   145–146
- 2:23   147
- 3:16   42, 43, 45, 191
- 3:22   18
- 4:7   45
- 4:26   125
- 5:2   12, 40
- 7:11   121, 123, 125
- 7:19   123–124
- 8:1   126
- 8:2   121
- 17:1   37
- 17:9–14   37
- 18:11   7
- 18:12–13   xii, 6, 82
- 18:23–32   67
- 21:6–7   xii, 5
- 24:65   83
- 35:11   35, 82, 163
- 38:14   83
- 49:25   35, 121
- 50:17   82

Exodus
- 1:15   59, 130
- 1:17   58, 64, 68
- 1:18   65
- 1:22   60
- 2:7   19
- 4:10   22
- 4:28   26
- 6:26   26
- 6:27   26
- 13:11–15   175
- 15:2   11, 14, 16
- 15:4   130
- 15:5   130
- 18:10   107
- 20:1   29
- 34:2   128
- 34:9–20   175

Leviticus
- 8:3   31
- 12:1–8   49
- 12:8   45
- 18:21   175
- 20:2–5   175

Numbers
- 11:12   29
- 20:7–8   31

20:10   31, 32
20:11   32, 160

Deuteronomy
   1:24   114
   1:35   32
   1:39   18
   4:12   29
   6:4   39, 45
   12:31   175
   23:19   101
   24:6   45, 50
   32:13   10, 11, 24

Prophets

Joshua
   2:1   106
   2:9–11   110
   2:10   104
   2:11   110
   2:15   103, 110
   2:16   114
   2:18   112
   3:9   32
   5:10   104
   8:33   32

Samuel
   I 2:8   125
   I 12:6   27
   I 15:3   160
   II 11:3   176
   II 15:12   140
   II 16:23   139
   II 17:23   176

Kings
   I 8:8   163
   II 22:14   112
   II 16:3   175
   II 21:6   175
   II 23:10   175

Isaiah
   5:1–2   134
   8:3   166
   28:9   19, 21, 34
   28:9–11   34
   28:10–11   21
   47:2–3   165
   57:5   175

Jeremiah
   23:29   156
   25:10   51
   33:6   27

Ezekiel
   16:4   10
   16:7   11
   16:20–21   175
   23:37   175
   26:19   121
   31:15   121, 127
   34:14   127
   38:12   135
   47:3–4   143

Hosea
   1:8   166
   7:1   27

Amos
   7:4   121

Jonah
   2:6   121

Nahum
   1:4   36

Zachariah
   13:1   143

Hagiographia

Chronicles
   I 22:7–10   138
   I 27:33   140
   II 33:6   175

Psalms
   36:7   126
   42:8   121, 122
   77:17   121

BIBLIOGRAPHY

78:15   121
85:11   87
106:37–38   175
135:6   121
124:4–5   124, 140
148:7   121, 124

Job
5:13   32
21:8   128
22:17   125
26:13   60
31:9–10   165
38:6   135

Proverbs
3:13–18   23
5:19   24

5:20   162
8:28   121
8:35   23
9:8   82
12:10   128
20:11   59

Song of Songs
1:13   163
7:2   133, 176
8:5   10
8:10   25

Ecclesiastes
2:5   135

Daniel
2:47   107
8:12   88

OTHER RABBINIC SOURCES

Mishna, Kiddushin 1,1   177
Mishna, Makhshirin 6, 7   160
Mishna, Avoda Zara 2, 1   20
Mishna, Yebamot 6, 6   82

Mekhilta de-Rabbi Yishmael Beshalah—Massekhta de-Shira parsha 5   130
Mekhilta de-Rabbi Yishmael Yitro—Massekhta de-Amalek parsha 1   110
Mekhilta de-Rabbi Yishmael Yitro—Massekhta de-ba-Hodesh parsha 8   29
Mekhilta de-Rabbi Shimon ben Yohai 6, 2   166
Mekhilta de-Rabbi Shimon ben Yochai 15, 1   160
Mekhilta de-Rabbi Shimon ben Yohai 15, 5   176
Sifri Bamidbar Piska 42   170
Sifri Bamidbar piska 115   173

Sifri Devarim piska 22   114
Sifri Devarim piska 317   24
Sifri Devarim piska 353   123
Sifri Zuta 10, 29 Horowitz p. 263   103

Palestinian Talmud, Ketubot 7, law 7, 31d   3
Palestinian Talmud, Ketubot 25c   165
Palestinian Talmud, Yebamot 6, law 6   169
Palestinian Talmud, Sanhedrin 10, 2:29b   158, 160
Palestinian Talmud, Hagiga, chapter 2, law 1   118
Palestinian Talmud, Sotah 10a   165

Genesis Rabba parsha 13, 13, Theodor-Albeck edition, p. 122   123

BIBLIOGRAPHY

Genesis Rabba parsha 17, 7, Theodor-Albeck edition, p. 158   146
Genesis Rabba parsha 20, 7, Theodor-Albeck edition, pp. 190–191   45
Genesis Rabba parsha 32, 7, Theodor-Albeck edition, p. 288   176
Genesis Rabba parsha 33, 1, Theodor-Albeck edition, pp. 298–300   127
Genesis Rabba parsha 53, Theodor-Albeck edition, pp. 563–564   6
Genesis Rabba parsha 60, Theodor-Albeck edition, p. 1040   83

Exodus Rabba 1, 13, Shinan, p. 56   60
Exodus Rabba 1, 15, Shinan, p. 61   65, 68
Exodus Rabba parsha 1   161
Exodus Rabba parsha 15   125
Exodus Rabba parsha 52   170–71

Song of Songs Rabba parsha 4   27
Song of Songs Rabba 7, 1   165

Ruth Rabba parsha 3, 4,   95

Babylonian Talmud, Bekhorot 7b   159
Babylonian Talmud, Bava Metzia 87a   159
Babylonian Talmud, Zebahim 116a   104
Babylonian Talmud, Hagiga 12a   36
Babylonian Talmud, Hagiga 15a   15
Babylonian Talmud, Yebamot 65b   76, 83

Babylonian Talmud, Yoma 11b   162
Babylonian Talmud, Yoma 54a   135, 163
Babylonian Talmud, Yoma 77b   143
Babylonian Talmud, Megilla 14b   112
Babylonian Talmud, Megilla 15a   106
Babylonian Talmud, Sotah 10a   165
Babylonian Talmud, Sotah 11b   11
Babylonian Talmud, Sotah 12a   166
Babylonian Talmud, Sotah 30b   14
Babylonian Talmud, Sukka 49a   134
Babylonian Talmud, Sukka 53a   137
Babylonian Talmud, Erubin 21b   162
Babylonian Talmud, Erubin 54b   24
Babylonian Talmud, Erubin 100b   43
Babylonian Talmud, Pesahim 87a   162
Babylonian Talmud, Pesahim 108b   160
Babylonian Talmud, Kiddushin 12b   90
Babylonian Talmud, Kiddushin 29b   165
Babylonian Talmud, Sanhedrin 39b   151
Babylonian Talmud, Sanhedrin 91b   177

Midrash Tanhuma (Warsaw) parshat Noah 7   128
Midrash Tanhuma (Warsaw) parshat Lekh-lekha 19   37
Midrash Tanhuma (Warsaw) parshat Hukkat 9   32

Yalkut Shimoni Torah parshat Noach 56   124
Yalkut Shimoni Torah parshat Vaera 182   10

INDEX

Aaron, 25, 26–28, 38
Abba, R.: injunction to procreate, 82; Song of Songs, 26
Abigail, 105
Abraham: Binding of Isaac, 69–70, 168n37, 175n31; circumcision, 37–38; hospitality, 68, 69; nursing miracle, 5–9; paternity of Isaac, 7, 9, 159n24; Sodom, 67–70
abstinence. *See* celibacy
adultery, 137, 140, 164n10, 170n26
aesthetics: creation of Eve, 148–49; legends of the Sages, 75, 89
age and sexuality, 7, 8
Aha, R.: on women's desire, 46
Ahitophel, 136–37, 139–40, 176nn47–48
Akiba, R.: on Flood, 126; on nursing miracle, 10
Amram, 60, 62, 63–64, 70
androgyny: drag, 78–79, 168n9, 168n11; of God, 12, 159n31
angel/whore stereotypes, 103, 113–14
anima and *animus*, 141–42
annulments. *See* divorce and annulments
anthropomorphism, 12
Apsu, 119–21
Ark: as center, 135; poles as breasts, 33, 162–63n84. *See also* Flood
Ashera, 35
axis mundi, 132, 133, 136

Babylon: creation myth, 36, 119–21; culture of, 154
Bakhtin, Mikhail, 8
Bathsheba, 140, 176n48
beauty, 2–3, 26, 27–28, 105–6
Beauvoir, Simone de, 54–55, 108, 109, 128
Berakhia, R.: on Eve's curse, 45–55
betrothals, 90–92, 177n6

Binding of Isaac, 69–70, 168n37, 175n31
biography, 89, 170nn30–32
biopower, 1
birth. *See* childbirth
birthstones, 130
blood and mucus, 148–49, 178nn10–11
body: control of female, 2, 8–9, 39, 41–55, 164n16; defects, 2–3; as feminine, 29, 30; feminist scholars, 2; Jewish, 2; power relations, 1, 168n11; split between erotic and reproductive, 102. *See also* modesty; *specific parts of the body*
boundaries: Creation, 132, 141; David, 139, 141; lack of in femininity, 36, 131
bound motifs, 89
Boyarin, Daniel, xx, 88, 154
breakthrough of sanctity, 132
breastfeeding: eroticism of, 16–17; by foreigners, 19, 20, 161n53; by God, 11–12, 13, 34, 35–36; importance of, 19, 20, 160–61n52; male anxiety about, 31; by men, 12, 13; miracles surrounding, 4–17, 31–34; of Moses, 18–22, 30; from rocks miracle, 9–15; Sarah, 5–9; striking of the rock, 31–34
breasts: Ark poles as, 33, 162–63n84; and beauty, 2–3, 26, 27–28; circumcision covenant, 37–38; compared to Torah, 23–30, 162n66; as evil, 17–18, 30–38; of God, 35–38; as good, 17–18, 23–30, 38; Moses and Aaron as, 25–28, 38; mountains as, 35, 163n92; and "otherness" of feminine body, 39; as primal pleasure, 18; puberty, 27, 162n72; sexuality, 3–4, 16–17, 160n47; Song of Songs, 25–28; striking of the rock, 31–34; tablets as, 29. *See also* breastfeeding
bride, debate over praise for, 170n26
Butler, Judith, 78, 108–9, 168n11

197

INDEX

Cain and evil, 45, 46, 47
Canaanite mythology, 35, 36, 163n92. *See also* Rahab
candelabrum and lamp imagery, 50, 51–54, 165n30
celestial pearl, miracle of, 93–99
celibacy, 48, 165n26, 167nn19–20
center: Temple as, 132, 135; Torah as, 26
chaos: the "deep" as, 119, 131, 132, 135, 139; as evil, 124; and Mother Earth, 128; primordial, 37, 38, 132, 138–39
characters, round and flat, 173n40
childbirth: absence of descriptions, 56; ambivalence toward, 46, 48, 66; avoiding, 46, 48, 74, 76–88, 90–92; compared to birth of nation, 71–73; Eve's curse, 41–55, 164n13, 164n16; male disgust, 148–49, 178nn10–11; political theories, 57; twins, 83. *See also* Hebrew midwives
circumcision, 37–38, 51
Cixous, Hélène, 22–23
Clément, Catherine, 22–23
collective versus individual. *See* individual versus collective
commandments: gender differences, 111, 169n21, 173n30; procreation, 74, 76–88, 165n26, 168n18, 169n17, 169n21; Rahab's breaking of, 111; tablets as breasts, 29; three, specific to women, 111
competition: between God and mother, 14–15; between Torah and secular life, 23–30, 162n66
conquest, 102–3, 111–13
context in legends of the Sages, 83
control: of female body, 2, 8–9, 39, 41–55, 121–22, 164n16; male sexual, 105, 106
conversions: and marriage, 173n35; Rahab's, 106, 109–11, 172n26
Creation: Babylonian myth, 36, 119–21; boundaries, 132, 141; the "deep" as feminine element, 118–20; of Eve, 145–56; as suppression of disorder, 132; truth and peace, 87–88
cross-dressing, 78–79, 168n9, 168n11

culture: as masculine, 14–15, 16, 121–22; versus nature, 72, 108, 121–22, 125, 126, 144

darkness: and chaos, 119, 124, 128; and the Flood, 127
daughter(s): and injunction to procreate, 84, 168n18; Miriam as, 61, 62, 63
David, 136–42, 161n60, 176n45
death: by drowning, 128–29, 130, 131; male/female morality, 70, 71; nursing and death drive, 31; by suffocation, 137, 176n46. *See also* infanticide
the "deep": as destructive element, 121, 125, 126–30; End of Days stream, 142–44; as feminine element, 118–20, 122–25, 126, 141; as life-giving, 121, 136; and the Temple, 131–44
defects, body, 2–3
dependence and desire, 54–55
desire: and breasts, 3–4; and dependence, 54–55; dominance over women's, 41–55; Freud and norms of, 108; God's desire for Jewish people, 47, 48; men's aversion to women, 149, 178n10. *See also* eroticism; sex and sexuality
destruction: as feminine, 120–21; by God, 36–38; and militarism, 71; by water, 121, 123–25, 126, 139
dialogistic readings, 76–77
dichotomous-hierarchical model, 22–23
didactics in legends of the Sages, 75
disguises: doubling and twins, 83; Judith, wife of R. Hiyya, 76, 77–79, 82, 86, 88, 92; Tamar, 168n8
divorce and annulments: to avoid childbirth, 90–92; and body defects, 2–3; from pregnant wives, 60, 63, 66
dominance. *See* control
doubling, 83. *See also* twins
drag, 78–79, 168n9, 168n11
drowning, 128–29, 130, 131
duality: dichotomous-hierarchical model, 22–23; and Rahab, 103, 113–14; water,

198

124; in women's sexuality, 3–4, 103, 113–14

Eleazar b. Simeon, R.: on injunction to procreate, 82, 86
Eliade, Mircea, 118–19, 131–32, 133
Eliam, 176n48
El Sha-dai, 12, 35–38
emperor's daughter and creation of Eve, 150–54
'Ena Saba, R.: on Rahab, 112
End of Days stream, 142–44
Enûma Eliš, 36
Epic of Gilgamesh, 113
eroticism: and nursing, 16–17; prostitution, 102; submission, 54–55; Temple shafts, 134. *See also* desire; sex and sexuality
essence, femininity as, 155
Esther, 13, 105
ethnic identity, 22, 161n62
Eve: creation of, 145–56; curse of, 41–55, 164n13, 164n16
evil: breasts as, 17–18, 30–38; and Cain, 45, 46, 47; as feminine, 124–25; and Flood, 124–25, 126
Exodus from Egypt: as birth of nation, 33–34, 71–73; Hebrew midwives, 56–58, 59–70; nursing miracle, 9–15; striking of the rock, 31–34
Exum, Cheryl, 58, 70, 73

faith: Abraham's and midwives' world changing, 68; Miriam's strength versus Amram's weakness, 63; proselytism, 106; Rahab's conversion, 109–12; recognition of God and God's power, 106, 109–10; reward in the world to come, 95–96; Sarah's nursing miracle, 6, 7–8; unity and recognition of God, 39
fathers: and infant identity, 14–16, 21; paternity, 8–9, 72, 159n24
fear of God, 68–69
female morality: Hebrew midwives, 67, 70, 73; Judith, wife of R. Hiyya, 77, 80, 87

female waters, 122–24. *See also* the "deep"
feminine voice, 96–99
femininity: angel/whore stereotypes, 103, 113–14; *anima* and *animus*, 141–42; beauty, 106; and the body, 29, 30; breasts as symbol of, 3; of David, 142; the "deep," 118–20, 122–25, 126, 141; dichotomous-hierarchical model, 22–23; as essence, 155; as evil, 124–25; and fertility, 123; and fluids, 36, 131; of God, xi–xii, 11–12, 13, 118, 131, 147, 159n31, 160n39; morality, 67, 70, 73, 77, 80, 87; myths, 117, 118; nature, 15, 30, 117, 118, 121–22, 153; of rabbinical perspective in Land of Israel, 154; Temple shafts, 134; Torah, 30; as the "uncanny," 99
feminist theory: about, xvii–xviii, xx; on the body, 2; sex, sexuality, and gender, xx, 107–8
fertility: and age, 8; El Sha-dai, 35; as feminine, 123; *keres* term, 80, 169n15; and morality, 102; sterilization, 76, 80, 82; twins, 28; and water, 123, 124, 139, 143. *See also* childbirth; procreate, injunction to
fire, 174–75n25
Fisher, Esther, 85, 86
Flood, 121, 123–29, 135
fluidity: element of, 125–26; as feminine, 36, 131; and gender, 174–75n25; Temple shafts, 134
folktales, 170n32
food: nursing from the rocks miracle, 13; Torah as, 23–25, 29; women as, 153, 178n15
foreigners: dialogues with Sages, 145–46, 151, 152, 177n5; as independent women, 109; and nursing, 19, 20, 161n53; and prostitution, 172–73n28
Forster, E. M., 173n40
Foucault, Michel, 1, 172–73n28
foundation stone, 135
Freud, Sigmund, 15–16, 18, 69–70, 98, 108

199

INDEX

Gamliel, Rabban: creation of Eve, 150–54; and Joshua, 171n12; as unaware of suffering of scholars, 171n12

Garden of Eden: breasts as, 18; and Eve's curse, 41–45; Song of Songs, 164–65n20

gaze and economy of desire, 3–4

Gehennom, the "deep" as, 127

gender: and commandments, 111, 169n21, 173n30; as continuum, 108–9; defined, 107–8; dichotomous-hierarchical model, 22–23; drag as metaphor, 78; and ethnic identity, 161n62; and fluidity, 174–75n25; and group identity, 113; as performance, 108–9, 111; research in rabbinic literature on, xx–xxi; as social product, 107, 108–9, 168n11. *See also* men; women

gezera shava, 104, 130, 175n32

Gilbert, Sandra, 103

Gilligan, Carol, 67, 77, 81, 96

God: androgyny of, 12, 159n31; as competition for mother, 14–15; denial of human aspects, 12; desire for Jewish people, 47, 48; as destroyer, 36–38; fear of, 68–69; femininity of, xi–xii, 11–12, 13, 118, 131, 147, 159n31, 160n39; Names of, 34, 35, 163n86; as nurser, 11–12, 13, 34, 35–36; prayers by Hebrew midwives to, 66–67; as rock, 34; symbolic paternity of, 9; unity and recognition of, 39

good breasts, 17–18, 23–30, 38

Goshen-Gottstein, Alon, 174–75n25

grinding of wheat, 51–52

grotesque, 8

group identity and gender, 113

Gubar, Susan, 103

guile, female, 57, 62

Gunkel, Hermann, 120–21

hak'hel, 33

halla, 111, 173n30

Hanina b. Dosa, R., and wife, 96

harlotry. *See* prostitution; Rahab

harmony: End of Days stream, 144; in marriage, 136; of mother and child, 14, 61–62; between twins, 28

Hartman-Halbertal, Tova, 158n10

Hebrew midwives, 56–58, 59–70, 71–73, 130–31, 166n13, 167n19

heresy and harlotry, 111, 113, 172n27

heterosexuality: heterotopia, 110, 172–73n28; as norm, 50, 107

highway robber's wife and desire, 45, 50–55

Hisda, R.: previous betrothals, 90–92; on Temple shafts, 136–37

Hiyya, R.: on miracle of pearl, 93–94, 95; wife's suffering, 74, 76–88, 90–92

Horeb, 163n92

hospitality, 68, 69

Hulda, 112

human sacrifice, 129, 175n31

Huna, R.: on End of Days stream, 142–44

idealism in legends of the Sages, 75

identity: *anima* and *animus*, 141–42; ethnic, 22, 161n62; group, 113; Judith, wife of R. Hiyya, 77, 88, 91; and marriage, 40; maternal legacy, 91; nursing and weaning, 14–16, 21, 22, 30–31; and the "other," 141–42; round and flat characters, 173n40; stages of women's, 81; twins and doubling, 83; women's identification with men, 115; women's voices, 96

idolatry and harlotry, 172n27

Ile'a, R.: on injunction to procreate, 82, 86

incest, 16–17

indiscriminateness, 100

individual versus collective: body and power relations, 1; childbirth and birth of nation, 72; God's desire for Jewish people, 47; nursing miracles, 5–9, 15

individuation, 81

infanticide: Binding of Isaac, 69–70; drowning, 128–29; and Hebrew midwives, 56–58, 59–70, 130–31

infants: development of, 19, 20, 30–31, 160–61n52; Song of the Sea, 14–16; wonder child, 161n60. *See also* breastfeeding

200

Irigaray, Luce, 3–4, 125–26, 174–75n25
irony: and celestial pearl miracle, 96, 98, 171n7; of contrast between Abraham and midwives, 69; of double moral standard, 153
Isaac: Binding of, 69–70, 168n37, 175n31; paternity of, 7, 9, 159n24
Isaac, R.: on beauty of Rahab, 105, 106; on foundation stone, 135
Isaac b. Abdimi, R.: on Eve's curse, 42, 44–45, 46, 164n13
Isaac Luria, R.: on Rahab, 172n23
Ishmael, R.: on Flood, 126; on injunction to procreate, 82; on Temple shafts, 133

Jacob's deathbed blessings, 35–36
Jael, 105
Jay, Nancy, 72–73
Jerusalem as center of Israel, 135
Jesus and Rahab, 112
jewelry, Temple shafts as, 134
Jochebed, 58, 59–60, 61, 62, 63
Johanan, R.: on Song of Songs, 25; on Temple shafts, 133, 136–37
Johanan b. Baroka, R.: on injunction to procreate, 82, 84, 86–87
Jose, R.: on Temple shafts, 133–34
Jose b. Halafta, R.: on creation of Eve, 146–50
Jose b. Isaac, R.: on Jochebed as Shifra, 60
Joseph, R.: on injunction to procreate, 82
Jose the Galilean, R.: Eve's curse, 45, 50–55; nursing from the rocks miracle, 14–15, 16
Joshua, R., and criticism of wealthy, 171n12
Joshua and Rahab, 112, 113
Josiah, R.: on Flood, 127
Josiah, 175n31
Judah, R.: on Ark pole as breasts, 162–63n84; on Flood, 127
Judah the Prince, R., and celestial pearl, 94–99, 171n12
Judan, R.: on Mordecai, 13
Judith, wife of R. Hiyya, 74, 76–88, 90–92
Jung, Carl, 141–42

keres, 80, 169n15
Klein, Jacob, 119–21
Klein, Melanie, 18, 30–31, 38
Kristeva, Julia, 14, 21

Lacan, Jacques, 21
lamp and candelabrum imagery, 50, 51–54, 165n30
language. *See* speech
law: exclusion of women from, 169n21; women as interpreters of, 79, 80, 169n12
Leibowitz, Yeshayahu, xvi
Levi, R.: on Hebrew midwives, 65; male and female waters, 122–23; on Sarah nursing miracle, 6
lies: Hebrew midwives, 62; Judith, 91; and peace, 86–88, 170n26; Rahab, 109
life: instinct and nursing, 31; male/female morality, 71; and water, 121, 136, 143
lighting Sabbath candles, 111, 173n30
liminal spaces, 104, 113, 131, 172n15
logos, 14, 22
Lorand, Ruth, xxii
Lubin, Orly, xvii
Lutzky, Harriet, 35
lying. *See* lies

MacKinnon, Catherine, 44, 54
maidservants and prostitution, 100–101
main sex organ, woman's, 3–4, 162n72
male morality, 67, 70, 71, 79
Marduk, 36, 119–20
marriage: adultery, 137, 140, 164n10, 170n26; ambivalence toward, 46, 48; and bodily defects, 2–3; and conversions, 173n35; millstone imagery for, 50, 51–52, 165n30; as norm, 40, 46; and previous betrothals, 90–92; robber's wife and desire, 45, 50–55; secret, 51
masculinity: *anima* and *animus,* 141–42; centrality of, 126; culture, 14–15, 16, 121–22; dichotomous-hierarchical model, 22–23; of God, 118; morality, 67, 70–71, 79; and oneness, 47, 122; of rabbinical perspec-

INDEX

tive in Babylon, 154; stones, 131; waters, 122–24
master and slave dependence, 54–55
maternal thinking, 70–71
matriarchy, shift from, 15–16
measure for measure: conventions, 175n34; drowning of Egyptians, 130, 131; post-childbirth sacrifices, 49
Meir, Ofra, 171n14
Meir, R.: on Hebrew midwives, 64
men: aversion to women, 148–49, 178nn10–11; circumcision, 37–38, 51; fear of God, 68–69; injunction to procreate, 84–85, 169n17, 169n21; nursing by, 12, 13; and sexual drive, 100, 101; women's identification with, 115. *See also* masculinity
menstruation, 43, 111, 148–49, 164n10, 178n11
Michal, 105
midrashim: about, xi; biography in, 89, 170nn30–32; context, 83; functions of, 76; interrelated teachings, 169–70n25; and minimalism, 74–75, 80, 88–89
midwives. *See* Hebrew midwives
militarism, 25, 71, 102–3
Millet, Kate, 40–41
millstone imagery, 50, 51–52, 165n30
minimalism in legends of the Sages, 74–75, 80, 88–89
miracles: breastfeeding, 4–17, 31–34; celestial pearl, 94–99; as change in order of Creation, 4; crossing of Jordan, 102; as imposing order, 8; splitting of Reed Sea, 14–16
Miriam: Hebrew midwives, 58, 59–60, 61; Moses's abstinence, 167n20; nursing of Moses, 19; as Pu'a, 59–60, 61, 62–64, 166n13
modesty, female: body, 3, 8, 17, 158n10, 164n10; sexual desire, 43–44
monotheism: feminist criticism of, 165n23; and patriarchal structure of sexuality, 47; use of myths, 117–18
monsters, women as, 103, 113–14

morality: female/male, 67, 70–71, 73, 77, 79, 80, 87; Flood, 126–29; legends of the Sages, 76; and motherhood, 70–71; and prostitution, 102
Mordecai's nursing of Esther, 13
Morrison, Toni, xviii–xix
Moses: breast imagery in Song of Songs, 25, 26–28, 38; as mother, 29; nursing of, 18–22, 30; parting blessings, 123; saving of, as female story, 58; stammering of, 21–22, 161n61; striking of the rock, 31–34; twinning with Aaron, 28
Mother Earth, 128
mothers: God as mother, 13; God in competition with, 14–15; and infant identity, 14, 15–16, 21; Jochebed as, 61, 62, 63; maternal thinking, 70–71; Moses as, 29; and sexuality, 4, 16–17; and wonder child, 161n60
mountains: breasts as, 35, 163n92; and the "deep," 126–29
mucus and blood, 148–49, 178nn10–11
multiplicity: of the "deep," 122; of rabbinic texts, 52–54; striking of the rock, 33, 34; symmetry as unifying, 27–28; women's sexuality, 3–4, 17, 38–39, 47
myths: Babylonian creation, 36, 119–21; and Judaism, 116–18

Nahman, R.: beauty of Rahab, 105–6; Hulda, 112
Nahman b. Isaac, R.: on injunction to procreate, 82
names: of God, 34, 35, 163n86; Judith, wife of R. Hiyya, 77; lack of women's, 74, 105, 168n6; Rahab, 105, 106; use of in midrashim, 61–62, 112–13
nation forming: conversion of Rahab, 110–13; Hebrew midwives, 57–58, 63, 71–73, 167n19; proselytism and subjugation fantasies, 106–7, 114; striking of the rock, 33–34
nature: versus culture, 72, 108, 121–22, 125, 126, 144; as feminine, 15, 30, 117, 118, 153

202

nidda, 111, 173n30
Noah. *See* Flood
non-Jewish people. *See* foreigners
notarikon, 46
nursing. *See* breastfeeding

object relations theory, 18
O'Brien, Mary, 57
Oedipal complex, 69–70
oneness versus multiplicity: breasts, 38–39; faith and, 39; feminine desire, 47; nursing from the rocks miracle, 13; patriarchal structure, 47; sexuality, 3–4, 122; striking of the rock, 33
oral stage, 11, 18
order: beauty as, 28; breastfeeding as part of natural, 5; changing of prevailing, 66; Creation as, 119, 132; father's symbolic, 15, 21, 92, 125; hierarchy as proper, 13; mother's semiotic, 15–22; oneness versus multiplicity in sexual, 3–4, 122; sacrifice and social, 72–73; symmetry as, 27
Ortner, Sherry, 121–22
the "other": angel/whore duality, 103; breasts, 39; the "deep," 141; and doubt, 99; and identity, 141–42; nursing of Moses, 22; Rahab, 103–4

Palgi-Hacker, Anat, 16–17
Pardes, Ilana, 47–48
parody, drag as, 168n11
paternity, 7, 8–9, 72, 159n24
peace: between husband and wife, 140, 176n48; lying and, 86–88, 170n26; male/female morality, 71
pearl, miracle of, 93–99
performance, gender as, 108–9, 111
petirah, 27, 162n71
Pharaoh and Hebrew midwives, 56–58, 62–67, 70, 130–31
Pharaoh's daughter, 20, 58
Phineas, R.: on End of Days stream, 142–44
Phoenician child sacrifices, 129
plurality. *See* multiplicity

poverty and wife of R. Simeon b. Halafta, 93–99
power: body as battlefield, 1, 168n11; childbirth and fertility, 84. *See also* control
pregnancy. *See* childbirth; fertility
procreate, injunction to: celibacy, 165n26; sons/daughters, 84, 168n18; suffering by Judith, wife of R. Hiyya, 74, 76–88; and women, 84–85, 169n17, 169n21
property, women as, 147, 177n6
proselytism, 106–7, 110, 172n19
prostitution, 100–107, 109–15, 172–73nn27–28
Pu'a, 59–60, 61, 62–64, 166n13
puberty, 27, 162n72
purity: End of Days stream, 143; and menstruation, 111; nursing by foreigners, 20–21
Pythagoras, 124

queer theory and drag, 78

Raba: on R. Isaac b. Abdimi, 42–43; on Song of Songs, 25, 26
Rahab, 102–7, 109–15, 172n23, 172n26
rain, 45, 46, 47, 48
rape, 50–51, 102–3
Rashi on Temple shafts, 134, 176n45
readers and reading, xv, xvii–xviii
Rebecca, veil and twins, 83
redactors and redaction, xxiii, 46, 59, 85
Reed Sea, 14–16, 130
reproduction. *See* fertility; procreate, injunction to
Resh Lakish: on El Sha-dai, 35–36; on righteousness and reward, 94, 96, 170n5
Rich, Adrienne, 50, 57
righteousness: celestial pearl miracle, 93–99; and Flood, 126–27; Hebrew midwives, 66; miracle of nursing rocks, 13; Miriam and Amram, 63; Sarah, 6, 9
robber's wife and desire, 45, 50–55
rocks/stones: birthstones, 130; foundation stone, 135; masculinity, 131; millstone

203

INDEX

imagery, 50, 51–52, 165n30; nursing miracle, 9–15; striking of the rock by Moses, 31–34
Romans: and harmony, 28; noblewoman, 146–50; and twins, 28
Rosen-Zvi, Ishay, xxi–xxii, 175n32
Ruddick, Sara, 70–71

sacrifices: Binding of Isaac, 69–70, 168n37; human, 129, 175n31; post-childbirth, 45, 46, 49–50; as pseudo-birth ceremonies, 72–73; water libation and Temple, 134
sanctity, breakthrough of, 132
Sanctuary as center of Temple, 135
Sarah, 5–9, 105
satire in emperor's daughter and creation of Eve, 153–54
Scholem, Gershom, 116–17
Schremer, Adi, 165n26
Scott, Joan, xxiii
sea in Babylonian creation myth, 36, 119–21. *See also* Reed Sea; the "deep"
secrecy: creation of Eve, 146–50; marriages, 51
selfhood. *See* identity
semiotic system, 14, 21, 22
separation of the sexes, 164n10
servants and prostitution, 100–101
sex and sexuality: body as fixed base for, 2; breasts, 3–4, 16–17, 160n47; circumcision covenant, 38; conquest, 102–3; defined, 107–8; dominance over women's, 41–55; female puberty, 27, 162n72; and feminist criticism, xx; grinding of wheat imagery, 51–52; heterosexuality, 50, 107, 110, 172–73n28; incest, 16–17; main sex organ, woman's, 3–4, 162n72; male sexual control, 105, 106; morality, 102; oneness and order, 5, 122; plurality of woman's, 3–4, 17, 38–39, 103, 113–14; prostitution, 100–107, 109–15, 172–73nn27–28; Sarah's, 7; secrecy, 147, 148; as social process, 44; and violence, 50–51, 54. *See also* desire; eroticism

Sha-dai, 12, 35–38
shafts, Temple, 133–34, 136–42, 176n45
Shekhina, 160n39
Shifra, 59–60, 61, 62, 166n13
Shifra, S., 119–21
silence, women's, 43–44, 54, 74. *See also* speech
Simeon b. Gamliel, R.: on Miriam and the Hebrew midwives, 59
Simeon b. Halafta, R.: on miracle of the pearl, 93–99
Simeon b. Yohai, R.: on Eve's curse, 45–55
Simon, R.: on Eve's curse, 45; on truth and peace, 87–88
sin: desire as, 46; post-childbirth sacrifices, 49–50
Sinai, 163n92
skepticism and wife of R. Simeon b. Halafta, 93–99
social awareness and celestial pearl miracle, 98, 171n12, 171n14
Sodom, 67–70
solidity: and gender, 174–75n25; stones, 131
Solomon, 135, 136, 138
Song of Ascent, 136–37, 138, 140–41
Song of Songs: breast imagery in, 25–28, 38; Temple shafts, 134
Song of the Sea, 14–16, 130–31
sons and injunction to procreate, 84, 168n18
sotah, 137, 164n10, 170n26
speech: desire, 43–44, 54; feminine voice, 96–99; Judith's lying, 91; nursing of Moses, 20–21; and self, 96; stammering, 21–22, 161n61
spies and Rahab, 102–5, 109, 113, 114
stammering, 21–22, 161n61
status: hero's family, 167n18; men's dominance in marriage, 51, 53–54
stealing. *See* theft
sterilization, 76, 80, 82
stones. *See* rocks/stones
striking of the rock, 31–34
style: context, 83; interrelated teachings,

204

169–70n25; minimalism, 74–75, 80, 88–89; order, xi
subversive intent and readings, 51–52, 64, 78–79, 99
suffocation, 137, 176n46
symbolic system, 14, 21
symmetry and breasts, 27–28
synagogues and study halls: frescoes of Hebrew midwives, 166n13; juxtaposition of, 162n70; Song of Songs, 25, 26; Tiberias, 93, 94, 170n3

Tamar, 83, 168n8
Temple and the "deep," 131–44, 176n45
Ten Commandments and breast imagery, 29
Tent of Meeting, 33
theft: in creation of Eve, 146–47, 149
Tiâmat, 36, 119–21
Tiberias, 93–94, 170n3
Torah compared to breasts, 23–30, 162n66
truth and peace, 86–87
twins, 28, 38, 83
tzur, 34

the "uncanny," 98
utopias, 172–73n28

Vashti, 105
violence: male/female morality, 71; and sexuality, 50–51, 54
voice. *See* speech

water: Babylonian creation myth, 119–21; End of Days stream, 142–44; and fertility, 123, 124, 139, 143; Flood, 121, 123–29, 135; and formlessness, 118–19; and gender, 174–75n25; male and female waters, 122–24; striking of the rock, 31–34; in Temple rituals, 132–33, 134; as threat to Temple, 131–44. *See also* the "deep"
wealth, criticism of, 97, 98, 171n12
weaning: Exodus from Egypt, 11; separation from mother, 14, 21; striking of the rock, 33–34. *See also* breastfeeding
wife of highway robber, 45, 50–55
wife of R. Hanina b. Dosa, 96
wife of R. Hiyya (Judith), 74, 76–88, 90–92
wife of R. Simeon b. Halafta, 93–99
women: creation of, 145–56. *See also* femininity
wonder child, 21, 161n60

Zadok, R.: on Flood, 123–24